PC Magazine
Guide to LANtastic

PC Magazine Guide to LANtastic

Frank J. Derfler, Jr., and Les Freed

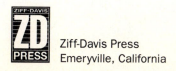

Ziff-Davis Press
Emeryville, California

Editor	Lyn Cordell
Technical Reviewer	Maria Forrest
Project Coordinator	Sheila McGill
Proofreader	Carol Burbo
Cover Concept	Carrie English and Ken Roberts
Cover Design	Tom Morgan/Blue Design, San Francisco
Book Design	Paper Crane Graphics, Berkeley
Screen Graphics Editor	Dan Brodnitz
Technical Illustration	Cherie Plumlee Computer Graphics & Illustration
Word Processing	Howard Blechman and Cat Haglund
Page Layout	Sidney Davenport and M. D. Barrera
Indexer	Valerie Haynes Perry

This book was produced on a Macintosh IIfx, with the following applications: FrameMaker®, Microsoft® Word, MacLink®Plus, Aldus® FreeHand™, Adobe Photoshop™, and Collage Plus™.

Ziff Davis Press
5903 Christie Avenue
Emeryville, CA 94608

Copyright © 1993 by Ziff-Davis Press. All rights reserved.

PC Magazine is a registered trademark of Ziff Communications Company. Ziff-Davis Press, ZD Press, and PC Magazine Guide To are trademarks of Ziff Communications Company.

All other product names and services identified throughout this book are trademarks or registered trademarks of their respective companies. They are used throughout this book in editorial fashion only and for the benefit of such companies. No such uses, or the use of any trade name, is intended to convey endorsement or other affiliation with the book.

No part of this publication may be reproduced in any form, or stored in a database or retrieval system, or transmitted or distributed in any form by any means, electronic, mechanical photocopying, recording, or otherwise, without the prior written permission of Ziff-Davis Press, except as permitted by the Copyright Act of 1976 and except that program listings may be entered, stored, and executed in a computer system.

THE INFORMATION AND MATERIAL CONTAINED IN THIS BOOK ARE PROVIDED "AS IS," WITHOUT WARRANTY OF ANY KIND, EXPRESS OR IMPLIED, INCLUDING WITHOUT LIMITATION ANY WARRANTY CONCERNING THE ACCURACY, ADEQUACY, OR COMPLETENESS OF SUCH INFORMATION OR MATERIAL OR THE RESULTS TO BE OBTAINED FROM USING SUCH INFORMATION OR MATERIAL. NEITHER ZIFF-DAVIS PRESS NOR THE AUTHOR SHALL BE RESPONSIBLE FOR ANY CLAIMS ATTRIBUTABLE TO ERRORS, OMISSIONS, OR OTHER INACCURACIES IN THE INFORMATION OR MATERIAL CONTAINED IN THIS BOOK, AND IN NO EVENT SHALL ZIFF-DAVIS PRESS OR THE AUTHOR BE LIABLE FOR DIRECT, INDIRECT, SPECIAL, INCIDENTAL, OR CONSEQUENTIAL DAMAGES ARISING OUT OF THE USE OF SUCH INFORMATION OR MATERIAL.

ISBN 1-56276-058-0

Manufactured in the United States of America
✆ The paper used in this book exceeds the EPA requirements for postconsumer recycled paper.
10 9 8 7 6 5 4 3 2 1

■ Contents at a Glance

Introduction		xiii
Chapter 1:	Networking Basics	1
Chapter 2:	Artisoft's Product Line	27
Chapter 3:	Planning Your Network	49
Chapter 4:	Installing LANtastic	63
Chapter 5:	Using LANtastic Every Day	87
Chapter 6:	Network Management and Security	107
Chapter 7:	Using LANtastic from the DOS Command Prompt	151
Chapter 8:	Expanding Your Network	181
Chapter 9:	LANtastic and Windows	207
Chapter 10:	LANtastic for NetWare	243
Chapter 11:	LANtastic and Third-Party Products	253
Glossary		275
Index		283

■ Table of Contents

Introduction   xiii
     How This Book Is Organized   xiii

Chapter 1: Networking Basics   1

Cabling   3
     Unshielded Twisted-Pair Wiring   4
     Shielded Twisted-Pair Wire for Token-Ring   7
     Coaxial Cable   8
     Fiber-Optic Cabling   9
     Wireless LANs   11

LAN Adapters   12
     The Adapter Makes the Network   15
     Wiring Hubs   18

Network Operating Systems   21

Chapter 2: Artisoft's Product Line   27

Operating System Software   28
     Standard LANtastic   29
     LANtastic/AI   33
     LANtastic for NetWare   33
     LANtastic Z   35
     ArtiCom   36
     The Network Eye   36

Artisoft's Hardware   38
     Two-Megabit LAN Adapters   38
     Peer-Hub   40
     Central Station   42
     Sounding Board and the ArtiSound Recorder   43

Chapter 3: Planning Your Network — 49

Taking an Inventory — 50

Defining Your Requirements — 52

Core Planning Issues — 52
- Crossing Adapters and Cabling 52
- Server Requirements 55
- Those Printers 57

Additional Planning Factors — 58
- The Server Directory Structure 58
- Menu Systems 59
- Backup 60
- Training 60

Chapter 4: Installing LANtastic — 63

Hardware Installation — 64
- Finding a Home for Your NIC Board 64

Installing the LANtastic Software — 68

Memory Management — 72
- The DOS 640k Memory Limit 72
- Responses to the 640k Problem 75
- Optimizing Your RAM for LANtastic 77

QEMM-386 — 84

Chapter 5: Using LANtastic Every Day — 87

What LANtastic Does — 88
- About Network Drives 88
- Logging into a LANtastic Network 90

Starting LANtastic 90

Using the Connection Manager Menu System 91
    Adding a Network Drive   92
    Adding a Network Printer   95
    Managing Print Queues   97
    Using LANtastic Mail   100
    Using the Chat Feature   103
    Other Connection Manager Functions   103

Chapter 6: Network Management and Security 107

LANtastic Security Features 108
    The Network Manager Program   109

Managing User Security 111
    Setting a User's Account Privileges   111
    Managing Group Accounts   113

Managing Shared Resources 114
    Access Control Lists   115
    Shared Disk Resources   115
    Shared Printer Resources   122

Managing Servers 130
    Server Startup Parameters   130
    Auditing Network Activity   133

Network Printing 136
    LANtastic Printing Facilities   136
    Queue, Stream, and Printer Management   137
    Printing to a File   140
    Printing Multiple Copies of a Document   141
    Network Printing Tips and Tricks   142

Networking Your Applications 145
    Networking and the Law   145
    Installing Networked Applications   147

Chapter 7: Using LANtastic from the DOS Command Prompt — 151

The Command-Line Interface — 152
- NET.EXE Command-Line Options   153
- NET_MGR Command-Line Options   170

Using DOS Batch Files with LANtastic — 175

LANtastic String Macros — 176

Chapter 8: Expanding Your Network — 181

Diskless Workstations — 182
- The Network Boot File   182
- Preparing Your Network for Remote Booting   183

The Sounding Board — 188
- The Sounding Board Hardware   188
- The Sounding Board Software   189

Sharing Modems on the Network — 189
- Artisoft's ACS: ArtiCom   190
- Installing the ArtiCom Software   192
- Using Shared Modems   197
- The ArtiCom Application Program   198
- Using ArtiCom with Third-Party Software   200

Sharing CD-ROM Drives — 201

Artisoft's Central Station — 202
- Connecting with the Central Station   202
- The StationWare Applications   203

Chapter 9: LANtastic and Windows — 207

Windows's Requirements — 208

Installing Windows with LANtastic — 208
    Installing Windows on Your Local Hard Disk   209
    Installing Windows from a File Server   209
    Windows, CONFIG.SYS, and AUTOEXEC.BAT   211
    SETUP and Printer Assignments   212

Running Windows with LANtastic — 212
    Controlling LANtastic from Windows   212
    Using Windows Applications on the Network   215

LANtastic for Windows — 215
    Installing LANtastic for Windows   216
    Using LANtastic for Windows   217
    The Windows Connection Manager   217
    The Network Manager Program   232

Chapter 10: LANtastic for NetWare — 243

What Is NetWare? — 244
    A Quick Tour of NetWare   244

The LANtastic for NetWare Software — 245
    Installing LANtastic for NetWare   246
    Using LANtastic for NetWare   249

Chapter 11: LANtastic and Third-Party Products — 253

Built-in Compatibility — 254
    Problems Common to All LANs   254
    Configuring Your File Structure   261
    DOS and Other Environments   264

Third-Party Network Boards 267

Network Your Network—On-Line Services 268
    CompuServe 269
    ZiffNet 272

LANtastic and Portable Computers 272

Working through Problems 274

Glossary 275

Index 283

■ Introduction

Our goal in writing this, our third book together, is to help make LANtastic work for you. It's a guide to using LANtastic efficiently, so we filled it with hints, tips, how-to instructions, and helpful information, and we also made it easy to read. We help you with tricky operations such as planning your network, printing on the network, using LANtastic with Microsoft Windows, linking to NetWare networks, and customizing network operations while maintaining security and flexibility. We'd like to make the point that this is a book for everyone—not just the network guru. Anyone who uses a PC attached to a LANtastic LAN can benefit from this book.

We have worked with LANs in a variety of circumstances. Les is a unique combination of expert programmer and successful businessman. He is the founder and former president of DCA's Crosstalk division and is intimately familiar with the technical side of PCs and networks. He knows how administrative support people, data entry personnel, warehouse and payroll clerks, programmers, and CEOs use networked PCs. He knows what real people want to do with their PCs in real business environments.

As the networking editor of *PC Magazine* and founder of the PC LAN Labs, Frank has dissected, evaluated, tested, and manipulated every network operating system running on practically every combination of servers, LAN adapters, and PCs. Frank also stays on top of news on products, version changes, patches, tricks, and tips.

Together, we've written a book containing all you need to know to make LANtastic work for you. If your company has recently installed a LANtastic system, you'll find this book to be a valuable tutorial on how LANtastic works and how to control the myriad options LANtastic offers. If you haven't installed your network yet, you'll find valuable information on planning, cabling, and installing the network hardware and software. If you're an old hand at LANtastic, you'll find hints and tips that can't be found in the LANtastic manuals.

■ How This Book Is Organized

Here is a rundown on what is in the book:

Chapter 1 is an introduction to networking basics. We explain what a network is and how a peer network like LANtastic differs from a server-based network like NetWare.

Artisoft, the makers of LANtastic, offer one of the broadest product lines of any LAN vendor. Chapter 2 provides a brief overview of all the Artisoft products and explains how the products relate to one another.

Planning a new network or reorganizing an existing LAN can be a major administrative headache. Chapter 3 tells you how to plan your network installation and how to run cables, as well as what the traps are and how to avoid them. We also cover the important but often-overlooked topics of network backups and power protection.

Much of the frustration of using and installing any network relates to the configuration of your PC's hardware and software. Chapter 4 begins the hands-on portion of the book with tips on installing network adapter boards and the LANtastic software. We show you how to avoid hardware-related problems, and we also show you how to make the most of your PC's memory resources.

Chapter 5 provides a detailed overview of the main LANtastic operations, including using network disks and printers, the electronic mail system, and the network chat facility.

Chapter 6 introduces you to network management and security—two topics that are often ignored or overlooked in other guides. LANtastic provides excellent security features, and we show you how to protect sensitive data without compromising the effectiveness of your network. We also show you how to share network resources effectively, and we offer some useful tips to help with the tricky topic of printing over the LAN.

Although LANtastic provides an effective, easy-to-use menu system, many users prefer to control the network software from the DOS command line. In Chapter 7, we show you how to control all of LANtastic's operations from the command line, and we explain how to write DOS batch files to automate many of these operations.

As your network grows, you'll probably want to add specialized services such as shared CD-ROMs, shared modems, and extra print servers. Chapter 8 explains the expansion options available for your LANtastic network and includes a close look at Artisoft's unique Central Station connectivity processor and the Sounding Board voice adapter.

Microsoft's Windows operating environment is taking over the world, but running Windows on a network can be like trying to mix oil and water. In Chapter 9 we tell you how to integrate the power of LANtastic with the power of Windows to use resources like files and printers. We offer hints on installing Windows on the network and show you how to use network disks and printers with Windows. We also take a close look at Artisoft's LANtastic for Windows product.

Despite the popularity of peer networks like LANtastic, Novell's NetWare is still the corporate standard in many organizations. In Chapter 10, we show you how to use NetWare and LANtastic together by running Artisoft's LANtastic for NetWare product.

To help you make your network a better place to work, Chapter 11 explores several third-party LANtastic enhancement products, including those that install and control applications on the network. We'll also describe how to take advantage of the information available on dial-in systems such as CompuServe and ZiffNet, how to use laptop computers on LANtastic, and tell you about some useful utility programs you can use with LANtastic.

Computer networks have changed the way many of us work. Certainly networks allow us to share resources such as printers and hard disks, but the real power of a network comes from the ability to share information. In this book we've used our experience to produce tips, tricks, and tools you can use to increase your access to networked information. Use them and become a corporate hero!

- *Cabling*
- *LAN Adapters*
- *Network Operating Systems*

CHAPTER

1

Networking Basics

"IF YOU'RE NOT CONNECTED, YOU'RE NOT COMPUTING." EVERY DAY, our favorite networking slogan moves farther from hyperbole and closer to fact. An increasing number of business, government, and service organizations use connected computers to gather, store, and produce information. The Gartner Group predicts that by 1995 the installed base of PCs will double and nearly three-quarters of all office PCs will be connected to LANs. If they are right, 30,000 PCs will be added to networks each working day during the next five years.

A LAN

👍 Allows file sharing among many PCs simultaneously

👍 Allows printer sharing

👍 Improves productivity

👎 Requires planning

👎 Requires management

It doesn't necessarily take a professional to install a network; anyone who's PC-savvy can do it. If you understand the concept of DOS subdirectories and aren't afraid to take the cover off a PC, you can install the LAN hardware and software required to link ten PCs together for less than $3,000, plus the cost of cabling.

Our second favorite networking slogan is "Networks are for sharing." In our broad definition, a LAN is a system that uses network adapter cards to interface between each connected PC's expansion bus and the network cabling system, and also uses some type of network operating system to deal with simultaneous requests for service from multiple client stations. In essence, you install a LAN to share files, printers, and links to other computer systems or networks. A LAN enhances its users' productivity with features like electronic mail and common databases; however, it takes careful planning and management to make a network run smoothly.

The subject of local area networks breaks cleanly into six sections:

- *Cabling*   Connects the computers, or *nodes*, of the network to each other

- *Adapter cards*   Connect the PCs to the cabling

- *Networking software*   Links the LAN adapters to the PCs

- *Network communications protocols*   Provide the software link between nodes

- *Off-LAN communications*   Connect the network to the rest of the world

- *Network applications*   Provide e-mail, scheduling, shared database, and other capabilities

These topics are interrelated, yet quite distinct. Adapter cards will typically work with many types of wiring, networking software like LANtastic can drive many different adapters, communications protocols carry data to many kinds of networking software, and application programs run over many different network operating systems. As you can see, modern LANs offer a rich, but often bewildering, menu of choices.

There are versions of the LANtastic software you can use with almost any brand of network adapter, but LANtastic operates fastest and most efficiently with Artisoft adapters. This is particularly true in terms of the amount of RAM the software uses; non-Artisoft LAN cards may require additional RAM-consuming software drivers. You can use Artisoft's adapters with coaxial cable, unshielded twisted-pair wiring, and (through special adapters) fiber-optic cabling.

In this book, we provide you with the best advice and information available on the installation and operation of networks using Artisoft's LANtastic network operating system and wide range of hardware. This first chapter provides an overview of network basics ranging from the selection of network cabling to the options you have for networking software. Later chapters will deal with off-LAN communications and network applications for LANtastic.

■ Cabling

The larger the area your LAN covers, the more critical cabling design becomes. You must look at the issue of cabling first to determine whether it will drive your network budget and planning cycles or is only a minor consideration. The type of cabling you have installed or want to use might be a deciding factor in the design and layout of your network, or it might be a minor factor that you can handle quickly.

Figure 1.1 shows the cabling choices: coaxial cable, fiber-optic cable, shielded twisted-pair, and unshielded twisted-pair. Wireless LANs, or at least wireless segments of LANs, provide a way out of difficult wiring problems in many installations, and we'll describe them later. First let's focus on physical cabling.

Figure 1.1

The major types of network media or wiring are (from left to right): thin coaxial cable with a BNC connector, fiber-optic cabling and connectors, shielded twisted-pair wiring with an IBM Token-Ring connector, and unshielded twisted-pair wire with a modular connector attached.

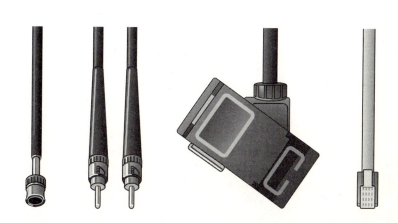

In simple networks of two to ten nodes it might be acceptable to run wiring along the wallboards, behind desks, and in false ceilings, but as a network grows, having a less visible wiring system that is more structured and probably more reliable becomes increasingly important.

The cabling used for local area networks is generally covered by building or fire codes. In certain cases you must use Teflon-coated cable called *plenum cable* as a fire precaution, because some non-Teflon cable generates poisonous gasses when it burns. Generally, you should make sure you're buying wire that meets the CMR (Communications Riser Cable) or CMP (Communications Plenum Cable) specifications of the National Electric Code.

You can have the wiring for your LAN installed by contractors as big as AT&T or GTE, by your local telephone company, by a local electrical contractor, or by your own employees, but be sure to consider the need for a final electrical inspection when you plan your installation. Also think about specific precautions like lightning protection on cables that stretch between buildings.

Major vendors including AT&T, Digital Equipment Corp., IBM, and Northern Telecom, as well as many smaller vendors have developed their own premise distribution system (PDS) plans. These cabling architectures provide for an integrated telephone and data cabling system using hardware components from a single supplier. The advantage of having one source of supply is that there is only one place to point the finger of responsibility; the disadvantage is that you become wedded to that vendor. If you are planning a new building or major renovation, shop for a PDS, but plan for a long-term relationship with the supplier you select.

Unshielded Twisted-Pair Wiring

Unshielded twisted-pair (UTP) wiring, which sells at a retail price of $110 for a 1,000-foot spool, is commonly installed in buildings for internal private branch exchange (PBX) telephone systems. Not all telephone wiring is twisted-pair, though. The telephone wire used in residences isn't, but it's improperly configured for network use anyway—residences are wired from room to room rather than in the star configuration required by PBXs and LANs. Other common types of telephone wire, such as the flat cable called "silver satin" for its shiny coat, aren't twisted either.

Figure 1.2 shows the two separate pairs of twisted wires in each twisted-pair cable. Their twisting provides an electrical self-canceling, or shielding, effect that helps keep desirable signals in and undesirable ones out. Only modern telephone systems use twisted-pair wiring that meets the requirements for data communications.

One way to make sure you are getting the right UTP cable is to ask if it conforms to the IBM Type 3 specification. This cable should have two pairs of 24-gauge solid copper wires, and should meet certain standards for electrical characteristics like distributed capacitance. The Institute of Electronic and Electrical Engineers (IEEE) has a standard for Ethernet UTP called 10BaseT, and you will also find cable with that designation.

Figure 1.2

Unshielded twisted-pair wire consists of two pairs of wires, each twisted together in a configuration that creates an electrical shielding effect.

A star wiring system

👍 **Provides excellent reliability**

👍 **Is flexible when people change offices**

👎 **Requires expensive hardware**

UTP wiring for LANs is installed in the star, or "home-run," wiring configuration shown in Figure 1.3. Each node on the LAN has its own dedicated wire run from the central wiring closet. With this configuration—or *physical topology* in LANspeak—if one wire is broken or shorted, only that node loses its network connection. Hub or concentrator equipment in the wiring closet isolates the rest of the nodes from disruption.

The star wiring scheme isn't unique to UTP; you can use it with all types of media. We strongly recommend that no matter what type of cabling you use, you arrange it in a star wiring pattern. If you are building a new house, insist that it be wired that way too!

Although unshielded twisted-pair wiring is very popular with network buyers, much of its appeal is based on misconceptions or outdated information. Before you decide to string along with UTP, you should ask yourself whether your decision is based on any of these ideas:

- *UTP is cheap.* Maybe, but while the wire itself is low in cost, the labor used to pull the wiring makes up the major portion of the bill. Fiber can cost ten times the price of UTP, but even at slightly more than $1 per foot, the cost of installation by a licensed electrical contractor can dwarf the cost of materials.

- *I can use the UTP already in the walls.* Again, maybe, but you need to analyze every wire run to see if it meets the length, noise, and other electrical specifications for the networking architecture you want to use. A device like the $2,495 PairScanner from Microtest Corp. or its bigger and more capable brother the Next Scanner will tell you which wire pairs you can trust.

- *UTP gives me the reliability of the star wiring scheme.* Sure it does, but this arrangement is not unique to UTP. Modern wiring hubs like the one shown in Figure 1.4 allow you to arrange any type of copper wire or fiber-optic cable in a star physical topology.

Figure 1.3

The star wiring topology uses a separate "home-run" cable between the central wiring hub and each network node. If one cable run is disrupted, the hub isolates the problem cable and the rest of the network continues to operate.

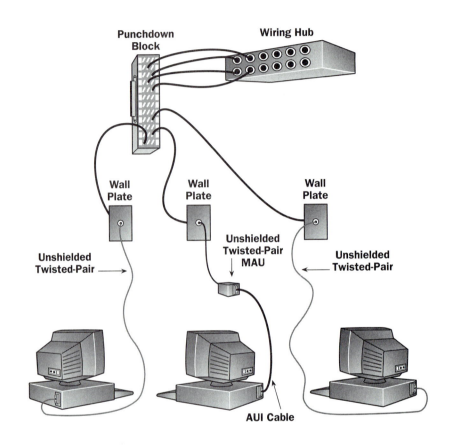

An organization called the UTP Developers Forum, whose impressive list of members includes Apple, AT&T, British Telecommunications, Hewlett-Packard, and Ungermann-Bass, is pushing a proposal for a standard that would provide a 100-megabit-per-second data rate over UTP. Unfortunately, despite the weight of these players, the laws of physics work against having many successful installations using typical cable runs installed for phone service. As network signaling speeds jump from today's 4 to 10 megabits per second to 100 megabits per second or higher, it will become much more difficult to use UTP.

On the bottom line, unshielded twisted-pair wiring can have unique appeal in certain installations, particularly those with relatively short wire runs—preferably no more than 100 feet and certainly no more than 300 feet—between the farthest node and the wiring closet. We know we're whistling in the face of a hurricane, but we think you should consider other wiring options before you settle for UTP. Many organizations will benefit from the decision to install fiber-optic cabling, coaxial cable, or shielded twisted-pair wiring as an investment in the future. If you do decide to use unshielded twisted-pair wiring, have a professional contractor test the system to be certain it meets the specifications for 10BaseT or Token-Ring installations.

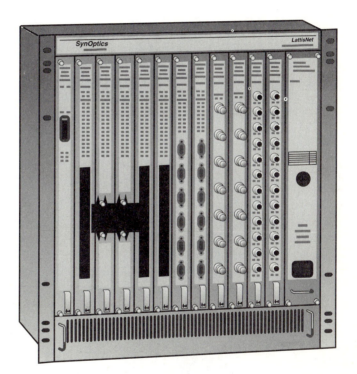

Figure 1.4

SynOptics LattisNet Model 3000 Concentrator allows you to configure a combination of wiring schemes in a physical star topology. This concentrator combines fiber-optic cable, 10BaseT wiring, and Token-Ring cabling. (Equipment and technical support courtesy of SynOptics Communications, Inc.)

Shielded Twisted-Pair Wire for Token-Ring

Shielded twisted-pair wire has been associated almost exclusively with Token-Ring network adapters. IBM has defined what they call Type 1 and Type 6 cables for Token-Ring networks. Type 1 cable is used in wire runs of more than a few feet. Type 6 cable is more flexible and is used in short runs, typically between a desktop PC and a wall jack. Both types wrap two pairs of wires inside a double layer of shielding to prevent electrical interference. This kind of cable is always installed as a home run between the wiring closet and each

Shielded twisted-pair

👍 Prevents electrical interference

👍 Provides high-speed capability

👎 Fills conduits quickly

👎 Requires experience to install

node, so installations using it benefit from the survivability of the star physical topology.

Shielded twisted-pair cables—particularly Type 1—are bulky, and it takes some skill to install the connectors properly. Type 1 cable sells for $396 in 1,000 foot rolls and Type 6 cable for only a few dollars less. The connector used on the end of each cable opposite the PC costs $11. You'll also find STP cable pairs in larger wire bundles with telephone UTP wiring and even with fiber-optic cable.

Aside from its use in Token-Ring, shielded twisted-pair wire is interesting because of the efforts of a group of companies including Advanced Micro Devices Inc., Chipcom Corp., Digital Equipment Corp., IBM, Motorola, and SynOptics to create an ANSI standard for 100-megabit-per-second signaling over this medium. Pushing data at 100 megabits over UTP is difficult—the degree of difficulty will vary with each installation—but signaling at 100 megabits per second over STP is relatively easy. So, while STP is expensive, it will work well for decades to come. Nonetheless, the popularity of unshielded twisted-pair wire has pushed the bulkier STP out of many new installations.

Overall, STP takes a lot of space in wiring conduits and closets and is expensive, but once it's in place it will serve your communications needs for years.

Coaxial Cable

Coaxial cable has been used for radio transmission lines since the 1940s. Its transition to local area networks occurred 30 years later, led by both the Ethernet and ARCnet LAN adapter systems. The name *coaxial* comes from the physical relationship between the cable's center conductor and its shield: The two parts have the same physical axis—thus, they are co-axial. All coaxial cable is not the same, however. For example, the RG-59 cable used in cable TV and other services, the RG-58 cable used for Ethernet, and the RG-62 cable used for IBM 3270 terminals and for ARCnet all look nearly identical, but differ enough electrically that they aren't interchangeable over runs of more than a few feet.

Ethernet uses two types of coaxial cable, commonly called thick Ethernet and Thinnet. The thick cable, known as "frozen yellow garden hose" for its rigidity, color, and size, is often used for long-run "backbone" cable in large installations. One thousand feet of this coax will set you back more than $1,000. You won't find new installations using thick Ethernet backbone cable because it's expensive and difficult to install.

Thinnet, nicknamed "cheapernet," uses a much thinner and more flexible type of coaxial cable. When Ethernet was first introduced, Thinnet was installed in a daisy-chain configuration (see Figure 1.5), with cable running from node to node and T-connectors at each one. The significant drawback to

Coaxial cable

👍 Provides freedom from interference

👍 Is easy to install

👎 Fills conduits quickly

this scheme is that one bad connector can disrupt the entire network. Since the late 1980s companies have offered ways to wire Thinnet systems in a star topology so that one outage doesn't take down the entire system.

Figure 1.5

The Thinnet coaxial wiring scheme uses T-connectors at each node and terminators at each end to soak up signals that would otherwise bounce and reflect throughout the cable. This wiring system limits the overall amount of cable you can use, and each T-connector is a vulnerable point in the network—any break or inadvertent disconnection results in total network failure.

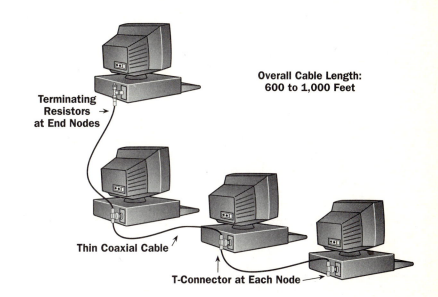

Coaxial cable has a long history and a strong future. Systems that use it are dependable and can carry data at rates of 100 megabits per second and higher. The major drawback of coax is that multiple runs of this relatively fat cable quickly fill available cable ducts and create physical wiring problems.

Fiber-Optic Cabling

Fiber-optic cabling, shown in Figure 1.6, is made of a hair-thin strand of glass surrounded by strengthening material such as Kevlar. Small lasers or light emitting diodes send pulses of light representing the 0s and 1s of the digital message through the fiber.

Fiber-optic cable has many advantages over copper wire including complete freedom from electrical interference, a small diameter so you can reclaim your building's conduits, and the potential for carrying large amounts of data at high speeds over longer distances. In some installations fiber can carry data over three kilometers—coaxial cable is usually good for about a kilometer, STP for 300 meters, and UTP for just 100 meters.

Figure 1.6

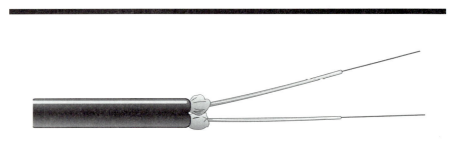

A typical fiber-optic cable contains two thin glass strands, each surrounded by a strong thread of Kevlar or stainless steel and an outer jacket. In operation, each strand carries a light wave in one direction.

Fiber-optic cabling

👍 Is immune to all forms of electrical interference

👍 Allows longer cable runs

👎 Requires expensive adapters

👎 Costs more per foot than copper cable

Practically all fiber LAN technologies use two strands of fiber going to each node, so some of the size advantage of fiber cable over small copper co-axial cable is lost in real installations. Each strand carries data in one direction for full-time, two-way communications.

All fiber is not alike. AT&T favors a fiber with a core diameter of 62.5 microns (a micron is 1/25,000 of an inch), while IBM specifies a 100-micron core. You must match the equipment and the fiber, but if you install fiber before you buy equipment you'll be safe specifying the 62.5 micron size. Expect to pay about $1,100 for a 1,000 foot roll of cable with two fiber strands.

The price of connectors and the skill needed to install them on fiber-optic cable is much less of a problem than it once was. In the late 1980s, installers needed specialized equipment and expensive training to properly attach a connector to a piece of fiber, but now AMP Inc. offers their LightCrimp system at a cost of approximately $6 to $7 per connector. Installation takes about two minutes per connector and installers can quickly learn to use the simple installation tools.

You may have heard the acronym FDDI, which stands for Fiber Distributed Data Interface. FDDI is a standard specified by ANSI, the American National Standards Institute, as ANSI X3T9.5 for transmission at 100 million bits per second. Don't assume that all LANs using fiber conform to the FDDI standard, because very few actually do.

The biggest use of fiber in LANs is still as a direct replacement for copper cable with the same signaling speed as copper. In most LANs, the fiber allows longer connections without requiring devices to repeat the signals at regular intervals and provides total immunity from interference in noisy electrical environments; however, it doesn't move data any faster.

Fiber systems that replace copper cable must use home-run wiring from a wiring center to each node on the network. Fiber is also widely used as backbone wiring to connect wiring centers located in different parts of a building or campus.

If you really want to connect all your PCs directly via fiber cable, be prepared to pay for the privilege. Codenoll Technology Corp., Proteon Inc., and

Pure Data Ltd. sell PC LAN adapters that use fiber in place of typical LAN cables. For example, the $695 Codenoll 8340 is an Ethernet adapter for ISA-bus computers that can drive signals over 1,600 meters of cable—more than half again the distance typically recommended for equivalent copper wiring.

Designed for reliability and flexibility as well as high throughput, the FDDI standard defines two physical rings that send data in different directions simultaneously. Codenoll Technology Corp. markets FDDI LAN adapters for ISA PCs priced at $4,995 and $7,395, depending on whether you want to take advantage of the standard's full dual-ring capability. Network Peripherals also offers an ISA-bus FDDI adapter for $1,995.

Optical Data Systems (ODS) is an excellent source of FDDI information and equipment. ODS carries useful adapters, transceivers, and other often overlooked pieces and parts that you need to make an FDDI system work.

Because the robust FDDI architecture is so appealing, companies like Crescendo Communications, Digital Equipment Corp., and Microdyne have announced products that use the 100-megabit-per-second architecture over different types of copper wiring; thus the standard becomes CDDI instead of FDDI.

As usual, speed doesn't come cheap. Microdyne's EXOS 505S is a CDDI adapter for PCs using shielded twisted-pair cable. It carries a $1,495 price tag, about five times the price of a typical 10Mb/sec Ethernet adapter.

The current high cost of devices like LAN adapters makes fiber-optic cable and FDDI in general 10 to 20 times more expensive than copper cabling alternatives. The prices will come down slowly, but it will be several years before FDDI becomes as economical as copper LAN alternatives (assuming it ever does), so fiber links aren't likely to reach every desktop soon.

Wireless LANs

The term *wireless* is misleading. Wireless LANs typically aren't totally wireless, but instead use either radio or infrared technology to connect a node or group of nodes to the main body of the network. It's difficult to categorize wireless LAN systems because they have several different architectures. Some products work only with Ethernet or Token-Ring cabling, while others replace the cabling on certain segments.

NCR's WaveLAN system uses $995 LAN adapters that function as UHF radio transceivers in each PC. WaveLAN can act as a link between cable segments of a LANtastic network, or you can create a complete wireless network using WaveLAN to link PCs. Figure 1.7 shows the WaveLAN architecture.

While the WaveLAN system uses radio waves to link network segments, InfraLAN, from BICC Communications, connects Token-Ring LAN segments using infrared light. InfraLAN costs $2,995 per device and you need two to get started. Because it functions as a simple repeater that literally

Wireless LANs

👍 Solve otherwise difficult or impossible cabling problems

👍 Allow flexibility for portable or mobile client computers

👎 Radio systems typically provide slower throughput than cable

👎 Optical systems require critical point-to-point alignment and are easily disrupted

extends the cabling over light waves, InfraLAN will work with any network operating system.

Figure 1.7

The WaveLAN system can weave individual nodes into a totally wireless network, but the cost of the wireless adapters will probably limit their use to nodes beyond the reach of an economical copper or fiber-optic cable system.

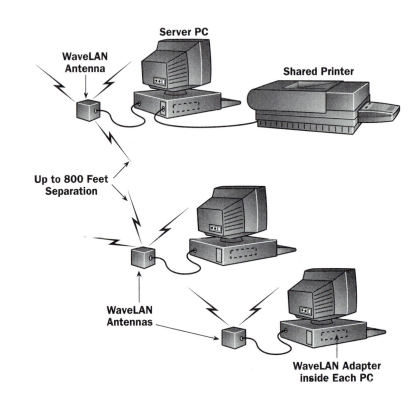

■ LAN Adapters

LAN adapters, also called *network interface cards* or *NICs*, translate between the low-powered signals moving in parallel over your PC's expansion bus and the more robust signals moving serially over the network media. A LAN adapter has two sides—the expansion bus side and the LAN cable side—and each side offers several technical alternatives. You have to find the right combination of alternatives in the system you buy.

Artisoft offers various models of LAN adapters, one of which is shown in Figure 1.8. LANtastic works best with these adapters, but in later chapters we'll explain how to use LANtastic over a variety of other adapters. (You can also use Artisoft's AE-2 and AE-3 adapters with Novell's NetWare and other network operating systems.)

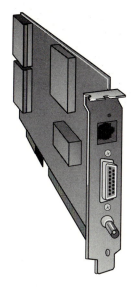

Figure 1.8

This Artisoft AE-3 LAN adapter has connections for unsheilded twisted-pair wiring and thin coaxial cable, and a multipurpose interface that can link to special transceivers for fiber-optic or thick coaxial cable.

On the expansion bus side, you must choose an adapter that is compatible with the architecture of your PC. Your choices include 8-, 16-, and 32-bit cards in versions designed for various bus systems, such as ISA (all PC AT clones), MCA (high-end IBM PS/2 computers), and EISA (high-end Compaq computers). Additionally, you can choose adapters with bus-mastering circuitry that takes much of the burden of servicing interrupts off the PC's CPU. Bus-mastering adapters are particularly useful in PC's acting as file servers, because they give the CPU time to run data-handling routines without interruption from the LAN adapter.

Tests run in PC Magazine's Labs show little difference between the throughput of 8- and 16-bit versions of Ethernet adapters in client PCs. On the average, you'll find a $40 to $50 price difference between adapters with an 8- or 16-bit bus interface. If $50 per PC is significant in your budget, you can safely save some money without sacrificing any visible performance by buying 8-bit adapters instead of the 16-bit versions; however, you should spend the extra money for a 16- or even 32-bit bus-mastering adapter for any PC that will act as a file server.

14 Chapter 1: Networking Basics

Internal adapters can be difficult to install inside crowded PCs, and some PCs—particularly the popular laptop and notebook models—don't have an expansion slot for a LAN card. Xircom Corp. led the industry in fielding an external LAN adapter (see Figure 1.9) that attaches to the parallel port on any PC. Accton Technology Corp., IQ Technologies, Megahertz Corp., and Xircom also make external adapters for both Ethernet and Token-Ring systems.

Figure 1.9

Xircom's external LAN adapter provides a way to connect any PC or laptop to a network without using an expansion slot. The Xircom adapter comes with drivers for Artisoft's LANtastic.

Typically, external devices are more expensive than internal adapters. For example, Xircom's 16/4 external Token-Ring adapter carries a $895 price tag and their Ethernet adapter costs $595. The throughput of an external adapter is typically 40 to 50 percent that of an internal adapter due to the relatively slow speed of the parallel port, but external models offer simple installation and, in some cases, network connections that you can't get any other way.

In late 1991, Xircom announced the development of a way to improve the throughput of external LAN adapters. The method uses an enhanced parallel port (EPP) that can move data in bursts at speeds as high as 16 megabits per second—approximately 30 times faster than the present parallel port speed of a PC. That speed will eventually open the bottleneck created by older external LAN adapter products, but you need new parallel port hardware in your PC to enjoy the accelerated throughput, so this will be a long-term development.

EPP is part of all laptops based on the Intel 25 MHz 80386 SL chipset that began shipping in the first quarter of 1992.

On the LAN side, it's typical—although not necessary—for the electrical circuitry and connectors on the adapter to determine what kind of cable the LAN uses; you buy an adapter designed for unshielded twisted-pair wiring, coax, or one of the other wiring schemes. Some adapters come with connections for more than one type of cabling. Several companies deliver Ethernet adapters for either UTP or coax connections, for example.

If you've already invested in adapters and you want to change the wiring, you can usually add an external device called a transceiver that will translate, for example, between a LAN adapter designed for coaxial cable and installed UTP wire or fiber-optic cable. On Ethernet adapters, the connection between the adapter and the transceiver is sometimes made using the Attachment Unit Interface (AUI) port, a 15-pin socket for special connection devices.

Transceivers and similar devices called *media filters* and *baluns* operate under the same general principles in Token-Ring networks. They range in price from about $40 to about $240, depending on what kinds of connections they make for copper cable systems. Prices for fiber-optic cable transceivers hover just under $500.

The Adapter Makes the Network

You've undoubtedly heard the names Ethernet, Token-Ring, and ARCnet before. Until the past few years, each of these terms encompassed a family of products that included specific types of wiring, connectors, network communications software, and adapter cards, but now the products within these families have evolved beyond the original definitions. For all practical purposes, these terms currently define the techniques adapters use to share the LAN wiring—the "media access control" (MAC) protocols in LAN lingo—and the type of signals they send. The adapters you choose determine what media-access control and signaling parameters you'll be using.

Interestingly, even the firm divisions between the hardware for these different networking schemes are breaking down. Chips and Technologies has introduced a chipset they call ChipsLAN that manufacturers can use to create both an Ethernet and a Token-Ring adapter in a single piece of hardware. The biggest use for these chips will be as LAN adapters built into PCs, a configuration that will make it easier and less expensive to connect PCs to a LAN.

In addition to compatibility with the cabling and the PC, you must consider one other area of compatibility when you choose your brand of network adapter: compatibility with the network operating system. All brands or models of adapters do not work under all LAN operating systems.

NDIS and ODI

👍 Provide interoperability

👍 Provide simplicity

👎 Sometimes slow throughput

Companies have taken several approaches to the problem of compatibility between the adapter and the operating system. Microsoft and 3Com developed the Network Driver Interface Specification (NDIS), which they hoped everyone would support. Their plan has been largely successful, and most LAN adapters now come with NDIS-compliant driver software. Working from a position of market domination, Novell has proposed what it calls the Open Device Interface (ODI)—a specification similar to NDIS in general concept, but not yet as widely supported by the market.

Some manufacturers of LAN adapters, like Standard Microsystems and Intel, try to insure compatibility by shipping a diskette full of drivers for various network operating systems with their products. Artisoft takes the opposite approach: they've cloned the operation of an adapter with a wide range of support—the Novell NE2000—to take advantage of the large library of software already published for that board. When you shop for LAN adapters, make sure the ones you buy have NDIS drivers, just as insurance against obsolescence.

Ethernet

Ethernet

👍 Proven

👍 Fast

👍 Inexpensive

👍 Flexible configurations

👍 Backed by many vendors

👎 Not the best choice for connections to mini/mainframes

The name Ethernet describes a broad set of standards with an evolutionary path that has a couple of branches. The main trunk of the Ethernet tree is defined by the Institute of Electrical and Electronic Engineers (IEEE) through their committee numbered 802.3. The IEEE 802.3 standard describes a listen-before-transmit media-sharing system called Carrier Sense Multiple Access with Collision Detection (CSMA/CD). Artisoft's AE-1, AE-2, and AE-3 adapters follow the Ethernet standard.

In simple terms, Ethernet cards share the common wire by transmitting only when the channel is clear and by quickly reacting to the situation when two stations start to transmit simultaneously because both heard the clear channel and had a message to send. Among network theoreticians, this is known as a *contention* protocol. Some academics look down their noses at such undisciplined operation. While contention media-access control systems work beautifully in the real world, they can be forced into a chaos of constant collisions in test environments.

Ethernet uses a signaling rate of 10 megabits per second. This rate sounds impressive, but because of contention and other overhead factors, even the busiest networks don't push more than about 8 megabits per second over the wire. Because of internal inefficiency, a single PC in the 386 SX/16 class will enjoy a little better than one megabit per second of effective throughput. Note that it takes only four to eight very busy PCs to saturate the capacity of a single wire. Fortunately, the PCs on a typical network access the wire briefly and infrequently.

Still, one of the best ways to improve the effective throughput of a busy Ethernet network is to break the cabling into segments and spread the busy nodes among them. Devices called *routers* can control the flow of traffic between LAN segments.

Despite the disdain shown its contention protocol in some circles, we strongly recommend Ethernet for modern network installations. A quick survey of the industry found 28 firms actively marketing Ethernet adapters in the U.S., and that number is very conservative.

Token-Ring

In marked contrast to Ethernet's contention protocol, Token-Ring systems use what is termed a *deterministic* media-access control system. The "token" in Token-Ring is a special message, passed from node-to-node, that gives a node permission to enter a message, or *frame*, into the ring. There is no contention for the wire—only an orderly rotation of the permission to transmit. IEEE standard 802.5 describes a system with a star wiring plan, but with a unique media-access control scheme using node-to-node token-passing and signaling at 4 or 16 megabits per second. Artisoft doesn't make Token-Ring adapters, but in case you want to run LANtastic over Token-Ring, we describe the technique in Chapter 8.

The "ring" part of Token-Ring comes from the way the wiring hub at the center of a Token-Ring LAN arranges all the nodes in a series electrically. The electrical impulses literally travel from node to node instead of being broadcast into the cabling as they are in the Ethernet and ARCnet plans.

Token-Ring

- Backed by IBM
- Carries heavy traffic
- Comparatively difficult to install
- Tends to be expensive

The argument between proponents of CSMA/CD and token-passing media-access control is parochial and largely academic. Here are some facts: First, the main reason to consider a Token-Ring installation is IBM's emphasis on Token-Ring as the best way to link PCs to mini- and mainframe computer installations. PCs and mainframe computers can function as peers on the same Token-Ring network and IBM functional software such as the Advanced Program to Program Communications (APPC) service can link applications on both kinds of systems. If you have to install a mainframe link, Token-Ring is practical; otherwise the lower cost of Ethernet adapters and wiring centers usually makes Ethernet a more economical choice.

Second, in most installations the people working at individual PCs won't perceive any difference in throughput between 10-megabit-per-second Ethernet, 4-megabit-per-second Token-Ring, and the newer 16-megabit-per-second Token-Ring. Finally, the difference between the Ethernet CSMA/CD access scheme and the token-passing access scheme only shows up under extremely heavy traffic conditions. A competent network manager will act to reduce the traffic load before it reaches the point where the difference between CSMA/CD and token-passing comes into play.

We did a nose count and found 20 companies marketing Token-Ring adapters. IBM sells the largest number of adapters, but products from Intel Corp., Madge Networks, Proteon, and Thomas-Conrad are widely accepted in the industry. IBM's ISA 4-megabit IBM Token-Ring adapter carries a retail price of $395. The IBM 16/4 adapter, a 16-bit ISA adapter for 4- or 16-megabit Token-Ring, goes for $895. Intel's ISA 16/4 LAN adapter costs $695 retail, and Compaq sells a high-performance, 32-bit DualSpeed EISA Token-Ring adapter for $1,299.

ARCnet

The Attached Resource Computing Network (ARCnet) system was developed by Datapoint Corporation in the mid-1970s. Originally, the system used 2.5-megabit-per-second signaling over coaxial cable configured in a star with a central wiring hub. ARCnet adapters control shared access to the wiring by using a polling scheme that shares some technical concepts with Token-Ring and handles heavy traffic without conflicts. More recent evolutions of ARCnet have moved it onto UTP and fiber, but the signaling speed hasn't changed.

ARCnet
- 👍 Inexpensive adapters
- 👍 Works well for small installations
- 👍 Backed by many companies
- 👎 Slower than other options

Despite the facts that Datapoint has not pushed to make its architecture an IEEE standard and has not upgraded its signaling technology, many organizations have settled on ARCnet because it is relatively inexpensive, works well, and can be installed over RG-62 coaxial cable previously installed for IBM 3270-series terminals.

Although Ethernet and Token-Ring are extremely popular today, ARCnet isn't dead. A group called the ARCnet Trade Association is behind a movement to make the ARCnet specification a standard endorsed by the American National Standards Institute. Datapoint is developing a 20-megabit-per-second version of ARCnet called ARCNETplus for release in 1992, and we found over 60 companies marketing ARCnet adapter products for the PC.

Although ARCnet networks perform well for most office environments and ARCnet is relatively inexpensive to install, the 2.5-megabit-per-second signaling rate will create a bottleneck on busy LANs populated with fast PCs. It will be interesting to see whether the introduction of 20-megabit ARCNETplus rejuvenates this aging technology. Until faster ARCnet signaling speeds evolve, we prefer Ethernet for first-time LAN installations.

Wiring Hubs

We've mentioned the star, or home-run, wiring scheme and the term *wiring closet* several times. You can install any type of cabling for any type of LAN adapters in the star physical topology, but you must configure the equipment at the center of the star—the wiring center, also known as the *hub* or *concentrator*—for a specific media-access control scheme like Ethernet, Token-Ring, or ARCnet, and for a specific type of cabling. Because it is literally at the center of the network, the hub is an excellent place to install network monitoring and management software.

At the low end, a hub is typically a simple device that fits in one cabinet and has little flexibility but a reasonable price—assuming you consider $400 to $800 for eight connections reasonable. A hub usually connects only to nodes with one specific type of cabling, although it isn't unusual to have a separate coaxial or fiber-optic cable connector for hub-to-hub links.

A high-end wiring hub has many pieces, parts, and options including a modular cabinet, power supply, and various connection modules. Each module, which is about the size of a hardback book, slides into the cabinet and connects to a data bus. Typically, you can insert modules with different cable connectors into the cabinet and add devices like bridges and routers. You might also select options for a high-end hub, like dual power supplies for reliability. In addition, you can add management modules and even LAN-to-LAN options like an interface to a high-speed, long-distance telephone circuit. A fully loaded, high-end hub able to handle 48 ports with sophisticated management and some fiber-optic connections could top $50,000.

One thing you don't have to worry about is compatibility between brands of hubs and brands of LAN adapter cards. It's perfectly okay to mix cards and wiring centers from different vendors, as long as they use the same cabling and media-access scheme.

As your network grows, the management capabilities of your cabling system become increasingly important. High-end devices called "managed hubs" often have their own microprocessors in the 80186 class and programming contained in ROM. These processors can count packets of data as they fly by, recognize errors in the stream of data, and generate reports. They hold data in a management information base (MIB) until it is polled by a computer running management software. These devices can protect the network by automatically disconnecting nodes generating bad data. In some cases, they can also enhance security by restricting the day of the week and time of day that specific nodes may enter the network. In addition, they can send special messages called *alerts* to computers running network management software.

A signaling and reporting scheme called the Simple Network Management Protocol (SNMP) provides an architecture for network reporting and management which includes agent devices that gather data in wiring centers and other network devices, and also includes computers acting as management stations. The management computers can be PCs, typically running Windows, or they can be other platforms like Sun workstations running Unix. Typically, SNMP uses the TCP/IP network communications protocol set to move alerts and MIB information between the agents and the management computers.

One exception is NetWorth, which runs SNMP over Novell's IPX protocol. While SNMP is still the most popular and widely supported management scheme, IBM's NetVIEW and the Common Management Information Protocol (CMIP) developed by the International Standards Organization are evolving to compete with it.

You usually install high-end wiring centers in a telephone wiring "closet." The term *closet* survives, even though the actual location may be a sizable room with its own power and air conditioning system. Whether your wires come together in a special room, in a real closet, or under someone's desk, we urge you to provide backup power for the wiring center—having backup power for the server and client PCs won't help if the wiring center fails.

In late 1991 some companies, including Novell and Artisoft, made provisions for the installation of wiring hubs in PCs acting as file servers. That's an interesting approach for a small office LAN, but in large LANs it's only practical when you're doing a new installation and can create a combined server room and wiring closet.

Various companies make hubs for Ethernet, Token-Ring, and ARCnet that offer different cabling options. Artisoft markets a low-cost Ethernet hub called Peer-Hub that mounts inside a PC and includes its own management software. A single card able to connect to five nodes costs $399, and you can add cards and connections until you run out of PC expansion slots. David Systems offers a wide selection of simple wiring hubs and sophisticated concentrators ranging from the VolksNet hub, which makes 12 10BaseT UTP Ethernet connections for $995, to the ExpressNET Intelligent Concentrator, which can cost over $10,000 for a sophisticated concentrator able to manage 48 connections.

We think highly of the DEChub 90 series of wiring concentrator products marketed by Digital Equipment Corp. This flexible concentrator system starts out with an $890 backplane that holds a series of plastic-cased modules. The 8-port DECrepeater 90T for 10BaseT wiring carries a $1,540 price tag. Other companies including AT&T and Hewlett-Packard, specialize in Ethernet wiring concentrators.

In the Token-Ring arena, the names of the products change a little. Because IBM calls their Token-Ring wiring center a Multistation Access Unit or MAU, this term is often used when referring to Token-Ring wiring center products. As with Ethernet, you can buy simple Token-Ring wiring hubs or much more complex management systems. For example, a 4-port Local Hub from Madge Networks costs $450, and an 8-port IBM 8228 goes for $630; on the other end, your budget is the only limit. Cabletron, IBM, Madge, SynOptics, Optical Data Systems, Thomas-Conrad, and other vendors make a variety of concentrators for Token-Ring with options that can push the costs over $50,000 for a 48-node concentrator.

At this time, there is no difference between Token-Ring wiring centers for 8- or 16-megabit-per-second Token-Ring; however, IBM and SynOptics have proposed a new standard for 16-megabit Token-Ring UTP wiring centers that would break the wiring into smaller segments electrically by using a retiming circuit on every port. The plan is to make the faster signaling of 16-megabit Token-Ring more viable over twisted-pair wiring, but at an additional cost.

ARCnet wiring centers typically carry much lower price tags than those for Ethernet or Token-Ring. Pure Data, Standard Microsystems, and Thomas-Conrad Corp. are among the dozens of companies selling ARCnet wiring centers. For under $100, you can buy a simple unpowered passive hub that will carry signals to four nodes over about 100 feet of coaxial to each node. Active hubs, available for a variety of cabling, run from $500 devices for eight ports of coaxial cable with a 2,000 foot range to a little over $2,000 for eight fiber-optic cable connections with a range of over a mile.

We recommend a star wiring system for all but the smallest network installations. When you've grown to a couple of dozen nodes, or anytime the network is running "bet the business," mission-critical applications like order taking, we also recommend wiring centers that have management capabilities.

■ Network Operating Systems

We've spent a lot of time discussing cabling and adapters because they are essential to any LAN. You must decide on a cabling architecture right up front, and your initial decisions are expensive to change. But after the initial installation, most of the time you spend working on the network will involve the networking software.

Although it's commonly used, the term *network operating system* can be confusing if you take Microsoft's MS-DOS as a model of an operating system. In many cases, so-called network operating systems run over DOS instead of replacing it, just as other applications do. For clarity, we'll use the term *networking software* instead of network operating system in the rest of this section.

The function of networking software is to set up some computers as hosts, or *servers*, and some computers as clients to those hosts. The servers make three categories of services available to clients across the LAN:

- File sharing

- Printer sharing

- Communications link sharing

Stated simply, PCs and other computers can operate in any or all of four roles: print server, file server, communications server, and client. Various modules from the networking software package running in the networked computers give them the ability to operate in those roles. For the bewildered, if you think that means one PC can act simultaneously as print server, file server, communications server, and client station, you're right!

For the most part, networking software packages are independent of LAN adapters and cabling. You can run any of them over Ethernet, Token-Ring, or ARCnet adapters. However, either the company selling the LAN adapters or the company selling the networking software must supply driver software to link the networking software and the adapters. As described earlier, some hardware companies go to great lengths to promote compatibility, and industry standards like NDIS and ODI go a long way toward marrying LAN adapters to different networking software packages. Check with the company who made the adapters, the networking software vendor, or your dealer to find out if a particular combination of software and hardware will work.

There are two major categories of networking software products: those that use DOS as the file system on the server and those that use some other file system, often Unix or some derivation of it. We'll call these categories DOS and non-DOS products. The non-DOS products include primarily Banyan's VINES, Microsoft's LAN Manager, and Novell's NetWare. Often, these products centralize the file server functions on one computer that runs the non-DOS specialized file-handling system.

LANtastic and other DOS-based products allow any PC on the network to make files, subdirectories, and entire disk drives available for sharing across the network. Each PC acting as a client loads two pieces of software: a *redirector* and a *driver*. The redirector fools DOS into thinking the PC has more hard disk drives attached than it really does. When requests from applications or the command line are sent to those drives, the redirector routes them out to the network. The redirector gets to the network through the driver, a set of software often called a *stack*, that is configured to communicate with the redirector on top and with a specific make and model of LAN adapter on the bottom. Typically, the client software takes less than 45k of RAM, and if you have room, you can load it into high memory with any memory manager.

The network communications software in the stack encapsulates the messages from the redirector into a packet of data containing specific identification and destination information. The network adapter then wraps that packet inside another packet (often referred to as a *frame*) for transmission across the wire. On the receiving side, the LAN adapter frees the communications packet from the transmission frame and passes it up through the stack to the networking software.

Typical formats for network communications packets include Novell's Internetwork Packet Exchange (IPX), the Network Basic Input Output System (NetBIOS) used and expanded by Microsoft and IBM, and the Internet Protocol (IP) originally developed by the U.S. government and now widely used in all sectors. Today, it is possible to load more than one communications protocol stack into a client PC and use servers running networking software packages from different vendors simultaneously.

A computer acting as any type of server has a driver stack to communicate with the LAN adapter and runs other modules that work in the background to receive and act on requests from client PCs. The actions of the server software include checking a user's rights to make the request and passing the request on to the local disk operating system in a format it will understand. DOS-based server software occupies between 50 and 150k of RAM; when it is busy, it takes time from other foreground tasks the processor is performing. In a DOS-based system, any PC on the LAN can load the client software, the server software, or both.

In non-DOS systems, the server software alone can occupy 4 or more megabytes of hard disk space and require 4 to 16 megabytes of RAM to run; however, most non-DOS server systems still provide some way to use the server to run local applications if desired. Various software modules in the server package allow the sharing of hard disk drives, printers, and communications ports. In a small network you might decide to put all three types of services in one PC, but in a larger network you would probably split the services between several PCs, so that each would act as a different type of server.

A networking software package for a DOS-based LAN usually contains one or two diskettes with a couple of programs that give a PC the ability to act as a server, as a client, or as both simultaneously. Many companies package the software in a starter kit with two LAN adapters, cabling, connectors, and a reasonable price tag. Artisoft's LANtastic is priced at $99 per node and the AE-2 LAN adapters are $299, but a two-node starter kit with software for 300 nodes carries a $699 price tag. To add more nodes you simply buy more adapters, and the price per node drops fast.

Typically, DOS-based networking software packages are less expensive for LANs of 2 to 12 PCs; they usually cost about $100 per node for the software alone. The price of non-DOS packages depends on the number of users on a server, so the per-user cost on a small LAN can be several hundred dollars, but can drop to $100 or less on a larger LAN. Prices are tricky to compare because when companies like Artisoft market their DOS-based package in a starter kit with adapter cards, they lower the price so much that it seems as if they're not charging for the software at all.

Before the introduction of MS-DOS 5.0 and the availability of reasonably priced PCs with 386 and 486 processors, there was a significant difference between the capabilities of the two categories of networking software. There were good reasons to employ the ability of non-DOS file systems like Unix to handle very large disk drives and to use memory above 640k; however, DOS 5 can handle disk drives of two gigabytes and has a good memory manager. DOS is still less powerful than Unix or OS/2 because it can't handle multitasking operations, but DOS-based networking software products add a time-shared multiprocessing capability to DOS, and the powerful CPUs in modern PCs don't miss a step, even as they service dozens of clients.

We don't mean to imply that DOS-based networking software products are the equal of non-DOS products in total power or features, because they aren't. The non-DOS products can handle several hundred client PCs on a single server. They also have facilities called *naming services* that make it easy to find and use resources over LANs with hundreds of servers. In addition, they can easily link Macintosh computers into the network, and they provide a solid base for sophisticated "client-server" applications, which split processing tasks between applications running on the client PC and those running on the file server to improve efficiency and reduce network traffic. Nonetheless, DOS-based networking software products like LANtastic can reliably and economically meet the needs of many organizations that have several dozen active client PCs on a network contained within one building or workgroup.

Artisoft's LANtastic is small, fast, easy to use, and relatively inexpensive. The recipient of numerous Editor's Choice awards and an Award for Technical Excellence from *PC Magazine*, LANtastic is popular and well supported. Artisoft also markets an excellent line of LAN adapters and innovative products like their new $595 Central Station Connectivity Processor, which acts as a complete print server and communications server on LANtastic and NetWare LANs. We'll take a closer look at Artisoft's product line in Chapter 2.

- *Operating System Software*
- *Artisoft's Hardware*

CHAPTER 2

Artisoft's Product Line

People who are aware of Artisoft generally know the company sells a network operating system and network adapters, but they may not realize that Artisoft produces an extensive line of interesting and useful products. Only a few of these are specific to the LANtastic operating system; most have applications across many different types of networks.

In this chapter, we'll describe Artisoft's principal operating system and adapters, but we'll also introduce some of their other innovative products.

■ Operating System Software

Increasingly affordable prices have made LANs more attractive to organizations of any size that are interested in sharing data and expensive peripherals and establishing a basic electronic mail system. Because smaller organizations usually do not have an in-house Management Information System manager or technical support, they need simple, functional networking products. Artisoft offers free unlimited technical support to registered end users and dealers and a 30-day, money-back compatibility guarantee on all Artisoft software. They also provide an unconditional 30-day, money-back guarantee and a five-year warranty on hardware.

LANtastic is easy to install, use, administer and expand. It also provides flexibility so that any PC in the network can act as a server, client, or server and client at the same time. Artisoft's target market is small to medium-sized businesses (under 500 employees)—as well as corporate and university workgroups—that need affordable and powerful network solutions. Although high-end networks with dedicated servers might be appropriate for larger LAN installations, many small businesses don't have the budget, technical expertise, or need to support a high-end network.

Artisoft's LANtastic network operating system (NOS), which is the heart of the company's business, comes in a couple of flavors and packages. To order exactly what you need, you have to understand the differences between the products.

The LANtastic software is available in the following forms:

- LANtastic Starter Kits, which come with two Artisoft adapters (either 2Mbps or Ethernet), the LANtastic software, and cables for a two-PC network

- LANtastic software-only kits, which include software that runs only on Artisoft's network adapters

- LANtastic/AI, an adapter-independent version of LANtastic that runs on LAN adapters sold by many companies

- LANtastic for NetWare, a specialized product that provides client PCs with the ability to use LANtastic and Novell NetWare servers simultaneously

- LANtastic Z, a two-PC "zero-slot" serial/parallel/modem version that requires no additional hardware

Standard LANtastic

The standard LANtastic operating system runs only on Artisoft's own network adapter cards. The company markets excellent network adapters that work with other network operating systems like NetWare, so the close tie between the LAN adapters and the software doesn't force you to invest in proprietary hardware that you can't use in any other network, but it gives the LANtastic operating system high throughput and small size.

As Figure 2.1 shows, the LANtastic software comes on a single diskette. People typically buy it in a starter kit that includes a software license for as many as 300 nodes and then add more hardware as they need it. You should budget about $350 per node for the software and hardware, plus the cost of cabling. We cover the installation and operation of LANtastic in detail in Chapters 3, 4, and 5. Anyone who knows DOS commands and isn't afraid to take the cover off a PC can install LANtastic.

You can configure the LANtastic software either by using the built-in menu-driven system or by creating batch files. Although the software can occupy as little as 12 to 15k on a client PC and 40k on a server, in a crunch you can easily unload it from memory.

You can run LANtastic on literally any type of PC with DOS 3.1 or later, and you don't need expanded or extended memory, even in a PC that will be a file server.

The standard installation process creates a "wide open" network in which everyone can access all the resources all the time. But you can and probably should add more levels of security by using password protection on subdirectories and storing special resources such as databases on CD ROM. You can also limit the access of specific individuals to certain times of day or days of the week.

The LANtastic system's audit feature monitors all access to subdirectories and printers, telling you who used a PC, printer, or other shared devices, when it was used, and for how long. It can even let you know if someone tries to enter a directory without the proper assigned rights.

One factor in LANtastic's high throughput is the very efficient disk cache system used on LANtastic servers. Like NetWare and other high-end network operating systems, LANtastic caches both reads and writes. Caching disk writes provides fast throughput, but if the server loses power before the cache writes its contents, you can lose data. It's always wise to equip any network server with an uninterruptable power supply. Because LANtastic has the ability to monitor an RS-232 serial port link to a UPS, it can gracefully shut down a server that's running on battery power. The software notifies anyone logged into the server that it is running on backup power, and then closes open files and limits further activity.

Figure 2.1

The LANtastic starter kit includes two adapter boards, the networking software, a manual, and connecting cable. The package provides everything you need to link two PCs except a screwdriver to install the adapters.

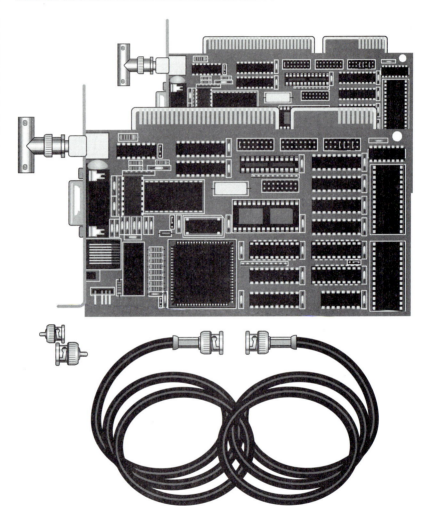

One easy menu lets you use the LANtastic system's Chat feature to exchange messages between two computers, just like a conversation. Another lets you send and save messages to read later. A small memory-resident program called LANPUP alerts you when you receive a new message.

Unlike many other LANs which move print jobs out to only one printer at a time, LANtastic automatically despools to two or more printers simultaneously. LANtastic also lets you create printer definition files to define draft, letter quality, different fonts, banner pages, tab expansion, and other printer options.

A feature called ALONE lets you dedicate a PC to act as a network server. You can start this stand-alone server program with a single command and reset the machine for operation as a client and server just as easily. By side-stepping DOS, ALONE allows true multitasking on a network server, so it can respond to more simultaneous user requests without reducing performance.

A huge body of data, ranging from graphic illustrations to demographic information and including many databases, is available on CD-ROM diskettes from commercial vendors and government agencies. It often makes sound economic sense to share CD ROM drives across the network. While some network operating systems require you to load the Microsoft CD-ROM extensions to DOS on every client PC, LANtastic only requires that you load the software on the computer acting as the CD-ROM server, which saves memory on each client PC.

LANtastic for Windows

Some programs simply run in Windows, while others take advantage of special features of the Windows environment like Dynamic Data Exchange, Microsoft's application-to-application protocol. Artisoft's LANtastic for Windows not only takes advantage of Windows's graphical user interface and DDE, but extends the power of DDE across the network. In effect, LANtastic for Windows is more of an extension to Windows than an add-in to LANtastic.

To run the program, you need LANtastic version 4.0 or later, Microsoft Windows 3.0 or 3.1, and DOS 3.1 or higher. LANtastic for Windows doesn't provide full networking services in itself; it tightly integrates the standard LANtastic network operating system and the features of Windows. A single $299 package of LANtastic for Windows covers the entire network; one purchase takes care of all your networked PCs.

The most exciting advantage of LANtastic for Windows is its ability, through the use of macros, to let programs such as Excel and Word for Windows exchange messages and data through their DDE interfaces. The LANtastic electronic mail program is "DDE-smart": It provides a way for applications to send data in real time between different nodes across the network.

For example, you can create a spreadsheet in Excel, a document or message in Word, or a graphic in Paintbrush and send it to people on the network through a DDE connection to LANtastic's electronic mail software. Typically, you'd create macros in any of the applications to use DDE's Hot Link and Execute mechanisms and to add other information such as addressing. The e-mail software moves the data to addressees described in the information passed by the DDE interface. When the person receiving the electronic mail message clicks on an item in the mail queue, the message addresses DDE and launches the application in which it was originally created.

People who use LANtastic under DOS depend on batch files to control the assignment of network resources to local DOS letters. This system works well, but lacks flexibility, because someone must edit the batch file to make changes. LANtastic for Windows makes the system more flexible by storing your PC's network configuration in a file called WNET.INI, and giving you the option of using that configuration or choosing another. You make the choice simply by dragging the icon representing the resource to the icon representing your PC.

Logging onto a LANtastic file server through LANtastic for Windows is as easy as dragging and dropping an icon designating your machine to another icon depicting the server. The same holds true for connections to shared CD-ROM drives, printers, plotters, and any other shared resources.

You can choose from a variety of icons to designate available network resources. As Figure 2.2 shows, you can assign separate icons to your dot-matrix and laser printers. You can also show icons depicting $5^1/4$-inch, $3^1/2$-inch, hard-disk, and CD-ROM drives. The user or network manager also has the option of examining server activity and throughput in either a text or a graphical format.

Figure 2.2

The LANtastic for Windows product gives the standard LANtastic software the ability to run as a real Windows program. You can create icons for special purposes and exchange data with other true Windows applications.

While LANtastic for Windows is just a utility program, it gives LANtastic all the capabilities of a "real" Windows application without forcing you to buy a completely different version of the operating system. You enjoy the Windows visual interface without sacrificing assured compatibility with the proven code of the network operating system.

LANtastic/AI

LANtastic's tight link between the program and the network adapters offers several advantages, including high speed and small memory requirements; however, there are times when you'll want the flexibility to choose different hardware or to link to network operating systems other than the standard version of LANtastic. To meet this need Artisoft markets LANtastic/AI, a version of the program that can run over the NetBIOS interface provided for some specific network adapters from other companies. LANtastic/AI is available for $99 per user or $2,499 for a network of up to 300 users.

Let's say you have an operational LANtastic network using the standard version of LANtastic and Artisoft's Ethernet adapters in a department that is undergoing consolidation. As a result of the consolidation, you need to add three computers already equipped with the popular Western Digital 8013 Ethernet Adapters (now sold by Standard Microsystems) to the network. You don't have to throw out the perfectly good Western Digital adapters to bring those PCs into the LANtastic LAN. You simply load Western Digital's NetBIOS software from the diskette that came with the adapters (or you can download the latest version from Standard Microsystem's bulletin board), and load a copy of LANtastic/AI on the same machine. All the machines on the network will interoperate, whether they're using standard LANtastic or LANtastic/AI.

The LANtastic/AI software also provides a way to use the LANtastic operating system over an existing hardware installation of ARCnet or Token-Ring adapters. The NetBIOS software layer insulates between the network hardware and the LANtastic software.

LANtastic/AI offers all the operational features of regular LANtastic, but the NetBIOS layer of software for the LAN adapter will probably use more memory than Artisoft hardware over Artisoft software. Also, the nodes using these software layers will probably show slightly slower throughput under benchmark tests, but most users won't see a major difference.

Unfortunately, all implementations of NetBIOS don't work together, so LANtastic/AI won't work with all adapters and NetBIOS programs. Some combinations might work together, but not with standard LANtastic and Artisoft adapters. You should check with Artisoft to be sure the software and hardware you plan to use are compatible. It's also a good idea to have the latest version of the NetBIOS program for the adapter you want to use.

LANtastic for NetWare

Like LANtastic/AI, LANtastic for NetWare runs on top of a special implementation of NetBIOS. In this case, LANtastic for NetWare runs over Novell's NetBIOS emulation program, allowing a PC to act as a client to both a

NetWare server and a LANtastic server at the same time (see Figure 2.3). Because LANtastic/AI is insulated from the network adapters by Novell's software, it will run over any LAN adapters NetWare can use. At $499 per network, LANtastic for NetWare is a bargain add-in product.

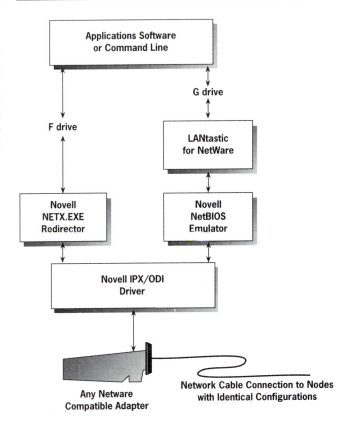

Figure 2.3

The LANtastic for NetWare software loads along with Novell's NETx redirection software and runs over Novell's NetBIOS emulation program. The Novell driver software (either adapter-specific IPX or ODI) moves data to and from the adapter.

If you have both NetWare and LANtastic for NetWare loaded on a client PC you might see the Novell file server as the DOS F drive and the LANtastic file server as the DOS H drive. Under this setup you can copy from one virtual drive to another and run applications using one or both networked drives. Similarly, a printer on the Novell server might be LPT2, while a printer shared through LANtastic might be mapped as LPT3. Note that many older applications don't include an option to address LPT3, so you must carefully plan how you will share resources.

Peer-to-peer networking allows any machine to act as a server or a workstation, affording independence from a dedicated server. Novell users can also add printers—up to five per PC—to any computer on the network and share them with others. In addition, LANtastic provides an easy way to add CD-ROM sharing to NetWare. And none of these activities interferes with the users' connection to Novell's dedicated server.

There are three drawbacks to LANtastic for NetWare. First, Novell's NetBIOS emulator is very large—it takes nearly as much memory as the whole LANtastic server software module—so the combination of LANtastic and NetWare occupies 60k or more of memory. Second, someone must administer totally separate network setup and management schemes for NetWare and LANtastic. Finally, Novell's NetBIOS is not compatible with Artisoft's, so PCs running LANtastic for NetWare cannot use the services of servers running regular LANtastic or LANtastic/AI. Servers or clients running LANtastic for NetWare can only interact with each other, not with standard LANtastic nodes. Despite these limitations, which make it a bit ponderous, LANtastic for NetWare works very well. On the whole, it is an inexpensive way to add impressive flexibility to your NetWare installation.

LANtastic Z

LANtastic Z is a $125 software and hardware product that lets you connect two PCs through their serial or parallel ports—the same ports usually used to connect printers and modems. Although these ports don't provide the high throughput of an Ethernet adapter, this system is fast enough for file transfers and many other applications, and it's easy to install. If you only need to link two PCs, LANtastic Z provides an inexpensive and efficient alternative to LAN adapters. The product is particularly good for linking laptop and desktop computers.

While many "serial" or "zero-slot" LANs are glorified file-transfer programs that tie up your PCs while data is going back and forth, the LANtastic Z software creates a true network with multitasking and virtual drives. You can expect actual throughput of 20 to 40kbps over parallel port connections and 8 to 10kbps over serial port connections.

Because it works through a serial port, you can use the LANtastic Z program across a telephone modem link. The system is slow because throughput over the modem drops to a few kilobits per second, but it's effective if you limit the amount of data you transfer. We recommend high-speed V.32bis modems with V.42bis data compression for this role.

The LANtastic Z kit, shown in Figure 2.4, comes with LANtastic NOS software on both $5^{1}/_{4}$-inch and $3^{1}/_{2}$-inch disks, a step-by-step LANtastic NOS user's manual, a 25-foot serial cable, and an 18-foot parallel cable. All you have to do is connect your two PCs with one of the cables, install the software, and you're up and running.

Figure 2.4

The LANtastic Z package includes everything you need to connect two PCs using either their serial or parallel ports. The parallel port connection is faster, but many machines don't have a spare parallel port. To install the system you simply connect either of the preconfigured cables and load the software.

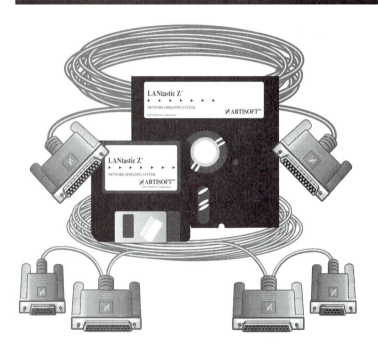

ArtiCom

ArtiCom is a memory-resident program that uses less than 6k of RAM and no additional hardware to dial out from your LANs, and gives any station on the network access to any modem across the network. The $399 ArtiCom package has the user-friendly interface of LANtastic, although it works on most NetBIOS-compatible systems. The system includes a communication program with terminal emulation, dialing directory, multiple upload and download protocols, as well as extensive security features. You can also use ArtiCom with most popular PC communications software.

Any PC on the network can be an ArtiCom workstation, server, or both. On the PC acting as an ArtiCom asynchronous communications server, modem communication on the LAN is as routine as network printing; however, ArtiCom is also designed for use with plotters, serial printers, or any other bidirectional peripheral devices on a serial port.

The Network Eye

The Network Eye (TNE) is what we call a "network remote control product," in contrast to modem remote control products, which operate more slowly, but over longer distances. With TNE, you can remotely view the screens and control the keyboards of every PC in your network, or allow those computers to simultaneously view and control your PC. TNE is a great classroom training product because it lets you view multiple remote screens at the same time as your local screen. The product costs only $199 for a network-wide license, and works across LANtastic or practically any NetBIOS network.

You can pop-up The Network Eye program, establish connections to other PCs, and view and control their screens—switching between windows with a keystroke—all without leaving your desk. As Figure 2.5 illustrates, each remote screen appears on your local screen in a pop-up window. You can size one window to take up the whole screen, or view up to 32 screens at once. With TNE, one person can run hundreds of programs at once on hundreds of remote PCs, and the program on each PC will continue running even after The Network Eye software connection with that PC is broken.

Figure 2.5

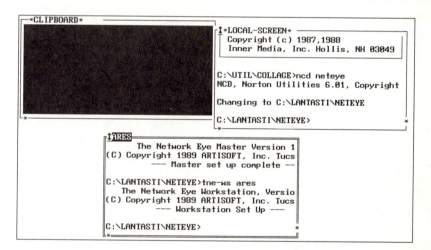

The Network Eye allows you to remotely control PCs from across the network. The screen of each remotely controlled computer shows up in a separate window on the controlling machine's screen, and the windows can be sized to provide different degrees of detail.

Using TNE, you can assist or train other users on their own PCs without leaving your computer. Teachers can share control of computers with students, monitoring their work and interacting without having to visit each individual workstation. Teachers can also broadcast their own screens, so students can see each keystroke an instructor makes without having to peer over each other's shoulders or strain to make out an overhead projection.

Many network operating systems provide no access to modem, fax, and plotter servers. TNE overcomes this limitation. When you use The Network Eye software, configuring a modem or fax board in a single computer makes it accessible to anyone on the network, and TNE also gives users direct access to plotters attached to remote workstations.

In addition, TNE lets you protect your PC from unwanted, unauthorized monitoring and control by displaying on-screen notification whenever someone is monitoring your computer.

■ Artisoft's Hardware

Although Artisoft's operating system software and network hardware are designed to work together, it is important to note that Artisoft's hardware is not dedicated to LANtastic. Except for the older two-megabit-per-second LAN adapter, the hardware can operate with networking products offered by many other companies including Banyan, Microsoft, and Novell.

Two-Megabit LAN Adapters

You can divide Artisoft's LAN adapters roughly into those that support the IEEE 802.3 specifications for Ethernet-like systems and those that use a proprietary signaling scheme. Using AT&T telephone-grade cable in a daisy-chain configuration, the LANtastic 2Mbps and 2Mbps micro channel adapters can connect up to 300 feet with as many as 32 nodes per cable segment. If you use the higher grade shielded cable sold by Artisoft, you can stretch the distance to 1,500 feet per network.

Both the Micro Channel Architecture (MCA) and Industry Standard Architecture (ISA) adapters include a 10Mhz coprocessor and 32k of on-board, dual-ported RAM. Artisoft's implementation of NetBIOS is loaded into and executed within the adapters, which cuts the memory requirements of NetBIOS on a PC's base RAM to just 2k, and off-loads network processing onto the adapter.

The cards are easy to install and use inexpensive dual twisted-pair cable. They are available in starter kits and individually with prices ranging from $199 for the ISA bus device to $699 for the MCA adapter.

Real 802.3 LAN Adapters

Designed to be a low-cost Ethernet solution, the $199 Artisoft AE-1/T Ethernet adapter uses the unshielded twisted-pair wire of the 10Base-T wiring scheme. The AE-1/T, shown in Figure 2.6, is an 8-bit adapter that is compatible with the NE1000 adapters first sold by Novell and now sold by Eagle Technology.

The Artisoft AE-2 Ethernet adapter is a highly capable adapter for IEEE standard 802.3 thin Ethernet and other cabling schemes that use the AUI port. The AE-2 intelligent network interface card configures itself, finding its own optimum settings; it adapts to the amount of memory on board and recognizes whether it is inserted in an 8- or a 16-bit slot. Artisoft's AE-2/T is a nearly identical adapter that is equipped with a transceiver for 10Base-T unshielded twisted-pair wiring. The AE-2 and AE-2/T come in an ISA version for $299 and in an MCA version for $399. Figure 2.7 shows both adapters.

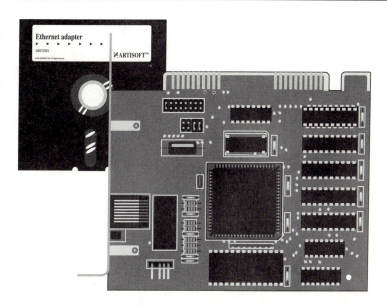

Figure 2.6

The AE-1/T adapter provides low cost but high-quality networking. You would typically use this 8-bit adapter in a PC acting as a client, but not as a server. It works with a wide variety of network operating systems in the 10Base-T cabling system.

The AE-2 and AE-2/T adapters clone the operation of the popular NE2000 adapters originally sold by Novell and now by Eagle Technology. In a diskless workstation, the AE-2 or AE-2/T adapter allows you to boot your computer across the network with Artisoft's programmable boot-ROM chips.

While it works like an NE2000 with NetWare and other network operating systems, the AE-2 or AE-2/T extends the capabilities of the NE2000 by providing additional IRQ (interrupt request) lines so it won't conflict with other expansion equipment. You can set up the AE-2 or AE-2/T to use IRQs 2, 3, 4, 5, 6, 7, 10, and 15; those above 5 are particularly useful in crowded PCs.

The Artisoft AE-3 Ethernet adapter supports three kinds of Ethernet cabling: thin, thick, and twisted-pair. This flexibility allows you to use a $349 AE-3 anywhere in your organization so you can be ready to join the migration to unshielded twisted-pair wiring. Aside from its wiring capabilities, the AE-3 offers the same NE-2000 clone operation, extended IRQ, and remote booting capabilities of the AE-2 family.

Figure 2.7

The Artisoft AE-2 and AE-2/T adapters provide high throughput and excellent reliability. You can use them in any networked PC with many different network operating systems.

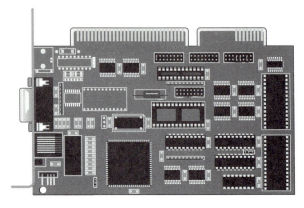

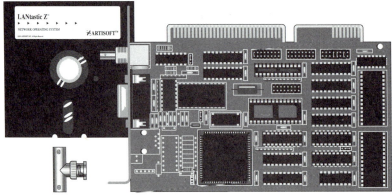

Peer-Hub

The IEEE 10Base-T specification calls for a star-configured network cabling system using unshielded twisted-pair wire. The star configuration is extremely reliable, since one interruption in the wiring doesn't take down the entire network, and the wiring hub is the logical point for network troubleshooting and management software; however, if you must put a separate processor in the wiring hub to run the management software, you increase its price significantly. To resolve this dilemma, Artisoft developed a 10Base-T wiring hub called Artisoft Peer-Hub that turns any PC into a managed wiring center in addition to its other tasks.

The $399 Peer-Hub concentrator, shown in Figure 2.8, works with any standard 10Base-T network and networking software, not just with Artisoft's products. It provides connections for five nodes, and you can add additional Peer-Hubs to increase the size of the network. With the addition of an AE-3 adapter, the Peer-Hub will connect a coaxial cable segment into the 10Base-T network without expensive bridging equipment.

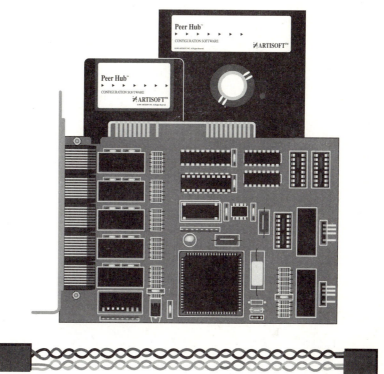

Figure 2.8

The Artisoft Peer-Hub slides into an expansion slot in any networked PC. The PC hosting this wiring hub should be at the geographical center of your office. A separate wire connects the Peer-Hub to each network node. For increased capacity, you can add more Peer-Hubs to the PC.

The Peer-Hub software running in the host PC displays the status of all ports and allows you to activate or disable each port individually. The software can either sound an alarm when the status of a port changes, or audit status changes to disk for later review.

On-board memory in the Peer-Hub concentrator saves your network configuration. If you have a power outage, your host PC can reconfigure the network because the Peer-Hub concentrator's programmable read-only memory remembers each port's name, physical and wiring location, and status.

Artisoft's $99 AUI Interface Kit combined with its Peer-Hub concentrator provide an internal bridge between 10BASE-T and coax Ethernet networks. The AUI Interface Kit includes two pulse transformer chips and an AUI interface cable. Installation is as easy as plugging the two transformer chips and the AUI interface cable into the Peer-Hub concentrator. You can then install a thin or thick coax Ethernet segment connected to an AE-3

Ethernet adapter in the same computer and marry all of the cabling segments. The AUI Interface Kit creates a bridge between the 10Base-T network on the hub and the coax Ethernet segment attached to the AE-3 Ethernet adapter.

In addition to the AUI connection, the Peer-Hub concentrator also has two other internal connectors designed to connect with other Artisoft products: One provides an internal 10Base-T connection to Artisoft's AE-1/T, AE-2/T, or AE-3 Ethernet adapters without using one of the five external RJ45 ports, while the others link multiple Peer-Hub concentrators together—up to four per PC.

Central Station

Artisoft calls Central Station, shown in Figure 2.9, a "connectivity processor." Pay close attention here, because this $595 device can play so many roles, it's easy to become confused. First, Central Station is a docking station in the purest sense—it connects to the parallel port of any PC and gives that machine a full complement of one parallel and two serial ports, along with a third serial port for configuration management and future features. This is particularly useful for expanding the capabilities of laptop computers.

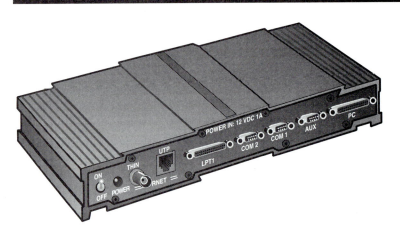

Figure 2.9

The Artisoft Central Station can be many things to many people. It acts as an external LAN adapter, a docking port for laptops, a stand-alone network access server, a print server, and a modem server. Central Station can do its tricks on both LANtastic and NetWare.

Second, Central Station is an external LAN adapter that functions like a Xircom external adapter, providing any attached PC with a high-quality Ethernet connection. Central Station has its own internal adapter—Artisoft's AE-3 circuitry—which emulates a Novell NE-2000 and includes both thin coax and 10Base-T RJ45 connectors.

Third, with the addition of a modem, Central Station becomes an access server. When the device is in this mode, people can load a modified version of the LANtastic networking software on their laptops, run applications and environments like Windows locally, dial into the LAN Central Station and have full access to all networked drives.

A slightly different twist for this flexible product allows a caller to remotely control the Central Station and run applications on the device's own NEC V50 processor and 520k of RAM. People on the network can also dial out through a modem attached to Central Station, so it acts as an asynchronous communications server.

Last, but certainly not least, Central Station can act as a print server all by itself. You can attach a printer to Central Station and allow any other PC to send it print jobs across the LAN. When it's acting in the remote control and print server roles, Central Station doesn't need a PC attached. You can be on the road with your only PC tucked into your briefcase and Central Station will stay behind and perform all its network server duties!

Central Station is a complete external CPU in a 2-inch by 12-inch by 5 ½-inch box. It has its own power supply and on-board programming that handles input/output tasks, particularly for laptop and notebook computers—even when they aren't present. On its front panel, Central Station has LEDs that monitor and display connections with the PC, parallel and serial ports, as well as the network. Although it comes from Artisoft, Central Station isn't limited to LANtastic networks. You can add software that let it work on NetWare too.

Artisoft calls software for Central Station StationWare. The StationWare Dial-Up LANtastic Connection allows you to dial into your existing LANtastic network through a modem. By attaching a modem to one of Central Station's serial ports and running the StationWare software, you can connect remote PC's to your network via modems, and the remote computers will operate as fully functioning network nodes. A similar package, the Dial-Up NetWare Connection, provides the same capabilities on a Novell NetWare network.

The LANtastic Print Server package provides support for making serial and/or parallel printers attached to Central Station available to the LANtastic network for printing, even without a computer connected to the PC port. Through the use of a TSR, a remote PC can control and monitor the printers attached to Central Station. The NetWare Print Server package provides the same kind of support on a Novell NetWare network.

Sounding Board and the ArtiSound Recorder

Artisoft has packaged an award-winning piece of hardware and a new and unique piece of software into a product that brings the world of sound to any OLE-compliant Windows program. Not only will this product work with any networking hardware or software, it doesn't even specifically require a network.

Artisoft's Sounding Board and ArtiSound Recorder system allow you to record sounds from a variety of sources and play them back or to play any prerecorded sound file in Windows-WAVE and PCM formats. Through the ArtiSound Recorder software you can link the sounds to spreadsheets, word processing program documents, electronic mail messages, and any other products created by programs compatible with Microsoft Window's OLE (Object Linking and Embedding) protocol.

The Sounding Board and ArtiSound Recorder package retails for $99 for an ISA card and $199 for an MCA package. Winner of the 1990 PC Magazine Technical Excellence Award, the Artisoft Sounding Board is an 8-bit adapter that digitizes and saves recorded voice or sound to disk. The Artisoft Sounding Board package includes a telephone-style handset that provides excellent sound clarity; audio in and out jacks for use in connecting the Sounding Board to external sound components such as CD players, tape recorders, and amplifiers; and the new ArtiSound software program.

In short, the ArtiSound Recorder application is an OLE server. With it, you can perform simple tasks such as playing and recording voice messages, as well as more complex tasks like interconnecting and implanting sounds into a client application. You can add background music to your written proposals, explain spreadsheet expenditures, leave greetings, or simply create voice mail messages. You can also use the ArtiSound program in conjunction with Sounding Board and a program like Microsoft's PowerPoint to create slide shows and demonstrations using your own voice, which allows you to present the material repeatedly without even being present.

Support for the Microsoft Windows OLE protocol is a powerful feature of the ArtiSound program. Using the ArtiSound menu, it's easy to embed and link the digitized sound bites into a Windows application as objects. You simply record a message or sound, and then cut and paste the icon where you want it in the desired application. The recorded message will appear as an icon within the selected application. When you or someone else later views the file, a click on the embedded icon will launch ArtiSound (see Figure 2.10) and replay the recorded message.

To take advantage of the ArtiSound Recorder's OLE support, you must run Microsoft Windows version 3.1 in each PC on your "sound" network, or purchase the multimedia extensions and add them to your Windows 3.0 application. Of course, you must also install a communications board such as the Artisoft Sounding Board, but if you already have a Creative Labs Sound Blaster, the ArtiSound software will work with it too.

The drawback to digitizing anything rich in content like sound or video is that the process results in large files. In this case, the Sounding Board uses about 8k of disk space per second of recorded voice. Artisoft's LANtastic local area network operating system has some ability to offset the problem of size when you send e-mail messages across a LAN: LANtastic's electronic mail application allows you to compress recorded messages created with ArtiSound with a 2:1 ratio, which helps cut down on the traffic running through your network cable.

Figure 2.10

The graphical interface of the ArtiSound menu makes it easy to record and play back sound. The control panel works like a simple tape recorder, and you can easily attach recordings to any document, electronic mail message, or spreadsheet.

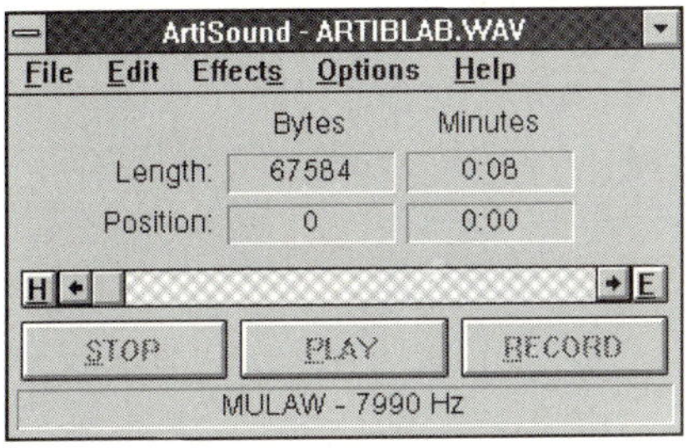

The Artisound Recorder not only lets you record digitized sound, it allows you to change recorded messages for fun and effect. You can increase or decrease volume, create an echo, or play the recorded message in reverse. For example, you can stress a particular word or phrase by increasing the volume on it. The ArtiSound program also includes a feature called Auto Replay that lets you repeat a sound or message indefinitely, thus eliminating the need for long recordings that use a lot of disk space.

You can use the ArtiSound Recorder to play, record, and convert between several digital audio formats, so you can accommodate several types of equipment, operating systems, or applications. For example, using the ArtiSound Recorder application, you can convert Windows WAVE (wave form audio files, or .WAV) files to Artisoft Sounding Board MULAW audio file format. You can also convert any 8, 11, 22, or 44kHz PCM (pulse code modulation) file formats—used by Sound Blaster and others—to Artisoft ArtiSound MULAW formats, and vice versa.

The Artisoft Recorder conversion software is easy to use and works like the document import/export capability built into many popular word processors such as Word or WordPerfect. You simply open a file, and the software automatically determines the format and converts the file. You can save a file in any of the supported formats just as easily.

The relatively low price of the Artisoft Sounding Board and ArtiSound Recorder package makes it practical to put one in every machine in a workgroup or organization. The effect of embedded sound on presentations and documents is dramatic, and voice e-mail messages are very effective. Support for OLE, LANtastic, and other electronic mail programs, and for different audio file formats make this product easy to use and incorporate into any system.

ArtiScribe for the Sounding Board

Artisoft's ArtiScribe is an add-on software package that doesn't need Windows. It turns the Sounding Board into a digital dictation system that allows users to dictate and transcribe spoken messages across a network. ArtiScribe works on LANtastic, Novell's NetWare, and any network operating system that runs on top of DOS.

ArtiScribe allows both the recording (dictation) process and the playback (transcription) process to take place in the background, so the foreground application remains fully accessible during these functions. The transcription process can even be controlled by voice commands spoken into the microphone of the headset, allowing hands-free operation and uninterrupted use of the main application program (typically a word processor for creating a transcribed document).

ArtiScribe's core software is the RAM-resident control pad. The control pad can be popped up over any text-mode DOS application at the press of a key, and used to record and play back voice files. The person creating the piece can attach a description before saving it in the ArtiScribe dictation repository. The control pad also provides users with the ability to see, hear, sort, and select from the set of all voice files accessible to them in the repository.

- *Taking an Inventory*
- *Defining Your Requirements*
- *Core Planning Issues*
- *Additional Planning Factors*

CHAPTER 3

Planning Your Network

The rule of the four Ps—Planning Precludes Poor Performance—should govern the early phase of every network installation. A little up-front work can save weeks of corrections and additions. In many cases we literally mean a "little" planning. Sometimes ten minutes of investigation is all you need, but any network with a dozen or more PCs will require you to spend a couple of hours and prepare a couple of pages of information before you place your first order for equipment and wiring.

The planning process has two critical components: the inventory and the statement of requirements. With these two packages of information in hand, you can plan the kind of server, wiring, memory, and client PC configurations you need.

■ Taking an Inventory

Before you start any network installation, you need a detailed inventory of the PCs and printers that will be in the network. Figure 3.1 is an inventory sheet that you should prepare for every networked PC.

Note that the inventory sheet asks for a great deal of information on the devices inside of and attached to each PC. Since each PC in a LANtastic network is capable of sharing all its resources with other PCs across the network, you need a detailed view of the available devices. Every piece of information is potentially valuable.

For example, you might not think the type of video adapter in a PC has anything to do with its networking capabilities, but information about the video adapter is important for several reasons. First, during installation you decide what benefits you'd realize from memory management software that loads network drivers above the portion of each PC's memory used by typical DOS applications. Some video adapters take up a great deal of the potentially free memory above 640k, leaving little room for pieces of the network operating system in that high memory, so you need to know what kind of adapter each PC has to make an informed decision about memory management software.

Second, it is often useful to remotely control a PC across a LAN network using a product like Artisoft's Network Eye, or across a telephone line using a modem remote control program like Norton-Lambert's Close-Up or Co/Session from Triton Technologies. These programs, which let you see and control what is happening on the client computer, are useful for training people on applications, troubleshooting problems, and configuring workstations. However, you often can't control a PC that has one type of video from a PC that has a different type, so it's important to know what kind of video board is in every PC.

HINT. *You should keep your inventory on a PC-by-PC basis, categorized by department, but you'll also find a cross index by type of PC valuable. A simple database program will let you sort on any factor and generate reports. We find that printed reports kept in a three-ring binder provide fast reference. Remember, you might not be able to access the server holding the database you need if the network is down!*

Figure 3.1

This detailed questionnaire helps you gather the information you need to plan the sharing of the network's printers, hard drives, and other resources. Information on the number of slots, memory address, and interrupt request (IRQ) lines available and in use is important when you're planning what adapters to buy and how to configure the networking software.

Network Survey Form   Date:
Name of this machine's primary user:
Extension number and department:
Brand name on the PC:
Brand name and model on the monitor:
If a printer is attached, brand name and model:
Is the printer connected via serial or parallel?
If a modem is attached, brand name and model:
    Speed:
    Internal or external modem?
What is the primary application used at the PC?
How many serial ports in this machine?
    COM1: 9 or 25 pin?
    COM2: 9 or 25 pin?
What is attached to the serial ports?
    COM1:
    COM2:
How many parallel ports?
How many free expansion slots?
Type of CPU: Speed:
Type of BIOS: Date:
Separate mouse board?
What size floppy disk drives?
    $5^{1}/_{4}$ Density?
    $3^{1}/_{2}$ Density?

What size hard disk drive?
Amount of free disk space:
How much total memory reported?
What is reported in memory? (Device drivers and TSRs?)
Other devices:
How could this PC be attached to a network cable?
Unshielded twisted-pair available?
Could we run coax to this location?

    A number of programs can provide you with the information you need to complete the inventory sheet. System Sleuth from Dariana Technology Group is a wonderful aid for anyone who has to install a LAN adapter in an already crowded PC. The program surveys the PC and provides information on all aspects of the system from the disk drives to the memory map, but its unique feature is the ability to scan for active and inactive IRQ locations and to help you determine where you can squeeze in a LAN card or other expansion device.

System Sleuth provides an excellent picture of the PC's interrupts, I/O port tables and device-driver tables. It can definitely help you with your survey.

Finding the inventory sheets when you need them is just as important as completing them in the first place. Keep the sheets someplace where you can always find them, and be sure to update them for every change. Although we suggest using a three-ring binder to hold all the inventory sheets, we've also seen successful installations in which each PC's inventory sheet was kept in an envelope taped to its side.

■ Defining Your Requirements

What do you and the other people who will use the network want it to do? Figure 3.2 provides a set of questions you can use to define your expectations and requirements. You might have to research some questions such as those concerning the amount of RAM required by TSRs, but such information is necessary. Despite the widespread use of memory management software, "RAM cram" is still a major problem in PCs, and you need to keep a close watch on the amount of free RAM below 640k in each machine.

HINT. *People often don't know what they want from a network before it's installed, and will sometimes suffer in silence once it's in because they think their problem is silly or their own fault. Talk to the people using the network frequently; many of their minor problems will be easy to solve.*

■ Core Planning Issues

Once you know what you have on hand and what you want to accomplish, you can begin looking at some specific planning issues. Three vital factors require up-front decisions that you'll probably have to live with for a long time:

- Physical configuration (adapters and cabling)
- Server(s)
- Printers

Crossing Adapters and Cabling

In the first chapter we described the various types of LAN adapters from which you can choose. If you have existing adapters and cabling, you should estimate the cost of staying with that system. If you have nothing, your primary concern will be whether you have existing unshielded twisted-pair wiring in the walls that conforms to the 10BaseT specifications and terminates in a central wiring closet. Note that Artisoft's AE-3 adapter can work with either unshielded twisted-pair wire in a 10BaseT star wiring arrangement or with thin Ethernet cable in a station-to-station wiring scheme, so if you use this adapter you have room for change in the future.

Figure 3.2

The answers to these questions will help you plan project needs for hard disk space, remote access connections, cabling, and other requirements.

We want to help you get the most value from your computer system. Please answer these few questions so we can give you enough resources to meet your needs.

Name:
Department and telephone extension:

How many sheets of paper do you print in an average week? If the number varies widely from week to week, please give a range:

Please list the programs you use. If you aren't sure of a program's name, enter its function:

Do you have to exchange files on a floppy disk or by some other means with anyone?   If so, how often and who is the other person(s)?

Are there files you need to see or use on any other PC within the organization? Please explain:

Do you ever have to move to someone else's PC to do a job? If so, what job and why do you have to move?

Are there some jobs you would like to be able to do on your computer, but can't? Please explain:

Do you know of any plans to change the location of your desk or computer in the near future?

You must look carefully at the quality of the cable used in any installation, old or new. It seems that every international and national organization even remotely concerned with networking has issued standards or guidelines for LAN cabling. The National Electrical Code describes various types of cables and the materials used in them, and IBM has its own family of cable specifications. In addition, the Electronic Industries Association/Telecommunications Industry Association (EIA/TIA) has issued EIA/TIA 568 and 569 standards for technical performance, and has an active program to extend their requirements. The IEEE also includes minimal cable requirements in their 802.3 and 802.5 specifications for Ethernet and Token-Ring systems.

HINT. *The star wiring configuration used in 10BaseT systems is generally more reliable than thin Ethernet cable installed in a station-by-station wiring scheme, simply because the long cable has so many potential points of failure. We strongly recommend you choose a star wiring configuration of coaxial or unshielded twisted-pair wiring for "bet-the-business" network applications.*

The Underwriters Laboratory focuses on safety standards, but the UL folks expanded their certification program to evaluate twisted-pair LAN cables for performance according to IBM and EIA/TIA performance specifications as well as National Electrical Code safety specifications. The program UL has established to mark shielded and unshielded twisted-pair LAN cables should simplify the complex task of making sure the materials used in the installation are up to specification.

The UL markings range from Level I through Level V. IBM's cable specifications range from Type 1 through Type 9 while the EIA/TIA has proposed categories of 1 through 5. It's easy to become confused by the similarly numbered levels, types, and categories: The IBM type specifications include descriptions of the configuration of each cable type, such as two pairs of 22 AWG shielded non-plenum cable. The UL level markings deal with performance and safety, but don't specify the details such as shielded or unshielded wire included in the IBM specifications. Like the UL levels, the emerging EIA/TIA categories will focus on performance.

Note that simply using the right materials doesn't guarantee that an installation meets performance specifications. Many factors, including how much the wire is untwisted before it reaches a terminal block, the type of terminal block, the electrical noise in various frequency bands, and the near-end crosstalk (NEXT) caused by wires in proximity to each other determine the quality of the total installation. You can get a good reliable start on a installation by using the correct cable, however.

Cables certified with UL Level I and II markings meet safety requirements, but the lower-level markings don't tell you much about performance. The primary difference between cables with Levels III, IV, and V UL markings is in the maximum amount of attenuation and crosstalk allowed in different frequency bands. Cables with higher UL number markings have lower attenuation and crosstalk and will typically allow higher practical signaling speeds through the wiring system. The crosstalk and attenuation have to get pretty bad before they slow the network noticeably, but these factors are the major cause of annoying network problems that seem to come and go mysteriously.

The UL certification marking level isn't all you need to know about a cable—you must provide other specifics to define its exact configuration. The UL certification program also begs the question, "What is the minimum UL certification level marking I need for the cables in my installation?" The answer is that UL Level III is probably good enough for all of today's installations, but if you someday plan to run 100 megabits per second over your copper cable system, price cables with higher certification levels to see if improved performance in the future is worth an investment today.

Our advice about fiber-optic cabling is clear and conservative. First, if you have a large installation or a noisy electrical environment like a manufacturing plant, always use fiber between wiring closets in the building and around the campus regardless of what cabling you run between the wiring closets and the desktops. Second, if you are planning a new building or doing a major rewiring and decide to install unshielded twisted-pair wire, pull as much fiber with it as you can afford and let the fiber sit dark and unused in the walls until the price of the adapters comes into reach. If you install coaxial cable or shielded twisted-pair wiring to each desktop, it isn't necessary to back it up with fiber.

In any case, we recommend using a wiring contractor or electrician who specializes in networking as at least a consultant for the work. Many large organizations supply in-house labor—people who know where the conduits and access points are—but to do the job properly you need some expertise.

Server Requirements

You must make several decisions about the PCs that will act as servers in your network: What type of CPU to use in each server, how much memory to install, whether to use the server for other tasks, and how much hard disk storage space to provide.

One primary advantage of LANtastic over other network operating systems (in addition to its simplicity and reasonable cost) is its ability to make any PC on the network act as a server while still running application programs. Under LANtastic, any PC can make its hard disk drives, printers, modems, CD-ROM drives, and other devices available to PCs across the network. In an extreme case, any single client PC can use dozens of servers. The hard disk drives of servers appear as different DOS disk drive letters to each client. Note, however, that handling requests for service from client PCs as a background task takes up space on a server's hard disk drive and slows the foreground processing of application programs.

You can create a network in which one or many PCs act as servers and run application programs simultaneously, or you can dedicate one or more PCs to the server role. Acting as a server creates a lot of overhead, so be sure any machine working in both roles simultaneously has enough processing power and storage space for both tasks.

It's impossible to specify what computer would be sufficiently powerful and the most economical as a server in every installation. The amount of work done at each client PC, the amount of data stored on the file server, and the load any particular application places on the server all vary widely. Nonetheless, we'll try to give you some rough rules of thumb.

Not all servers are file servers. Under LANtastic you can set up some PCs as only print servers or communications servers. File server actions create the most overhead on a PC because they occupy the PC's processor for many milliseconds at a time. A very busy print server will also bog down if it is feeding a slow printer, but the large amount of memory available in modern printers usually speeds the throughput of print jobs.

If you're creating a file server that will be used by more than 2 or 3 client PCs and will run a low-demand application like a lightly used DOS-based word processor at the same time, that server will need a processor in at least the 80386SX 20MHz class. If you want to support 4 to 12 client PCs with file service from the same machine, its processor will have to be in at least the 80386DX 33MHz class. If the PC is going to run a more demanding application, you will either need to moderate the client stations' loads or provide a powerful processor in the 80486 33MHz or better class. We also recommend using a top-end machine for a file server if you plan to support a dozen or more clients.

HINT. *Don't scrimp on the hard disk drives for a PC that will act as a file server. Buy the biggest and fastest drive(s) you can afford. You'll always find uses for the storage space, and a fast drive is more important to network performance than a fast processor.*

Some applications that you might not immediately classify as demanding can slow the network operation on a shared-use file server simply because they involve a lot of keystrokes. Keystrokes create hardware interrupts that can delay network processing, so even if the application on the shared server is a simple word processing program, try to assign that machine to someone who doesn't pound the keyboard all day. Similarly, we recommend you avoid using a computer running Microsoft Windows as a shared server for more than a few clients due to the burden Windows places on the machine's processor.

Although LANtastic servers don't need a lot of memory compared to other network operating systems, they benefit from having several megabytes of memory for a disk cache. Considering the low cost of RAM, it makes sense to have four megabytes of memory in the file server. With that much extra memory, you can probably load some network drivers or terminate-and-stay-resident programs into upper memory and still get fast disk access service from a disk cache.

You should also consider two other issues when you plan your servers: power and security. Every PC acting as a server should be protected by an uninterruptable power supply (UPS). People are often confused by the ratings of UPS systems and PC power supplies. UPS systems are typically rated in "volt/amps" (VA) while PCs are rated in watts. You can usually find a PC's power consumption in watts on a plate or sticker on the back of the machine. As a quick rule of thumb, you should choose your UPS with a VA rating at least twice the wattage rating of the PC power supply it is to support. UPS systems rated at 600 VA are commonly available, and that is about the lowest rating you should accept for the UPS protecting a server.

HINT. *Don't forget to provide a small UPS for the wiring center if you use a star wiring system outside the server. A 10BaseT network will fail completely if the wiring center loses power.*

It's common to overlook physical security for important network file servers. Most managers limit access to important data across the network with a password protection scheme, but many forget that anyone who can touch the server's keyboard can access all the files on its hard drives. If you have sensitive financial or personnel data, consider providing the same level of physical security for the file server PC that you would for the documents it contains. Putting the unit in a private office is usually sufficient, but in some cases you might have to put it in a closet or room that locks. If you do, remember to allow for environmental control of that space to prevent overheating.

Those Printers

Printers are valuable, necessary, and troublesome. Because they are electromechanical devices, they break. Since they are often physically distant from the people who use them and can't send messages like "PAPER OUT" back through the network, networked printers can create unique administrative problems.

Programs create print jobs in many formats. Sometimes they send the job in a configuration meant for a specific make and model of printer. Sophisticated programs may generate printed output in a page description language like Adobe's PostScript or Hewlett-Packard's PCL. To avoid problems, you must carefully link the application to the printer through the redirected LPT or COM port in the client PC. The combination of various printers and applications can create a complex matrix for any network planner.

HINT. *Load your laser printers with the maximum amount of memory they will hold. Printers with more memory unload print jobs from the print server faster, so printer memory is a good investment in performance.*

Along with pairing programs and printers, you must also consider the physical location of the printers. People don't want to walk too far to pick up a print job, and jobs that lay in a printer's output tray too long can get lost. Fortunately, LANtastic lets you attach a printer to any networked PC, so you have some flexibility in physical placement. Artisoft's Central Station can also act as a print server without a PC, so you can attach printers to a Central Station anywhere along the network cable.

HINT. *Our experience shows that people like to hear the printer start their print jobs. The sound seems to give users a sense of accomplishment (Done at last!), so try to place shared printers at a convenient distance from the people who use them.*

■ Additional Planning Factors

You'll live with the physical configuration of the network, the server, and the printers you set up for a long time, but other up-front choices are relatively easy to change:

- The server directory structure
- Network security
- Menus
- Backup
- Training

The Server Directory Structure

Where you put your subdirectories does make a difference. A sound up-front decision on the logical structure of your server's hard disk drives makes training and backup easier and simplifies the management of the server.

First, don't put everything into the root directory of the server. Watch the installation programs contained in the applications you install and override them if they don't start from a subdirectory you designate.

For backup and security purposes it is often useful to store files created by applications under a major subdirectory name that describes the person or department using those applications. Therefore, all the data files for the spreadsheet, word processing, and accounting programs used in the accounting department could be stored in subdirectories under the major heading "accounts." You can either put the files containing the programs themselves in subdirectories under the same major subdirectory or group them logically by function. If you want to reduce the load on the network, load as many applications as possible from each PC's local C: drive.

HINT. *Many word processing programs have large overlay files, sometimes in excess of 600k, which they refer to while performing special tasks like spelling checks. Loading at least these overlay files on the local drives of networked PCs reduces the load on the server and improves performance. You might have to check with the company who wrote the software to determine the best configuration for the program's files on a network.*

Menu Systems

Menu Systems

👍 Make applications easier to use

👍 Simplify training

👍 Enhance security

👍 Help protect against viruses

👎 Often require customization

The issues of ease of use, security, and protection against viruses are all legs of the same elephant. Fortunately, several companies market excellent menu programs that provide tools for handling these problems.

There's a famous computer-industry adage: "Easy to use is easy to say!" Many people using PCs on a network don't want to know much about computers. The best thing you can do for them is arrange their systems to start up in the application they'll be using. The catch is, most people use more than one application, so the next best thing you can do is provide a menu that starts applications with a single keystroke.

In its simplest form, a menu program contains a series of commands or batch files that change the command line to the proper drive and subdirectory, start applications, and return the user to a selection screen when applications terminate. More complex menuing programs check for viruses in the programs they run and prevent users from circumventing the menu system.

Fortunately, some of the best menu programs on the market are compatible with LANtastic. PC Tools from Central Point Software, Inc., Direct Net from Fifth Generation Systems, Inc., and Norton Commander from Symantec are all excellent multipurpose programs that include strong menu systems. Using these tools, you can create a menu system customized to each individual or workgroup. You can even deny access to the DOS command line to prevent copying and protect the system from computer viruses.

Network security is an on-going task that faces every administrator. New people come in, others leave, and some change jobs within the organization. Each action requires a reaction from the network administrator. If you organize the subdirectories and files on your network in a logical and disciplined order, you can easily give people use of the files they need and change their access when they change their jobs.

But there is more to network security than assigning passwords to users and granting access to specific files; viruses are an important subcategory of the security issue. While a few companies have unknowingly shipped commercial programs containing viruses, they typically enter organizations and networks through illegally copied and pirated software. Your first defense against viruses is a ban against loading any software that you haven't provided and checked yourself. A menu program that prevents unlimited access to DOS can help to enforce such a ban. You can set up menu selections that perform needed DOS functions such as formatting a diskette or copying a predefined set of files to or from a floppy diskette, but you can also protect the entire network from harm with a menu system.

In addition, we suggest you run a high-quality and frequently updated virus scanning program from the AUTOEXEC.BAT file of every PC in your organization.

Backup

A good backup system can save your job. Hard disk subsystems break and people make mistakes, so you can lose data. Early in the network planning cycle, you should decide whether you need special equipment to back up your data files. The choices range from floppy disk drives to an 2-gigabyte DAT tape systems. In the middle ground, many people are happy with a quarter-inch tape cartridge (QIC) system that has 120 megabytes of storage (typically called a QIC 120 system). We've also had good results with removable-cartridge disks like the SyQuest SyDOS and Iomega Bernoulli units. When you choose a backup storage system, you measure storage capacity and speed against cost.

We suggest you make a regular, periodic backup—perhaps weekly—of all application program files and data files on the file server. Then you can make faster daily backups of only changed data files. This technique saves a lot of time overall. If you have to restore the server's drive, you first use the full set of files and then the latest set of changed files.

HINT. *You can use the network to back up all the files in all the client PCs, too. During a period of low activity, run a batch file to load the LANtastic server software in each machine. Then one machine equipped with a storage device can—again, under the control of batch files you've created—draw down the changed files from each PC.*

Training

We strongly suggest you plan a short but formal training program for people who will use the network. If you have asked for requirements, planned carefully, set up menus and batch files, and automated the backup process, the training should be painless, but it's still necessary. To make people feel comfortable and confident, you must introduce them to their new set of shared resources.

- *Hardware Installation*
- *Installing the LANtastic Software*
- *Memory Management*
- *QEMM-386*

C H A P T E R

Installing LANtastic

As we saw in Chapter 1, every LAN is a combination of hardware and software components. While LANtastic is generally easy to install and configure, today's complicated PC systems open up a world of possible conflicts and incompatibilities. In this chapter, we'll take a close look at the installation of the LANtastic hardware and software.

■ Hardware Installation

Each PC on a network needs some type of physical connection to the other PCs on the network. This is most often accomplished by a *network interface card*, or *NIC*. A NIC is a printed circuit board that installs inside a PC, in one of the PC's expansion slots. The board connects to the PC's internal data bus, and a connector on the board attaches to the network cable. For the most part, network boards can only be installed in desktop PCs—most laptop and notebook portables don't have the expansion space required by a network board, but those computers can still attach to the network through an external LAN adapter. We'll look at some external LAN adapters in Chapter 11.

Finding a Home for Your NIC Board

If your PC is fairly basic, installing a network interface board is usually a simple matter. In most cases, you can simply remove the PC's cover, find an empty expansion slot, and plug the board into the slot. If your PC falls into this category, you don't have to concern yourself with the nitty-gritty details of hardware installation.

If your PC is already full of expansion boards, you may find that installing a network board causes problems with other boards in your system. The number of expansion interface slots, memory addresses, IRQ lines, and DMA channels in a PC is limited, and video adapters, disk controllers, mouse ports, and other communications boards all consume these resources.

The more expansion options your PC has, the more likely you are to encounter a problem. If your network board attempts to use the same I/O port addresses, memory addresses, or interrupt request (IRQ) lines as another component already in your system, one or both of the devices won't operate. The resulting conflict can cause you to learn more about the inner workings of your PC than you ever wanted to know.

Depending on the type of network board you are using, you'll have to select an I/O port address, a memory address, an IRQ line, and possibly a Direct Memory Access (DMA) channel to use for the board's operation. If you are using a board with an on-board boot ROM, you'll also need to select an address for the boot ROM.

I/O and Memory Addressing

All network interface boards fall into one of two groups: I/O mapped or memory mapped. These two categories define how the computer's CPU communicates with the board. In the case of I/O-mapped boards, the board occupies several I/O port addresses on the CPU's I/O bus, much like a serial or parallel port. Data coming from the network appears to the computer's CPU as a stream of data coming in one of the I/O addresses; data being sent to the network is sent to another, usually adjacent, I/O address. Memory-mapped boards are similar, but use a reserved area of the PC's main memory instead of I/O ports.

Neither method is inherently better than the other. Memory-mapped operation is somewhat faster than I/O-mapped operation, but the memory on a memory-mapped card usually occupies some of the precious below-640k "low DOS" memory. Most newer network boards—including all of Artisoft's—are I/O mapped.

Some professional network installers consider the techniques they use to avoid interrupt and memory address conflicts trade secrets, but the real secret is organization. Having a quick reference to the I/O and interrupt addresses used in each machine can avoid frustration and save hours of installation time.

The first piece of advice we can give you about network adapter installation is to use the defaults recommended by the adapter's manufacturer. The company chose those defaults to avoid typical problems.

In case the adapter doesn't work at the default memory or I/O address, most installation manuals list at least two alternative settings. Adapters designed for the standard IBM PC AT expansion bus (the Industry Standard Architecture, or ISA, bus) usually use jumpers or switches to determine the shared RAM address and IRQ line. Adapters designed for the Microchannel Architecture (MCA) and Extended Industry Standard Architecture (EISA) change these parameters through special configuration programs provided on a diskette that's shipped with the adapter.

Table 4.1 shows some of the I/O addresses and IRQ lines used by standard PC devices. These settings commonly interfere with the operation of LAN adapters. If you try the LAN adapter with the default settings and they don't work, look for other unused combinations.

There is one especially important point to remember: If you change the board's settings, you must reconfigure the LANtastic software to match the address and IRQ set on the board. The software won't be able to find the adapter unless it knows where to look.

Interrupt Request (IRQ) Lines

Virtually all network boards use one of the PC's interrupt request (IRQ) lines. An *interrupt* is a signal sent to the CPU indicating that a particular piece of hardware or software requires its immediate attention.

The first installation tip you should know concerns interrupt request line IRQ3. The COM2 serial port on all PCs uses this IRQ line. However, most LAN adapters (including Artisoft's) come with this same IRQ line set as the default. If you install a LAN adapter using IRQ3 in a PC with a COM2 port, the serial port will probably stop working. If you have a modem or serial mouse attached to COM2, and the modem or mouse doesn't work when you're logged into the network, this may be your problem. Try moving the network adapter to another IRQ line.

Table 4.1

IRQ Addresses and Memory Locations

IRQ LINE	DEVICE
2	Interrupt controller (use with care in AT-type systems)
3	Serial ports COM2 and COM4, many network boards
4	Serial ports COM1 and COM3
5	Second parallel port, most XT disk controllers, some tape backup controllers, SCSI disk controllers (including CD-ROM controllers), Adlib and Sound Blaster sound boards, Microsoft's InPort mouse board
6	Floppy disk controllers
7	First parallel port (LPT1), tape backup controllers, SCSI disk controllers (including CD-ROM controllers), Adlib and Sound Blaster sound boards

I/O ADDRESS	DEVICE
1F0h	AT hard disk controllers
320h	XT hard disk controllers
220h	3270 emulation boards, Adlib and Sound Blaster sound boards
240h	HP scanners, some CD-ROM interface boards
278h	Second parallel port (LPT2)
280h	Tape backup controllers
2E8h	Serial port COM4
3E8h	Serial port COM3
2F8h	Serial port COM2
3F8h	Serial port COM1
3F0h	Floppy disk controllers
378h	First parallel port (LPT1)
3b0h	Mono, EGA, and VGA video boards
3c0h	EGA and VGA video boards
3d0h	CGA and MCGA video boards

If you don't need the COM2 port, you can probably disable it. Many PC manufacturers provide either a software or hardware method to disable an on-board COM2 port, but there is no single standard technique.

Because so many IBM PC/AT clones come equipped with an internal COM2, many installers avoid IRQ3 and use IRQ5 whenever they put LAN adapters in these computers. But don't try this setting in an older IBM PC/XT or clone because the hard disk controller in an XT will conflict with IRQ5 every time. Similarly, the LPT2 port used in many PCs acting as network print servers also uses IRQ5. As they do for the COM2 port, most PC vendors provide a way to disable the LPT2 port if you don't need it.

Selecting IRQ2 for the LAN adapter usually works on AT-type machines. However, this IRQ line is used to relay requests for IRQ lines 8 through 15, so you may encounter conflicts if any devices in the AT use these higher-numbered interrupts. IRQ2 conflicts often sneak up on you when you try to add an internal device to a PC that's been operating happily with a LAN adapter at IRQ2.

All of Artisoft's newer AE-2 and AE-3 network boards allow selection of IRQ10 and IRQ15. These interrupt request lines aren't used in many PCs, and may be a good choice if you're installing an Artisoft Ethernet board in a crowded PC.

Selecting an I/O and Memory Address

Due to the lack of industry standards, there are no hard and fast rules about which I/O port and memory addresses you can use. In most cases, the default I/O port address of 300h will work, unless you have another device installed there.

Remote boot ROMS let you use diskless workstations to boot from the server. The autoboot ROMs use higher addresses and can conflict with the ROMs in some video adapters. In the PC Magazine LAN Labs, we've had good success using CC00h as the boot ROM address in many computers with VGA video systems.

A few LAN adapter boards use a technique called Direct Memory Access (DMA) to speed the transfer of data between the CPU and the network board. At present, all Artisoft boards support DMA operation, but the LANtastic software doesn't use the DMA features. If you must install an adapter using a DMA channel, try DMA channel 3 on an AT-style machine. On an XT, use DMA channel 2 to avoid conflicts with the XT's hard disk. All PCs use DMA2 for the floppy disk drive controller, however, so someone trying to use the floppy disk drive and a LAN adapter set to DMA2 simultaneously may experience problems.

Generally, you won't have a problem setting up a LAN adapter in a typical client workstation if you use the default settings; however, the challenge comes when you want to put a LAN adapter in a PC equipped with a special adapter for a mainframe connection or with a tape-drive controller. These devices, and to a lesser extent internal mouse adapters, often default to the same IRQ and memory locations used by LAN adapters. Some conflicts are insidious. For example, you might not see a problem until you try to do a tape backup and pull files across the network at the same time. In this case, one of the conflicting products would have to move to a different address and/or IRQ line.

Getting multiple boards to work together in tricky installations is often a matter of experience and luck. That's why many system integrators support only product lines that have a proven ability to work together. The craft of LAN installation involves some art, but it's primarily a skill that has specific rules and a roadmap of the PC's architecture for you to follow.

Installing the LANtastic Software

Installing the LANtastic software is a fairly simple operation that normally takes only a few minutes. This section covers the basics; we'll show you how to customize your LANtastic installation in Chapter 5.

The entire LANtastic system comes on one diskette. To install the software, place the LANtastic diskette in a floppy drive (usually A:), and type **A:INSTALL**. After displaying an initial sign-on screen, the INSTALL program asks you to name your PC, as shown in Figure 4.1 below.

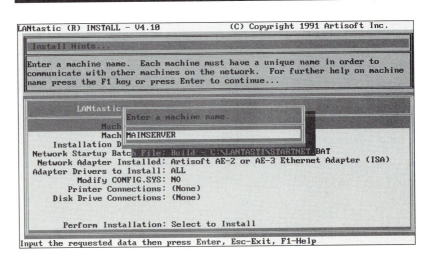

Figure 4.1

Naming a new LANtastic PC. The machine name allows other users to identify your PC by a unique name.

In our example, we've chosen the name MAINSERVER. You can use virtually any name you like for your PC. If your installation has a large number of PCs, you may want to give the servers meaningful names like "Accounting," "Engineering," and so on.

After you've entered the machine name, INSTALL displays the main installation screen. This screen shows all the major LANtastic options. You can change any option by using the arrow keys to move the highlight bar to the desired option, and then pressing Enter. Figure 4.2 shows the main INSTALL screen.

Figure 4.2

The main INSTALL screen, from which you can view and change most of LANtastic's options.

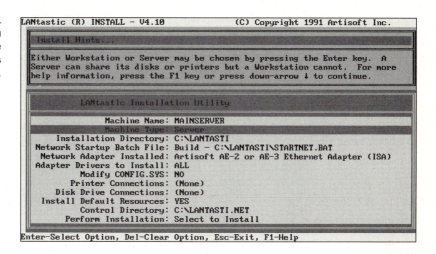

The first item on the INSTALL screen is Machine Type. The INSTALL program initially assumes that you want to install only the workstation (client) part of the LANtastic software. If you won't be sharing your disk or printer with other network users, leave Machine Type set to Workstation. If other network users will need access to your disk or printer, change Machine Type to Server, as in the previous figure.

The next item on the INSTALL screen is Installation Directory. This directory is normally set to C:\LANTASTI, and we recommend you use the default setting. If your machine boots from a drive other than C:, change the directory name to point to the \LANTASTI directory on your boot drive.

The Network Startup Batch File option contains the name of the DOS batch file you'll use to start your network software. LANtastic automatically creates this batch file for you. The default name is STARTNET.BAT, and INSTALL normally places the batch file in the same directory as the LANtastic software. If you want a different name for the batch file, you can use this setting to specify the directory and name to use.

The Network Adapter Installed option specifies the type of network adapter board in your computer. If you've already installed an Artisoft board, the INSTALL program will automatically detect it. If you haven't installed a board, you'll have to select the proper network adapter type. Move the highlight bar to Network Adapter Installed, press Enter, and select your board from the pop-up list that appears.

The next selection, Adapter Drivers to Install, tells INSTALL which drivers to install on your PC. The default setting is ALL, which copies all available network drivers to your hard disk; however, you really need only the drivers for your particular board.

The Modify CONFIG.SYS selection tells INSTALL to make any necessary modifications to your CONFIG.SYS file. We're usually skeptical of programs that want to mess with our CONFIG.SYS files and INSTALL is no exception. If you let it, INSTALL will set the LASTDRIVE setting to drive Z:. While this setting works fine with LANtastic, it may cause problems if you want to install a CD-ROM drive or if you use NetWare or another network system in addition to LANtastic. We've found that setting LASTDRIVE to N: usually works fine.

You can use the next two settings, Printer Connections and Disk Drive Connections, to have your PC connected to specific network printer(s) and/or disk drive(s) automatically when you start LANtastic. Initially, we recommend you leave these settings blank.

The final two settings, Install Default Resources and Control Directory, appear only if you're installing your machine as a server. We'll examine network resources in detail in Chapter 5. Basically, the default resources allow you to share your floppy drive(s), your entire hard disk, and your printer with other network users. If you want other users to have access to all these resources, select YES. If you'd rather have more control over what files other users can access, select NO, and see Chapter 6, "Managing Your Network." The Control Directory is where LANtastic records who has access to what devices on your PC. We recommend you use the default setting of C:\LANTASTI.NET.

Once you have the INSTALL settings the way you want them, select the last item on the screen, Perform Installation, to copy the LANtastic software to your hard disk. After INSTALL copies the files, it creates the STARTNET.BAT network startup file. At this point, installation is complete and LANtastic is ready to run, but before you actually start LANtastic, check the STARTNET.BAT file to be sure it contains the proper commands for your installation. Figure 4.3 shows the contents of a typical STARTNET.BAT file.

Before we go into the specifics of using LANtastic, it will be helpful for you to understand what each command in the STARTNET.BAT file does, so let's take a line-by-line look at our example STARTNET.BAT file.

Figure 4.3

A typical STARTNET.BAT file for a LANtastic server. This file contains all the commands necessary to load LANtastic on your PC.

```
@ECHO OFF
PATH C:\LANTASTI;%PATH%
SHARE /L:200

AEX IRQ=15 IOBASE=300 VERBOSE
AILANBIO
REDIR MAINSERVER LOGINS=3
SERVER

NET LOGIN/WAIT \\MAINSERVER MAINSERVER
NET LPT TIMEOUT 10
```

The first line,

```
@ECHO OFF
```

tells DOS not to echo the remaining batch file commands to the screen. As a result, you don't see each DOS command (PATH, SHARE, and so on) as it is processed. The @ before ECHO tells DOS not to echo the ECHO command itself.

The second line,

```
PATH C:\LANTASTI;%PATH%
```

adds C:\LANTASTI to your existing DOS PATH statement, which allows DOS to find the LANtastic software directory.

The third line,

```
SHARE /L:200
```

loads SHARE.EXE, the DOS file sharing and record locking program. In a network environment, several users may try to access the same file at the same time; SHARE acts as a sort of network traffic cop, managing access to the shared files. SHARE loads as a terminate-and-stay-resident (TSR) program.

The next four lines actually load the LANtastic software as TSR programs. The first of these lines,

```
AEX IRQ=15, IOBASE=300 VERBOSE
```

installs the driver software for the Artisoft AE/2 and AE/3 Ethernet boards. The statements IRQ=15 and IOBASE=300 tell the AEX program where to find your Ethernet board. If you've moved your board from its default settings, you may need to change these statements to reflect the actual IRQ line and I/O address used by your network board. The VERBOSE setting tells the AEX driver to report the network board's configuration on the screen.

The next line,

```
AILANBIO
```

loads Artisoft's NETBIOS software, which is the heart of the network software. Virtually all the LANtastic programs use NETBIOS to communicate with one another.

The REDIR command loads the LANtastic redirector program. REDIR watches for DOS disk and printer requests, and reroutes them to the appropriate network drive or printer. The option MAINSERVER defines the server as having the name MAINSERVER, and LOGINS=3 tells LANtastic that this PC will access a maximum of three servers at once. If your network will have more than three servers, increase this number to reflect the actual number.

The command SERVER loads the LANtastic server program. This line won't be present on workstation-only installations.

The last two lines,

```
NET LOGIN
```

and

```
NET LPT
```

actually connect your PC to the network. We'll examine these commands in Chapter 5.

■ Memory Management

As we just saw, the LANtastic networking software consists of several TSR programs. Although it uses much less RAM than other networking software, once LANtastic is loaded, you still may not have room for some memory-hungry application programs. In this section, we'll show you how to conserve your system's DOS memory and parcel out RAM in a style that would make Scrooge proud. In the process, we'll examine the types of memory used in PCs, and decipher the alphabet soup of acronyms used to describe memory management techniques. Most importantly, we'll show you how to get your RAM back.

The DOS 640k Memory Limit

Because of its design, DOS is inherently limited to using only 640k of memory. The complete LANtastic software including the server and client software can consume up to 70k of memory. In addition, you may have TSR programs or special device drivers that further reduce the amount of memory available to DOS and application programs. Obviously, there's a problem here.

Like so many things in the PC industry, the notorious DOS "640k barrier" owes its origin to decisions made way back in 1980 when a team of IBM engineers was designing IBM's first Personal Computer. At that time, the most popular computer on the market was Apple's wildly successful Apple II. One key to the Apple's success was that the Apple could display text and graphics in color. Most Apple II systems came with 16k of RAM, but could be upgraded to 48 or even 64k.

Second to the Apple in popularity were a group of machines from a large number of manufacturers, including Xerox, Osborne, Kaypro, and Northstar. These systems had two things in common: They all used Intel 8080 or compatible CPU chips, and they all ran an operating system called CP/M. In a number of ways, the CP/M machines were the true forerunners of today's PCs. Most CP/M systems could run each other's programs—providing one system could read another's (usually incompatible) disk.

A large number of CP/M systems were based on a common hardware architecture called the S-100 bus, and expansion cards designed for that architecture would work in most S-100 computers. However, the CP/M systems had one major drawback: They had no standardized color or graphic display capability. Even though most CP/M systems were faster and more powerful than the Apple II, none of them ever approached the success of Apple's system.

Assessing this situation, the IBM engineers took the strengths of both the Apple and CP/M systems, added a few new goodies of their own, and the IBM PC was born. The original PC had five expansion slots, a nonproprietary bus, an optional color display, and an operating system that looked and worked a lot like CP/M. Since RAM was very expensive, IBM offered a basic model with 16k of memory, upgradable to 64k.

The original IBM PC was built around Intel's 8088 microprocessor chip. The 8088 can address 1Mb of memory, so IBM's engineers wisely decided to put the system ROM area at the "top" of the 1Mb address space, leaving the lower area free for the RAM used by application programs and for memory-mapped expansion boards. The engineers decided that the address space from address A000 (640k) to address FFFF (1Mb) would be reserved for ROMs and expansion boards. This arrangement left 640k of free address space for DOS and programs. Remember, 640k was *ten times* the maximum memory capacity of the Apple II. The classic definition of a minicomputer at the time was a machine that had a megabyte of memory and cost less than a million dollars. No wonder the designers felt safe providing nearly a megabyte for growth in these "personal" computers. Figure 4.4 shows how the PC's lower 1Mb of memory is organized.

Figure 4.4

This memory organization chart shows the areas used by DOS, the system ROMS, and expansion boards.

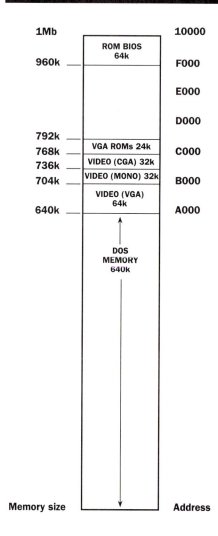

Meanwhile Bill Gates and his crew at Microsoft were preparing the operating system for the new IBM machine. (At the time, Microsoft was not known for their operating system expertise. There are many legends about why IBM chose Microsoft over Digitial Research, the creators of the popular CP/M operating system, but that's another story.) Given the specifications from IBM, Microsoft designed DOS to run in the lower 640k of memory space. Microsoft also created a ROM version of the popular BASIC programming language for the new machine.

When the IBM PC was announced in August 1981, it was an immediate hit; however, users quickly discovered that 64k of memory just wasn't enough for serious business applications. Almost overnight, an entire industry was born. Companies like Quadram and AST Research were quick to the market with memory expansion boards for the new PC. With one of these boards in the system, the original design could be expanded to hold 544k of RAM.

In early 1983, IBM announced an improved PC called the PC XT. The XT held 256k of memory on the motherboard, but could accommodate 640k with the addition of a memory expansion board. In addition, the XT was available with a 10Mb hard disk. At the time, 256k was more than enough memory for most applications, and many programs required less.

When Lotus 1-2-3 was released in 1983, the rules changed dramatically. Lotus 1-2-3 liked memory—the more, the better. Around the same time, TSR programs like Rosesoft's SOFTKEY and Borland's SideKick became popular. These programs remain resident in the lower 640k of memory, thus reducing the amount of RAM available to other applications.

Responses to the 640k Problem

In 1985, on the original PC's fourth birthday, IBM announced the PC AT, based on the Intel 80286 processor chip. The 80286 processor has a 24-bit address range and can accommodate 15Mb of *extended memory* in addition to the usual 1Mb of conventional memory. Extended memory begins at the 1Mb boundary, just above the system ROMs; however, this memory is only accessible when the 80286 processor operates in *protected mode* with operating systems like OS/2, Unix, and Novell's NetWare. Unfortunately, DOS runs all processors in *real mode* for software compatibility, so DOS can't use extended memory. To maintain compatibility with the large installed base of PC's and XT's, the system ROM and video addresses remained where they were, starting at the 640k boundary. While the new PC AT machines could hold a heap of memory, DOS applications were still confined to the first 640k.

Since the introduction of the AT, IBM and dozens of other PC makers have designed new systems around the Intel 80286, 80386, and 80486 CPU chips. Most newer 80386SX, 80386, 80486SX, and 80486 systems have all the capabilities of the 80286, and the DX-series processors add 32-bit addressing, allowing them to handle up to four gigabytes of RAM. Despite the capabilities of the chips, DOS applications still can't use all this RAM by themselves.

Converting Extended Memory to Expanded Memory

In 1985, Lotus, Intel, and Microsoft (LIM) mounted the first full-scale assault on the 640k barrier. They created the EMS expansion technique—also known as *expanded memory*—which allows EMS-compliant programs working with EMS-compliant hardware to put data into the extended memory area above one megabyte. This extended memory can then be overlaid or "mapped" into the DOS memory area as needed.

Originally, EMS was designed primarily to store data from spreadsheets. Recognizing the limitations of EMS and feeling the pinch of competition, AST, Quadram, and Ashton-Tate soon developed what they called the Extended Expanded Memory Specification (EEMS). Then, in 1987, pushed by Intel's need to add support for the 80386 processor in the LIM EMS specification, the LIM team enhanced the original EMS to include larger page-mapping abilities. This new product, named LIM EMS 4.0, operates similarly to EEMS.

The original Lotus-Intel-Microsoft EMS specification allowed remapping of only a single 64k chunk of memory. LIM EMS 4.0 allows programs to swap the entire 1Mb address range in and out with data contained in the special LIM EMS 4.0 memory. Programs can only access EMS memory through a special region called a *page frame*, which typically occupies 64k in the first megabyte of address space. The software driver included with EMS memory cards manages the memory by swapping the RAM requested for DOS applications from a holding pool of expanded memory to the page frame.

A major benefit of EMS 4.0 memory is its ability to fill in unused sections of the high-DOS memory area. In many systems, there are "holes" in the lower 1Mb of address space. Although the area above 640k is reserved for expansion boards and ROMS, that doesn't mean the entire address space is actually in use. Figure 4.5 illustrates the address space in a typical PC equipped with a scanner board, a VGA video board, and a memory-mapped network interface board.

Some EMS manager programs automatically search out these unused areas, "backfilling" or "remapping" them with EMS memory, which is called high-DOS memory. After remapping such an area, special "loadhi" programs like QEMM, 386MAX, and NetRoom can load and execute most DOS programs or drivers in this memory. The load-high feature is built into DOS 5.0.

In modern PCs, there's often very little room free in the high-DOS area. The variations between video boards and specific versions of drivers for mouse, memory, fax, LAN, and other adapters make trying to use this area a different challenge on every PC. On some, the combination of ROM BIOS, video adapter interface, and a 64k page frame makes it impossible to move any other useful blocks of software from conventional memory into high-DOS memory.

Alphabet Soup

A number of sometimes confusing terms are used to describe the various memory types and management techniques. Different hardware and software manufacturers may use different terms to describe the same thing. Table 4.2 defines some of the more common terms.

Figure 4.5

This memory map diagram illustrates how adapter boards occupy pieces of the lower 1Mb address space, leaving "holes" in the area between 640k and 1Mb.

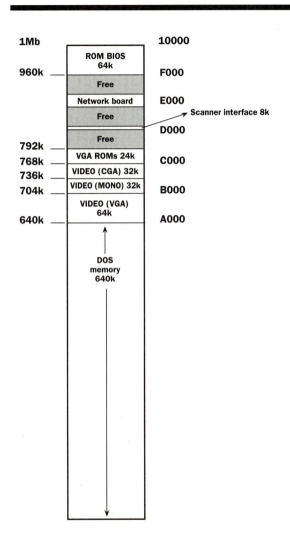

Optimizing Your RAM for LANtastic

Now that you understand the 640k problem, we'll show you several ways to get around it. There are a number of tools and techniques you can use to expand the amount of memory available to DOS applications. All these techniques assume your PC has at least one megabyte of memory—640k of low memory and at least 384k of high memory.

Table 4.2

Common Memory Management Terms and Definitions

TERM	DEFINITION
Extended memory	Memory installed in an 80286, 80386, or 80486 system, above the 1 Mb boundary. This memory is not directly accessible by DOS.
Low-DOS memory or DOS memory	The memory between 0 and the 640k boundary. This is where DOS and application programs actually reside.
High-DOS memory or high memory	The memory area between the 640k and 1Mb boundaries.
LIM or LIM EMS	The Lotus-Intel-Microsoft specification for managing expanded memory. Memory managed by an EMS-compatible program is called "EMS memory."
Expanded memory or EMS memory	Memory managed by a LIM compatible driver.
Microsoft Extended Memory Specification, or XMS	A specification designed by Microsoft as a standard method for programs to access extended memory and high-DOS memory. There are three sources of XMS memory, each with its own acronym: EMBs (extended memory blocks)—Memory above the 1Mb boundary UMBs (upper memory blocks)—Memory "stolen" from the high-DOS area HMA (high memory area)—The 64k of memory beginning at the 1Mb boundary.

Taking an Inventory of Your PC

Before you can optimize your PC's memory, you have to find out what's in your computer. To do this, you need a *system analyzer program*. These programs typically show the amount and type of memory installed in your PC, as well as the amount of memory that is being used by DOS, device drivers, TSR programs, and system overhead. Memory manager programs like 386Max, QEMM, and NetRoom all include system analyzers. In addition, both PC Tools and The Norton Utilities include excellent analyzer programs.

To give you an idea of how memory is allocated in a typical system, we'll use QEMM's MANIFEST.EXE program to take a look at the memory organization of a typical 80386-based computer.

Initially, we'll be running DOS 5.0 with ANSI.SYS and DOSKEY installed. ANSI.SYS is the standard DOS screen driver, and DOSKEY is a keyboard utility provided with DOS 5.0. We'll also load the LANtastic REDIR, AEX, and AILANBIO programs, the three components of the LANtastic workstation software. Figure 4.6 shows MANIFEST's analysis of our example PC's memory in this "normal" configuration.

Figure 4.6

MANIFEST's picture of our test 80386 system in its standard configuration. The first section shows 525k available for DOS, with 42k being used by LANtastic and other TSR programs. Notice the "Unused" areas above the 640k boundary. The second part of the report shows which TSR programs are using the 42k of memory.

```
First Meg / Overview
        Memory Area     Size    Description
        0000 - 003F     1k      Interrupt Area
        0040 - 004F     0.3k    BIOS Data Area
        0050 - 006F     0.5k    System Data
        0070 - 11F3     70k     DOS
        11F4 - 1C78     42k     Program Area
        1C79 - 9FBF     525k    [Available]
        ===Conventional memory ends at 639k====
        9FC0 - 9FFF     1k      Extended Bios Area
        A000 - AFFF     64k     VGA Graphics
        B000 - B7FF     32k     Unused
        B800 - BFFF     32k     VGA Text
        C000 - C7FF     32k     Video ROM
        C800 - DFFF     96k     Unused
        E000 - E7FF     32k     ROM
        E800 - EFFF     32k     Unused
        F000 - FFFF     64k     System ROM

First Meg / Programs
        Memory Area     Size    Description
        11F4 - 130A     4.4k    COMMAND
        130B - 130F     0.1k    [Available]
        1310 - 1320     0.3k    COMMAND Environment
        1321 - 1377     1.4k    [Available]
        1378 - 147A     4k      DOSKEY
        147B - 155F     3.6k    AEX
        1560 - 1914     14k     AILANBIO
        1915 - 1C78     13k     REDIR
        1C79 - 9FBF     525k    [Available]
```

As you can see from the first part of the MANIFEST analysis, with DOS and the LANtastic workstation software loaded, only 525k of free memory is available for DOS applications. In the following section, we'll "tune up" this system and show you how to regain some memory for applications.

Microsoft's Solution

The key to using expanded or extended memory effectively is to use a memory manager program. Both DOS 5.0 and Windows 3.1 include Microsoft's HIMEM.SYS and EMM386.EXE. Together, these two programs provide expanded and extended memory management. Once they are installed, you can load TSR programs into the high-DOS memory area using the DOS command LOADHIGH. To load the LANtastic software into high memory, we had to modify the STARTNET.BAT network startup file, as shown in Figure 4.7.

Figure 4.7

The modified STARTNET.BAT file

```
@ECHO OFF
PATH C:\LANTASTI;%PATH%
LOADHIGH SHARE /L:200

LOADHIGH AEX IRQ=15 IOBASE=300 VERBOSE
LOADHIGH AILANBIO
LOADHIGH REDIR MAINSERVER LOGINS=3

NET LOGIN/WAIT \\MAINSERVER MAINSERVER
NET LPT TIMEOUT 10
```

After installing HIMEM and EMM386 on our example system, we loaded the network software and reran the MANIFEST analysis. The results are in Figure 4.8.

As you can see, the HIMEM/EMM386 combination increased the available memory from 525k to 614k. Most of this gain came from moving the LANtastic programs into high memory.

You'll find complete instructions for installing HIMEM and EMM386 in Chapter 12 of the MS-DOS 5.0 manual, but before you install these programs you should know about a few caveats: First, they don't work 100 percent on every machine ever made. We've seen big-bucks PCs from reputable manufacturers that simply won't run HIMEM and EMM386 correctly.

Second, installing HIMEM and EMM386 isn't always easy. You must modify your CONFIG.SYS and AUTOEXEC.BAT files manually to include the HIMEM and EMM386 commands, and these changes don't take effect until you reboot the PC. You'll probably have to go through several iterations of the edit-reboot-test cycle before you get it right, but if you make an error while changing the CONFIG.SYS and AUTOEXEC.BAT files, you may not be able to restart your system. We strongly recommend that you create a bootable floppy disk before you install HIMEM and EMM386. Then if you mess up the CONFIG or AUTOEXEC file on your hard disk, you can always boot the system from the floppy.

HIMEM.SYS and EMM386.EXE

- Work well with LANtastic
- Leave more RAM for DOS programs
- Are free with DOS 5.x and Windows
- Can be difficult to install

Figure 4.8

MANIFEST's analysis of our example system's memory configuration with HIMEM.SYS and EMM386.EXE installed. Notice that 614k is now available for DOS programs.

```
First Meg / Overview
    Memory Area      Size    Description
    0000 - 003F      1k      Interrupt Area
    0040 - 004F      0.3k    BIOS Data Area
    0050 - 006F      0.5k    System Data
    0070 - 05C0      21k     DOS
    05C1 - 066B      2.7k    Program Area
    066C - 9FFE      614k    [Available]
    9FFF - 9FFF      0k      High RAM
    ===Conventional memory ends at 640k====
    A000 - AFFF      64k     VGA Graphics
    B000 - B7FF      32k     Unused
    B800 - BFFF      32k     VGA Text
    C000 - C7FF      32k     Video ROM
    C800 - CCE4      19k     Unused
    CCE5 - DFFF      76k     High RAM
    E000 - E7FF      32k     ROM
    E800 - EFFF      32k     Unused
    F000 - FFFF      64k     System ROM
         HMA         64k     First 64k Extended

First Meg / Programs
    Memory Area      Size    Description
    05C1 - 0655      2.3k    COMMAND
    0656 - 065A      0.1k    [Available]
    065B - 066B      0.3k    COMMAND Environment
    066C - 9FFE      614k    [Available]
    ====Conventional memory ends at 640k=====
    CCE5 - CDEB      4.1k    ANSI
    CDEC - CDF5      0.2k    [Available]
    CDF6 - CEF8      4k      DOSKEY
    CEF9 - D10B      8.3k    SHARE
    D10C - D1F0      3.6k    AEX
    D1F1 - D1FB      0.2k    [Available]
    D1FC - D5B0      14k     AILANBIO
    D5B1 - D918      13k     REDIR
    D919 - DFFF      27k     [Available]
```

Third-Party Memory Managers

There are several excellent memory manager programs on the market, including QEMM (Quarterdeck Expanded Memory Manager), 386Max, and NetRoom. These programs are similar to the HIMEM/EMM386 combination but are generally easier to install and more flexible.

All three perform these functions:

- Convert extended memory to expanded memory
- Act as a LIM, XMS, and EEMS memory manager
- Fill "holes" in conventional memory with EMS memory
- Load TSR programs including LANtastic in high memory
- Load device drivers (like ANSI.SYS) into high memory
- Copy slow ROMS into faster RAM

As we saw with HIMEM and EMM386, memory manager software can be complicated to install. Virtually every PC has a different combination of memory, video boards, network boards, and adapter addresses. Improperly installed memory manager software can create a myriad of problems, from lost memory to system crashes. Fortunately, all three of the programs mentioned above include installer and optimizer programs that make installation as simple as possible, and programs like 386Max's ASQ and Quarterdeck's MANIFEST can also help guide you through the installation process.

Since our example system is an 80386, we'll use Quarterdeck's QEMM-386 to show how an expanded memory manager can increase your DOS memory. (Quarterdeck produces a similar product called QRAM—pronounced "cram"—for 8088 and 80286 systems.) The techniques discussed here will work on 80386SX and all 486-equipped PCs.

QEMM includes the excellent MANIFEST system analysis program and a memory optimizer program called OPTIMIZE. Typically, you install QEMM-386 using the INSTALL program provided with the product, and then run OPTIMIZE. The OPTIMIZE program inspects your computer's hardware, software, and memory, and then maximizes the amount of free memory. Normally, you run the OPTIMIZE program only once; it automatically changes the QEMM settings in your CONFIG.SYS file.

Our example system had 525k of free memory in its standard configuration. After installing QEMM-386 and running the OPTIMIZE program, the available DOS memory increased to 612k, as shown in Figure 4.9.

Memory Management

Figure 4.9

MANIFEST's display of available memory for our example system with QEMM-386 installed.

```
First Meg / Overview
        Memory Area      Size     Description
        0000 - 003F      1k       Interrupt Area
        0040 - 004F      0.3k     BIOS Data Area
        0050 - 006F      0.5k     System Data
        0070 - 062F      23k      DOS
        0630 - 06DA      2.7k     Program Area
        06DB - 9FFF      612k     [Available]
        ===Conventional memory ends at 640k====
        A000 - AFFF      64k      VGA Graphics
        B000 - B7FF      32k      High RAM
        B800 - BFFF      32k      VGA Text
        C000 - C7FF      32k      Video ROM
        C800 - CDFF      24k      Unused
        CE00 - DFFF      72k      High RAM
        E000 - EFFF      64k      Page Frame
        F000 - FFFF      64k      System ROM
             HMA         64k      First 64k Extended

First Meg / Programs
        Memory Area      Size     Description
        0630 - 06C4      2.3k     COMMAND
        06C5 - 06C9      0.1k     [Available]
        06CA - 06DA      0.3k     COMMAND Environment
        06DB - 9FFF      612k     [Available]
        ====Conventional memory ends at 640k=====
        B000 - B7FE      31k      [Available]
        CE00 - CE0B      0.2k     [Available]
        CE0C - CF0E      4k       DOSKEY
        CF0F - CFF3      3.6k     AEX
        CFF4 - D3A8      14k      AILANBIO
        D3A9 - D70C      13k      REDIR
        D70D - DFFF      35k      [Available]
```

■ QEMM-386

QEMM-386

👍 Works well with LANtastic

👍 Leaves more RAM for DOS programs

👍 Is easy to install and optimize

👍 Can move slow ROMs to faster RAM

If you compare QEMM's results to those attained by HIMEM/EMM386, you'll see that they are quite similar. But QEMM has an additional feature that sets it apart from HIMEM. When QEMM first loads, it scans the system memory area looking for ROMs. Since ROM chips are very slow compared to RAM, QEMM copies the contents of the ROMs into extended memory and then maps the extended memory into the area previously occupied by the ROMs. This technique, called *ROM shadowing*, improves system performance noticeably.

Some systems (but not our example machine) employ two ROM chips that contain redundant information. QEMM recognizes these "split ROMs" and eliminates the redundant data, thus compressing them to half their original size. In some Compaq machines, ROM BIOS chips that previously required 64k of address space can be compressed to 32k, leaving 32k of extra free space for programs in high memory.

- *What LANtastic Does*
- *Starting LANtastic*
- *Using the Connection Manager Menu System*

CHAPTER 5

Using LANtastic Every Day

This chapter begins the "hands-on" section of the book. We've designed it as a tutorial for people who have a working knowledge of DOS, but no specific knowledge of LANtastic or networks in general. You can do most of the example exercises in this and following chapters on your own system. If you don't have access to a PC on a LANtastic network system, you can still follow along by referring to the screen illustrations.

Like all network systems, LANtastic is very complex. Many of the most difficult LANtastic procedures are related to security and network management, so we'll save those topics for Chapter 6. Here we'll focus on the basic LANtastic operations you're likely to do every day.

■ What LANtastic Does

Essentially, network operating systems do one thing: They make disk drives, printers, and other shared devices available to other users on the network. If you need access to files residing on a computer down the hall, the network software enables you to access those files as if they resided on drives in your own machine. Similarly, LANtastic lets you use printers located thousands of feet away as if they were attached to your own LPT1 port. Finally, LANtastic allows you to use network modems or connections to minicomputers as though they were connected to your own COM1 port.

In Chapter 1, we introduced the concepts of servers and clients. Basically, a machine containing a shared resource—a disk drive, modem, or printer—is a server, while a machine making use of a shared resource is a client. Some network operating systems (Novell's NetWare, for example) use dedicated servers. In a dedicated server network, file servers provide print and file sharing services for all the clients on the network.

LANtastic is a *peer-to-peer* system, meaning that all the PCs on the LAN are peers. Any networked PC can be a server, a client, or both a server and a client at the same time.

Network files and programs can be shared by several users, so several people can have simultaneous access to the same data. For example, a large central customer database could be stored on a network and accessed by dozens or even hundreds of people at once. Before the advent of the LAN, such sharing of important data wasn't possible without a large, expensive mainframe or minicomputer system.

In its simplest sense, LANtastic adds one or more disk drives and printers to the PCs connected to the LAN. As a LAN user, you can control how those disk drives and printers work. You can add drives, remove drives, and assign different printers to your computer. All these tasks are controlled by the network software. By learning a few basic LANtastic operations, you can tailor the network to suit your needs.

About Network Drives

Your PC probably has a floppy disk drive designated as drive A: and a hard disk named drive C:. These are *physical* drives; they actually exist in your computer. LANtastic also allows you to use disk drives located on someone else's computer as though they were on your own machine. When you use one of these *logical* drives, it shows up on your PC with a name like F: or X:. The LANtastic redirector software essentially tricks your PC's DOS into thinking that it has another drive or two.

Similarly, when you attach a network printer, LANtastic tells DOS to send all printer output to the network printer instead of sending it to the PC's own printer port.

To a user on a client PC, a LANtastic network drive looks very much like a regular DOS drive. LANtastic drives have volume names, just as DOS drives do, and LANtastic volumes have subdirectories containing individual files, just like DOS disks.

Access Privileges

For all their similarities, there are also some major differences between logical network drives and physical drives.

If you have a hard disk on your PC, you have access to all the files on that disk. You are free to view files, create files, delete files, change existing files, or even format the entire hard disk. On a network drive you may or may not have any of these rights, or *privileges*, as they are called in LANtastic. File and printer privileges are controlled by the system manager, who can delegate access privileges to other users as necessary. Rights are assigned on a directory-by-directory basis. Rights to a given directory may be assigned on a user-by-user basis, or may be given jointly to a group of users.

We'll take a detailed look at privileges and network security in Chapter 6. For now, you need to know that you may not have rights to all the files on the LAN, and that no one else (except the system manager) has rights to the files on your PC unless you grant them those rights. If you've just installed a new LANtastic network, you'll find that all network users have full rights to all shared files on the network. This approach works well for small networks of only two or three users, and it allows you to learn LANtastic without learning the ins and outs of network security, but before you begin using LANtastic for day-to-day work, we strongly advise you to implement the program's security features.

File Sharing and Record Locking

There is one more important difference between network disks and "real" disks. On a network, it is possible for more than one user to have access to the same file at the same time. This doesn't normally happen on a non-networked PC, since only one user at a time can use the machine, but on a network, dozens of users may have access to the same file simultaneously. If all the users are only reading the file, there's no problem; they all see the same data. However, if more than one user tries to write to the same file at the same time, there's obviously a potential for conflict. To prevent problems caused by multiple users trying to write to the same file simultaneously, LANtastic uses the record locking mechanism built into DOS version 3.1 and higher. This feature allows the network to block access to a portion of a file while a user writes data to it.

Logging into a LANtastic Network

All network operating systems provide security features, and LANtastic is no exception. Typically, each user on the network has a unique user name and password. The user name identifies the user to the network operating system, and the password verifies that the user is an authorized user of the network. In most other network systems, you must enter the user name and an optional password when you first connect to the network. LANtastic doesn't require your user name and password until you actually try to use shared network resources.

Before you can use resources on another networked PC, you must establish a connection to that PC. This process is called *logging in*. Once you've logged into another PC, you can use any resources on that PC as long as you have sufficient privileges.

■ Starting LANtastic

As we saw in Chapter 4, The LANtastic INSTALL.EXE program automatically creates a batch file named STARTNET.BAT to start the network software. STARTNET.BAT contains all the commands necessary to load the LANtastic software, but doesn't normally add any remote drives or printers to your PC. To gain access to network drives and printers, you use the LANtastic Connection Manager program named NET.EXE, which is normally located in your C:\LANTASTI directory.

The Connection Manager won't run unless the LANtastic software is installed. To start your LANtastic network, switch to the C:\LANTASTI directory and type **STARTNET**. As each program named in STARTNET loads, it displays a sign-on message. Figure 5.1 shows the result of a typical STARTNET run.

The Connection Manager has two modes of operation: a menu mode and a command-line mode. In menu mode, you pick options from a series of on-screen menus, and the Connection Manager performs the operations you choose. In command-line mode, you enter an entire command to NET.EXE at the DOS command prompt and NET carries out your instructions. Command-line options can be used in batch files, while menu options can't.

Figure 5.1

The LANtastic STARTNET.BAT file in operation. STARTNET loads the components of the LANtastic networking software.

```
C:\LANTASTI>startnet
SHARE installed
AEX AI-LANBIOS(R) driver V3.01 - (C) Copyright 1992 ARTISOFT Inc.

Command line               IRQ=15 IOBASE=300 VERBOSE
IEEE 802.3 node address    00006E2F68E7    Network packet size     1500
MPX interface number       C7              IO base address         0300
Interrupt request (IRQ)    15              Network buffer size     16384
Packet type                IEEE 802.3      Transmit buffers        20
Bytes of memory used       3648
            ---- AEX driver installed ----
Adapter Independent AI-LANBIOS(R) V3.01 - (C) Copyright 1992 ARTISOFT Inc.
AEX AI-LANBIOS(R) driver V3.01 - (C) Copyright 1992 ARTISOFT Inc.
            ---- AI-LANBIOS(R) Installed ----
LANtastic (R) Redirector V4.10 - (C) Copyright 1992 ARTISOFT Inc.
U.S.A. version only - NOT FOR EXPORT.
            ---- LANtastic (R) Redirector Installed ----
LANtastic (R) Server V4.10 - (C) Copyright 1992 ARTISOFT Inc.
U.S.A. version only - NOT FOR EXPORT.
            ---- LANtastic (R) Server Installed ----
C:\LANTASTI>
```

The menu mode is easiest to learn, because all possible choices are presented on the screen. The command-line options take a while to master, but once you've learned them, they're faster to use than the menu system.

In this chapter, we'll examine the menu mode of operation; we'll show you how to use the command-line options in Chapter 7. The LANtastic for Windows product also includes a Windows version of the Connection Manager, which we'll examine in Chapter 9.

■ Using the Connection Manager Menu System

To start the Connection Manager program in menu mode, type **NET** from the DOS command prompt. The main menu will appear, as shown in Figure 5.2.

The Connection Manager main menu provides access to all of LANtastic's features. Before we dig into the specifics of the menu items, let's take a look at the menu choices.

- *Network Disk Drives and Printers* is the most important and frequently used item on the menu. This choice lets you add and remove network drives and printers.

- *Printer Queue Management* lets you view and control network printers.

- *Mail Services* lets you exchange electronic mail messages with other users on the network.

- *Chat with Another User* allows you to conduct a real-time, back-and-forth keyboard conversation with another user on the network.

Figure 5.2

The main Connection Manager menu. From this menu, you can add and remove network drives and printers, send mail to other users, and perform several network maintenance operations.

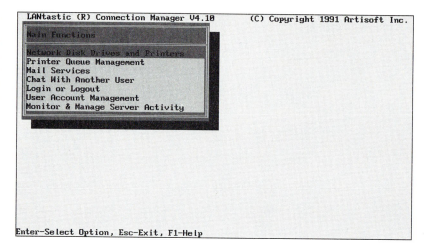

- *Login or Logout* lets you make or break connections with the servers on your network.

- *User Account Management* lets you change your network password, check your network access privileges, and monitor the status of your network account.

- *Monitor and Manage Server Activity* lets you see who is using which network resources.

To select any of the Connection Manager menu choices, use the arrow keys to move the highlight bar to the desired item, and then press Enter. Not surprisingly, each of the menu choices represents a major feature of LANtastic. In the following sections, we'll investigate each menu item and show you how to use the Connection Manager to manage your network activities.

Adding a Network Drive

We'll begin our tour of the Connection Manager menu system with the first item, Network Disk Drives and Printers. As its title implies, you use this menu choice to add and delete network drives and printers. When you select this item from the main Connection Manager menu, you'll see a display like the one in Figure 5.3.

This screen shows the active network drive and printer assignments. If you aren't using any network drives or printers, there won't be any entries on the screen, as in the previous figure; however, notice that the screen does identify drives A:, B:, and C: as physical drives.

Figure 5.3

The Network Disk Drives and Printers display screen, from which you can view, add, and delete network drive and printer assignments.

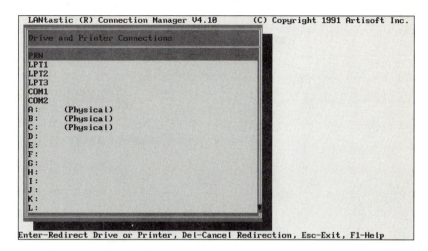

The example network we'll be looking at has two servers named ALR486 and LTE386. Initially, server names are displayed in parentheses on the Network Disk Drives and Printers screen to indicate that a server is active but you haven't yet logged into it. Once you log into a server, LANtastic removes the parentheses and adds two backslashes to the server's name.

To use a network disk drive, follow these steps:

1. From the Network Drives and Printers screen, select the drive letter to use for the network drive. To select a drive letter, use the arrow keys to move the highlighted bar to the desired drive letter, or simply type the letter. In either case, you'll need to press Enter after you make your selection. Since our example system has physical drives in drives A: through C:, we'll select drive D: as our first network drive. When you type **D** and press Enter, LANtastic displays a list of available network servers.

2. Select a server from the list. If the server you want to use isn't on the list, press Ins and type the name of the server, as shown in Figure 5.4.

3. Once you've selected a server, you'll be asked to enter your user name and password.

4. LANtastic will ask if you want to set your PC's clock to the server's clock. This feature is useful if your PC doesn't have an internal clock (most do), or if you want to make sure your PC's clock is set correctly.

5. Select a network drive to use and press Enter. The newly assigned drive will appear in the window on the left side of the screen. In our example, we've mapped drive D: to the C: drive on server \\LTE386 (see Figure 5.5).

Figure 5.4

Specifying a server on the Network Drives and Printers screen.

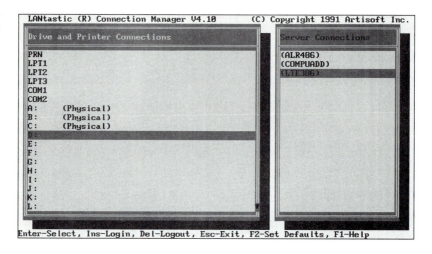

Figure 5.5

In this example, logical drive D: has been assigned to physical drive C: on server \\LTE386.

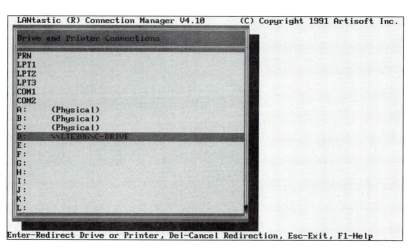

6. To add another network drive, repeat steps 1 through 5. When you're finished adding network drives, press Esc to leave the Network Drives and Printers menu.

You can add as many network drives as you need. As a rule, you should connect only to drives that you'll actually be using. Each server has a predefined maximum number of connections, and each drive mapping uses one of those connections.

If you'll always be using the same user name and password, you may want to take advantage of the default user name feature. With the list of servers on the screen (see step 2), press the F2 key. LANtastic will ask for a user name and password, and will then use that user name and password for all future logins.

Adding a Network Printer

To add a network printer, you follow the same basic steps as for adding a network drive: Select a printer port to use, and then select a network printer from the list of available printers. If you're not already logged in, LANtastic will ask for your user name and password.

Sharing a printer among several users is easier than it sounds. Most application software in use today is designed to send printer output to one of the PC's built-in printer ports. LANtastic intercepts this output and routes the print data to a network printer.

The parallel printer ports on your PC are called LPT1, LPT2, and LPT3. You don't actually need to have a printer port installed in your PC to use a network printer. Even if you have only one physical port (LPT1), you can still use all three logical parallel ports for network printing. If you have a "local" printer attached, you can still use the network printers, through the same printer port your local printer uses.

In addition to the three parallel ports, DOS supports printer connections on serial ports COM1 and COM2. By connecting a network printer to each of the serial and parallel ports, you can use as many as five network printers at once. By connecting each available printer port to a different network printer, you can send print jobs to multiple network printers from your workstation. As Figure 5.6 shows, you can use the same network printer or a different one for each port.

Since many users share network printers, LANtastic must deal with several people trying to use the same printer at once. It does this through the use of *print queues*, which are "holding areas" for print jobs on their way to the printer. Each server may have a print queue, and each queue can service several printers.

As users send jobs for printing, LANtastic places them in the appropriate queue. This process (also known as *spooling*) allows an application program running on a client PC to dispense with printing very quickly, because the software does not have to wait for the printer. The print data flows from your PC to the server at a very high speed, and once your print job has been sent to the server, your PC is free for other work.

When a user's application program signals that it is finished printing, the server sends the queued print job to the appropriate printer. This may take some time, depending on the number of jobs already in line. Print jobs are normally handled on a first-come, first-served basis.

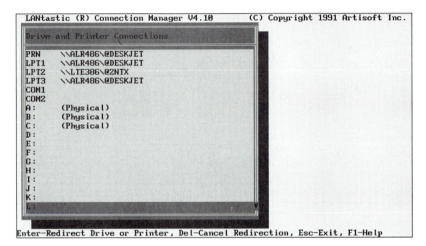

Figure 5.6

LANtastic's printer redirection function catches and redirects print jobs sent from application programs to the local printer ports on a client workstation. You can link each printer port to a different network printer. In this example, printer ports LPT1 and LPT3 are connected to the HP Deskjet printer on server ALR486, and port LPT2 is connected to the LaserWriter NTX on server LTE386.

Printing Pitfalls

Network printing seems to be the one part of LANtastic that causes users the most grief. Our experience has shown that nothing prints right the first time, even on a printer attached directly to your PC, and using a networked printer adds another layer of frustration. When you use a shared network printer, you might send a big file to the print server, wait for the job to make its way through the queue behind print jobs from seven other people, and then find that the right margin is too wide, that it's printed on the wrong type of paper, or... you get the picture.

You can take one simple step to help reduce this frustration, and it doesn't have anything to do with LANtastic. If your software provides a "print preview" feature, use it! Many word processor and spreadsheet packages offer some sort of print preview function. While you may not be able to see all the details of the document, most print previewers will reveal glaring problems like bad pagination, wrong margins, and other formatting errors. Previewing saves time, effort, energy, paper, printer ink, and frustration!

One thing to keep in mind when using a network printer is that you don't "own" the printer, even if it's attached to your PC! You are sharing the printer with several other users. If you are accustomed to printing on a printer dedicated to your PC, you expect paper to start churning out as soon as you start printing. This is not the case with network printers. When you send a print job to a network printer, several other print jobs may be ahead of yours.

It is important to make sure you are sending your print job to the right printer. If you're using WordPerfect and your copy is set up for a NEC Laser printer, you must send your print job to that type of printer. If you send it to a line printer, you'll get pages and pages of PostScript data. Conversely, if you send non-PostScript output to a PostScript printer, nothing at all will happen, because PostScript printers don't print anything that's not sent in PostScript format! The printer takes the data, looks at it, decides it's not PostScript, and ignores it.

Another problem occurs frequently with Hewlett-Packard Laser printers. If you mistakenly send HP printer output to a dot-matrix printer, you may get dozens or even hundreds of pages of gibberish. This happens because these printers use a series of special characters to control printer functions, and one frequently used control character happens to mean "eject the current page" to most dot-matrix printers.

You can avoid most of these problems by organizing your network resources carefully. We'll offer more tips for managing your network printers in Chapter 6.

Managing Print Queues

As you learned in the previous section, your print jobs go to a print queue on the server when you print to a network printer. Since other users may also have jobs in the queue, LANtastic provides a convenient way for you to check on the status of your print job. The Printer Queue Management screen shows the status of all the jobs in the print queue. To see the jobs in a print queue, select Printer Queue Management from the main LANtastic menu, and then select a file server from the list of servers that appears. Next, you'll see the printer queue display. Figure 5.7 shows a printer queue display with several jobs in the queue.

Although the printer queue display looks simple enough, you can perform dozens of operations from this screen. Typically, most of these tasks are performed by people designated as *queue managers*, who can control other users' print jobs; if you're not a queue manager, you can control only your own jobs. We'll examine the queue manager options in Chapter 6.

The Printer Queue Display

As you saw in the previous figure, there are three windows on the Printer Queue Management screen. Let's begin with the main window at the top of the display.

Chapter 5: Using LANtastic Every Day

Figure 5.7

A typical printer queue display. In this example, several jobs are waiting for the printer, and one job is being printed. The jobs will print in the order shown.

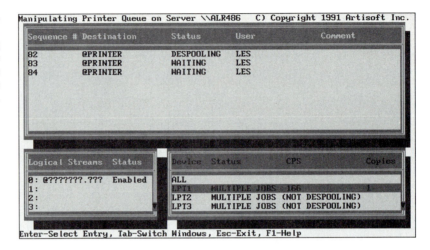

Each job waiting in the queue is represented by a line in the print jobs window that shows its sequence, destination, status, user name, and an optional comment.

The server normally prints incoming jobs in the order they are received. The Sequence # column shows the order in which the server received the current print jobs.

Each server (and therefore each print queue) can manage up to five printers. The Destination column shows the destination printer for each print job.

The Status column shows the status of each job in the queue. A job's status can be one of the following:

Status	Meaning
Deleted	This job has been deleted.
Despooling	This job is currently being printed.
Held	Either the user or a queue manager has placed this job on hold. It will remain on hold until it is released for printing.
Immediate	This print job is using the immediate despooling option. The job will begin printing even though the application program is still sending print data to the spooler.

Rush   This job has been rushed by a queue manager. It will print next, even though other jobs are ahead of it in the queue.

Waiting   This job is waiting for a printer, probably because another job is using the target printer.

The User column shows the user name of the person who placed the print job in the queue.

The Comment column displays any comments related to each print job.

The two windows at the bottom of the Printer Queue Management screen are provided for queue managers. The window at the bottom-left of the screen shows the printer streams status. *Printer streams* provide a convenient way to separate print jobs bound for the same printer. For example, you can establish a stream for letterhead and another stream for plain paper.

The window at the lower-right corner of the Printer Queue Management screen shows the status of each printer attached to the selected server. Queue managers can use this window to stop, start, and pause selected printers. We'll discuss queue management and printer streams in detail in Chapter 6.

Controlling Printer Queues

Remember, as a print queue user, you can control only print jobs that you placed in the queue. Unless you've been granted the queue manager privilege, you can't delete or modify jobs other users have placed in the queue.

To delete a print job from the queue, select the job with the arrow keys and press the Delete key. LANtastic will confirm that you really want to delete the job. If the job is already printing, LANtastic will print a "CANCELLED" message on the document.

To modify a print job waiting in the queue, select the job with the arrow keys and press Enter. You'll see the menu of options shown in Figure 5.8. Note that you can't change a job once it begins printing; you can only modify jobs that are waiting to print.

When you select a print job from the queue, a pop-up menu appears listing the operations you can perform on the selected entry. They are as follows:

Menu Item   Function

Copy   Copies the queue job to a disk file. Use this choice when you want to keep an on-disk copy of the print job. The saved file will contain all the printer formatting codes.

Delete   Deletes the job from the queue. Use this option to cancel a print job.

Hold	Holds the entry but does not delete it. Use this feature when you want to temporarily delay printing of a job already in the queue.
Release	Releases a print job that has been placed on hold.
Rush	Marks this job entry as top priority. If you have several jobs in the queue, the "rush" job will print first.
Show	Shows detailed information about the print job including time printed and amount of data.
View	Displays the selected print job in a window on the screen.

Again, if your user account has the queue manager privilege, you can perform these operations on all print jobs in the queue.

Figure 5.8

Managing a job in the print queue. The pop-up menu shows the actions you can perform on the selected print job.

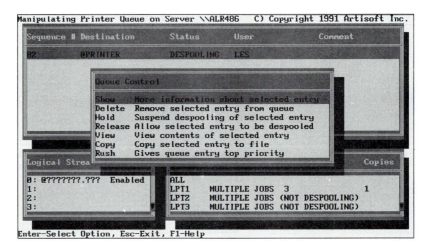

Using LANtastic Mail

LANtastic includes a simple, but very flexible, electronic mail system. As a network user, you can exchange electronic mail messages with any other user on the network. A mail message may be a simple text message, a voice message (if you have an Artisoft Sounding Board), or a disk file.

Each server contains its own set of mail files. When you send network mail to another user, the mail message is stored on a particular server of your choice until the recipient retrieves it. One twist you need to know is this: If you send a mail message to someone via a server that the recipient doesn't log into, he or she will never receive the message. In most cases, we recommend that all users use the same server for all mail messages. In larger organizations with heavy mail-message traffic, you may want to consider adding a dedicated mail server to your network.

Reading Your Mail

To access the LANtastic mail system, select Mail Services from the main Connection Manager menu. The Network Manager will ask you to select a server; choose a server from the list or type the name of the desired server. If you aren't currently logged into the selected server, you'll be asked to enter your user name and password. Once you're connected to a server, you'll see a display like the one in Figure 5.9.

Figure 5.9

Checking incoming mail messages. The top window shows incoming messages; the lower window shows undelivered outgoing messages.

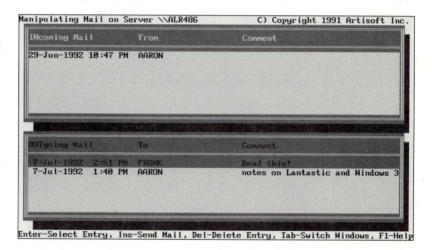

To read an incoming message, move the highlight bar to the desired message and press Enter. A pop-up menu will appear, as shown in Figure 5.10.

As you can see, the pop-up menu allows you to read, delete, forward, or save incoming mail messages. If you have more than one incoming message, you can use the arrow keys to move through the list of incoming messages; you don't have to read them in any particular order. Mail messages remain in your mailbox until you delete them.

LANtastic handles voice messages exactly the same way it handles text-based messages. Voice mail messages appear in your mailbox with a (V) in front of the comment field. You must have a Sounding Board (see Chapter 8) installed to send or play voice mail messages.

Figure 5.10

Selecting an incoming message. The pop-up menu allows you to read, forward, delete, or save the incoming message.

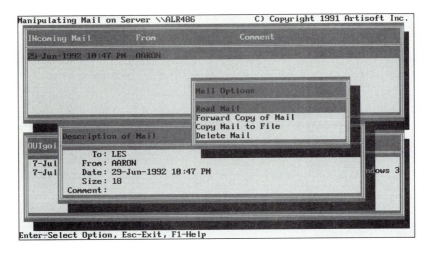

Sending a Mail Message

There are three ways to send a mail message to another user: You can create a text-based message with the mail editor, you can send an existing disk file as a mail message, or you can record a voice mail message.

To send a mail message, select Mail Services from the Connection Manager menu, and then press Ins. A pop-up menu will ask if you want to use the mail editor, send a disk file, or send a voice mail message. Figure 5.11 shows the Send Mail pop-up menu.

Figure 5.11

The Send Mail pop-up menu. From this menu, you can create a message, send an existing voice or text file, or record a new voice message.

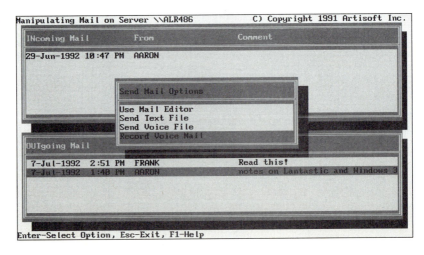

To send a message with the mail editor, you simply compose your message on the screen, and then press the F2 key to send it. LANtastic will ask you to select a user to receive the message.

You can also send a disk file to another user as a mail message. The file must already exist, and you must supply its full path name. Normally, you'd use this feature to send a text file as a mail message, but you can also use it to send binary (nontext) files like spreadsheets, programs, and word processor documents.

To use LANtastic's voice mail functions, you must have an Artisoft Sounding Board and the SOUNDBD.EXE driver (see Chapter 8) must be installed. Then you can record voice mail messages directly from the Send Mail menu and use the mail system to send them to other Sounding Board-equipped users on the network.

Using the Chat Feature

The LANtastic Chat feature allows you to carry on a keyboard-to-screen "conversation" with another user on the network. If both users have a Sounding Board installed, you can speak handset-to-handset over the network.

To use the Chat feature, select Chat with Another User from the Connection Manager main menu. Then press Ins, and type the name of the machine you want to call. If the other machine is logged in, a pop-up message will appear on its screen, telling the user that you wish to chat.

To answer an incoming Chat alert, the called user must start NET and select Chat with Another User from the main menu or type **NET CHAT** from the DOS command line. Once a Chat session has been established, each user's typing appears in one of the two windows on each computer's screen. Figure 5.12 shows a Chat session in progress.

Either user can end a Chat session by pressing Esc or Del.

Other Connection Manager Functions

The last three items on the Connection Manager screen are rarely used system management tools. Login or Logout allows you to log into or log out from additional servers. User Account Management lets you change your password, temporarily disable your user account, and check your access rights on any shared network device. Monitor and Manage Server Activity provides a way for you to monitor the activity on your server, and to shut it down. You'll learn more about these tools in Chapter 8.

104 Chapter 5: Using LANtastic Every Day

Figure 5.12

A network Chat session in progress. Each user can see what the other is typing.

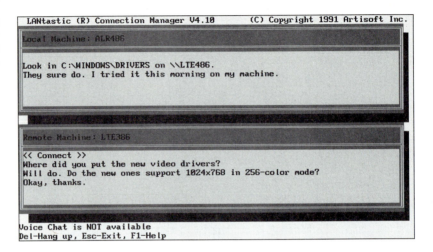

- *LANtastic Security Features*
- *Managing User Security*
- *Managing Shared Resources*
- *Managing Servers*
- *Network Printing*
- *Networking Your Applications*

CHAPTER

Network Management and Security

Because Lantastic is so easy to set up and use, people sometimes overlook an important fact: Networks must be managed. We're not saying a three-user network needs a full-time network administrator, but even small networks need occasional attention.

The old adage about too many cooks spoiling the broth still holds true in the information age. As a network grows larger, it becomes harder to manage. We've found that it's usually best to designate one person or a small group of people as the primary network manager(s). That person or group should be responsible for setting up and maintaining user accounts, keeping track of shared network devices, making backups of network files, and installing new software on the network.

One of the main reasons companies install networks is to promote fast and convenient data sharing. As a network manager, you must make sure users have access to data. Conversely, data security is an important issue; even the smallest company is likely to have sensitive or confidential data stored on one or more PCs on the network. Keeping sensitive data private is an important element of network management.

In this chapter, we introduce the basics of good network management. Because most network management tasks require a solid understanding of network security, you'll find that much of the information in this chapter deals with LANtastic's security features. We'll also point out some common network management problems, and offer solutions to them.

■ LANtastic Security Features

Many people think small networks don't need security, and in a way, Artisoft encourages this attitude; by default, all LANtastic users have full access to all the files on every server. But even the smallest companies probably have some files that should be restricted to access by a few users, and fortunately LANtastic includes a comprehensive set of security features.

LANtastic provides three basic levels of security:

1. *User Security* Each user can be required to provide a unique user name and password before accessing any network resources. This level of security prevents unauthorized users from gaining access to the network and allows LANtastic to uniquely identify each network user. This is your front-line security tool; if unauthorized people can't access the network, they can't get to your data.

2. *Access Control* Each server maintains an *Access Control List,* or ACL, for each shared device on the server. The ACL tells LANtastic which users have access to each shared resource on that server. You can allow access to some users, while protecting a resource from other, unauthorized users. The ACL is a key LANtastic feature; we'll explore it in detail later in this chapter.

3. *Audit Trails* An optional audit trail can keep track of each user's access to any shared device. You can use this feature to monitor access to any network device and to detect attempted security violations.

With a little planning, you can tailor these three tools to provide the level of security appropriate for your organization.

The Network Manager Program

You use the LANtastic Network Manager program to manage shared network resources. LANtastic stores all account and shared resource privilege information in a special directory called the control directory. Each server maintains its own control directory, usually named C:\LANTASTI.NET.

The control directory on each server can have an access password assigned to it, and we strongly advise you to use this feature. The control directory password is separate from any user's account password, and provides the network a sort of "master key" protection.

If you choose to password protect the control directory, you'll be asked to enter the password each time you start the Network Manager program, or whenever you change control directories.

After you start the program and enter the password, the main Network Manager menu, shown in Figure 6.1, appears.

Figure 6.1

The main Network Manager menu. You can control most LANtastic network configuration and security options from this menu.

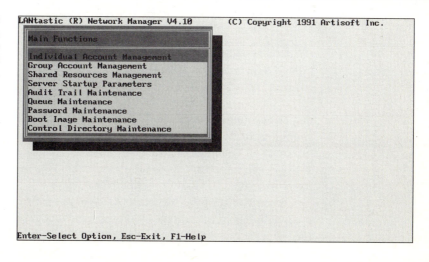

Chapter 6: Network Management and Security

The Network Manager controls all major LANtastic network management and security options from a single menu. The choices on this main Network Manager menu are as follows:

- *Individual Account Management* lets you create, delete, and modify accounts for individual users on the network.

- *Group Account Management* lets you create, modify, and delete group accounts. Group accounts are similar to individual user accounts, but allow several users to share the same account information.

- *Shared Resources Management* manages shared network resources like disks and printers. You can create, delete, or modify security privileges for each shared device from this menu.

- *Server Startup Parameters* controls performance and configuration related settings for servers.

- *Audit Trail Maintenance* controls network auditing.

- *Queue Maintenance* lets you specify the location of print queue files.

- *Password Maintenance* lets you change or delete the master password for the current control directory.

- *Boot Image Maintenance* creates a disk *boot image* used by diskless network workstations.

- *Control Directory Maintenance* lets you select a control directory to use, and make a backup copy of the control directory.

As you can see, many of the items on the Network Manager menu are related to network security. We'll look at the security-related items first, and cover the remaining items in the next section.

It's important to remember that each server contains its own list of user names, account privileges, and access control lists. If you create a user account named BILL on server A, Bill doesn't automatically have an account on server B. You must create a user account on each server a person will use. If Bill doesn't need access to the shared resources on server B, there's no need to create an account for Bill on that server.

When you start the Network Manager program, it assumes you wish to work with the control directory on the local machine. To use a control directory on a different server, choose Control Directory Maintenance on the main Network Manager menu, and select the other server's control directory. If the control directory you select is password protected, you'll be asked to enter the password.

Managing User Security

When you log into a LANtastic network, the network software requires you to enter a user name and password. The user name identifies you to the server, and the password insures that you are who you say you are. This basic level of security prevents unauthorized users from gaining access to the network.

When you enter your user name and password, LANtastic looks them up in the control directory on the target server. Each user account record in the control directory contains detailed information about the user, including password, account expiration date, and any special privileges.

Setting a User's Account Privileges

You control account-related information from the Individual Account Management menu. To add, view, or change a user account record, select Individual Account Management from the Network Manager main menu. A list of all user names will appear. To add a new account, press the INS key. To edit a user account, select a name and press Enter. In either case, the user account information screen will appear. Figure 6.2 shows a sample user record.

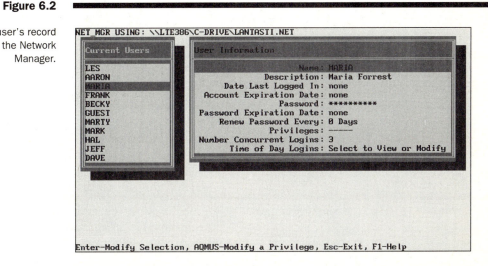

Figure 6.2

Editing a user's record with the Network Manager.

To change any item in a user's information record, move the highlight bar to the desired field and press Enter. LANtastic will prompt you to provide the new information for the field.

The Name field contains the user's account name, which can be up to 16 characters long and must not contain spaces, question marks (?), or asterisks (*). LANtastic always displays user names in uppercase, even if you type them in lowercase or mixed case characters.

The Description field contains a longer descriptive name for the user, usually his or her full name. This name can be up to 32 characters long, and can contain mixed upper- and lowercase.

Date Last Logged In shows the date this user last logged in to this server. If the user has never logged in, this field will be blank.

Account Expiration Date displays the date this user account will expire. This field is optional; it allows you to create temporary accounts that automatically expire after a certain date. Once an account expires, the user can no longer access the server.

The Password field contains the user's password, which can be up to 16 characters long. As with user names, LANtastic automatically converts passwords to all uppercase. Note that the password is hidden from view to protect its confidentiality.

Password Expiration Date is an optional field that contains an expiration date for the user's current password. If you enter a date in this field, the user's password will expire on that date.

The Renew Password Every field sets an automatic password expiration interval. If you activate this feature, the user will be required to enter a new password periodically.

The Privileges field determines any special privileges assigned to this user. The privileges are

Privilege	Purpose
A (access control list)	Prevents LANtastic from checking the access control list for each shared device, effectively granting the user full access to all shared resources on the server.
M (mail manager)	Allows a user to see all mail in the server's mail queue. Normally, a user can only see his or her own mail; this privilege allows the user to read and delete mail for any user on the server.
Q (queue manager)	Allows the user to control other user's print jobs in the print queue. Without this privilege, the user can control only his or her own print jobs.
S (system manager)	Allows a user to issue commands that affect the file server, like NET RUN and NET SHUTDOWN.
U (user audit)	Allows the user to add audit entries to the server's audit log.

The Number of Concurrent Logins field sets the number of simultaneous logins allowed to this user. Normally, this field will be 1, meaning that the user can log into this server from only one workstation at a time. If a particular user needs to log in from several workstations at once, set this number higher to allow more logins.

Time of Day Logins determines when a user is allowed to log in to the server. By default, all users have access to the server 24 hours a day, 7 days a week. You can use this option to control each user's access to the system—for example, you could prevent access to the LAN after business hours. To see the allowed login times, select Time of Day Logins from the Individual User Account menu and press Enter. A chart of login times will appear, as shown in Figure 6.3.

Figure 6.3

Setting the allowed login times for a user. In this example, the user may not log in on Saturday or Sunday, or after 5:00 p.m. on Friday.

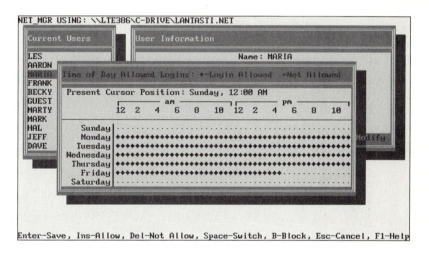

To change the allowed login times, move the cursor to the desired time and press DEL to disallow logins or INS to reallow them. To select a block of times, move the cursor to the start of the block and press B; then move the cursor to the end of the block and press INS or DEL to allow or disallow logins for the selected block. Once you've set the allowed login times, you must press Enter to save the settings.

Managing Group Accounts

If your network has a number of users who need identical network access and privileges, you can create a group account for those users. A group account is a shared network account that allows many users to use the same basic account information and password. Group accounts are convenient, because they allow the system manager to administer many users under the umbrella of one account.

Group account names must end with an asterisk (*). LANtastic uses the asterisk as a "match any name" character. For example, if you created an account named WRITERS_*, anyone could log in using a name like WRITERS_LES or WRITERS_FRANK. A user must know the group account password to gain access to the network. If a shared resource allows rights to the group WRITERS_*, all users in that group inherit those rights.

By default, the LANtastic INSTALL program creates a group account named * that has all privileges and full access to all shared network resources. Because the * means "match any name," any user can log in with any account name. If you plan to use LANtastic's security features, you will need to delete the * account on each server, or reduce the privileges assigned to it.

You create, delete, and modify group accounts with the Group Account Management menu. The Group Account menu looks exactly like the Individual User Accounts menu, and all of the options described earlier for individual user accounts also apply to group accounts; however, there are four subtle differences between group accounts and individual accounts:

- Several users may be using the group account at once, so you need to set the Number of Concurrent Logins to a number large enough to accommodate all the group users.

- Group users cannot change the group password; this must be done manually through the Network Manager program. Because many users will be sharing the same password, we suggest that the network manager change group passwords fairly often.

- The order in which groups appear in the group account list is important. When looking for a group name at login time, LANtastic scans the group account list from the top down. If, for example, the default account * were the first item in the group accounts list, LANtastic would find a match for any group name and log the user in as a member of the * group.

- Similarly, the order in which groups appear in the access control lists is important. When attempting to match a user name to an ACL, LANtastic starts at the top of the ACL. If you wish to grant special rights to a specific group user (like WRITERS_LES), that user's name must appear in the ACL *before* the group name. We'll cover ACL rights in more detail later in this chapter.

■ Managing Shared Resources

The major purpose of any network is to provide a means for sharing resources. With LANtastic, any disk, disk directory, or printer on any server can be shared by the users on the LAN.

Access Control Lists

Network security plays an important part in the management of shared resources. As mentioned earlier, each shared resource has an access control list associated with it. The ACL contains information about the resource, as well as information that tells LANtastic which users are allowed access to the resource.

Each server maintains its own set of access control lists in the control directory. There are access control lists for three types of shared resources:

- *Network Disks*   Each shared network disk or network directory is treated as an individual resource with its own ACL. For example, you can grant some users full access to drive C: on a server, but restrict other users' access to a particular subdirectory on that drive.

- *Network Printers*   Each network print queue has an associated ACL. (Print queue names must start with @.)

- *Network Mail Queues*   The mail queue on each server has its own ACL. (Mail queue names must be @MAIL.)

The access control list for each shared resource can have any combination of rights. Each right grants the user a particular type of access to the shared resource, as shown in Table 6.1. Note that all these rights apply to shared disks, but only the read, write, create, and lookup rights apply to mail queues and printers.

Each access control list can contain an entry for each user or group on the server. In addition, each ACL includes an entry for the ∗ group, which determines the default rights for users who aren't specifically named in the ACL.

If you selected the Install Default Resources option when you installed LANtastic, the INSTALL program automatically created an access control list for each shared disk on your system. By default, the ∗ group has all rights to the files on these disks, except the I and P rights.

To create, delete, and modify shared resources and access control lists, you use the Shared Resource Management menu choice on the Network Manager menu. In the following sections, we'll use the Network Manager to modify the shared resources on a server. We'll start with a standard "out-of-the-box" LANtastic server set up by the LANtastic INSTALL program.

Shared Disk Resources

A shared disk is a disk or directory on a server that has been made available for use on the network. Before a disk can be shared, you must create a shared disk resource to describe the disk.

The LANtastic INSTALL program automatically creates a shared disk resource for each disk drive it finds on the server. Normally, these would be

Table 6.1

Access Control List Rights

RIGHT	ACTIONS ALLOWED	NOTES
R	Open and read data from files, print queues, or mail queues	Grants the user permission to read data from existing files, but does not automatically grant the ability to see those files in a directory listing. The user will be able to open a file only if he or she knows the name of the file. If you want the user to be able to search through a list of files, you must also grant the L right.
W	Open and write data to files, print queues, or mail queues	Does not automatically imply that the user may read data from the file or queue.
C	Create new files, print jobs, or mail messages	Allows the user to create new files, but does not imply that the user can write data to those files.
M	Create new subdirectories	The user can create new subdirectories beneath the current directory, but cannot create files in the new directory unless you also grant the C right.
L	Perform directory lookups, print queue lookups, and mail queue lookups	For files, this right allows the user to perform directory lookups (DOS DIR command, and so on) on the files in the directory. For queues, this right lets the user see the available queue names.
D	Delete existing files	Allows users to delete existing files.
K	Delete directories	Allows the user to delete any subdirectory.
N	Rename files	Allows the user to rename existing files.
E	Run programs	Allows the user to run programs (.EXE, .COM, and .BAT files) from the shared disk.
A	Change the attributes of files in a shared directory	The user may change the DOS file attributes (read only, system, hidden, archive, and so on) of files on the shared disk. Note that many file backup programs change the archive attribute of each file after a backup.
I	Use indirect files	Allows the user to create and use indirect files on the shared disk.
P	Physical access	Allows the user to connect directly to a DOS device, usually a printer.

the A: and B: floppy drives and C:, the server's hard disk. To see the existing shared resources on a server, select the Shared Resources Management menu item from the main Network Manager menu. You'll see a display like the one in Figure 6.4.

Figure 6.4

Viewing the shared resources list with the Network Manager. This list shows the standard resources created by the INSTALL program.

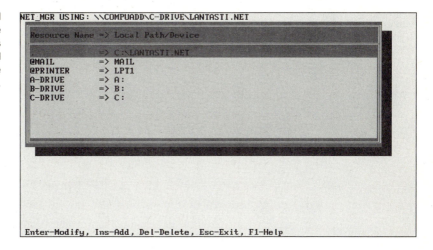

As you can see from the figure, our example server has six resources:

Name	Shared Resource
•	The server's network directory resource. This resource must be present on all servers, and may not be deleted.
@MAIL	The server's mail directory. If a server will be used for electronic mail, this resource must be present, and must be named @MAIL.
@PRINTER	The server's LPT1 printer port.
A-DRIVE	The A: floppy drive.
B-DRIVE	The B: floppy drive. This resource appears only in systems that have two floppy drives.
C-DRIVE	The server's hard disk.

The network directory resource allows users to treat the three shared disk drives (A-DRIVE through C-DRIVE) as though they were subdirectories on the same drive. In our example server we'll map a workstation's E: drive to the server's directory resource. Figure 6.5 shows how the directory of the newly mapped E: drive will look.

Figure 6.5

Using the server's network directory resource. The server's shared disks appear as subdirectory entries beneath the top-level server directory.

```
Volume in drive E is TEST_SERVER
Directory of E:\
.            <DIR>       07-14-92    8:40p
..           <DIR>       07-14-92    8:40p
@MAIL                450 07-14-92    8:40p
@PRINTER             450 07-14-92    8:40p
A-DRIVE      <DIR>       07-14-92    8:40p
B-DRIVE      <DIR>       07-14-92    8:40p
C-DRIVE      <DIR>       07-14-92    8:40p
       7 file(s)         900 bytes
                     2981888 bytes free
```

The @MAIL resource is the server's electronic mail. This resource must be present on all servers that will handle electronic mail, and it must be named @MAIL.

The @PRINTER resource is the LPT1: printer port on the server. A single printer port may have more than one printer resource, but each one must have a different name. We'll show you how to add and delete printer resources later in this chapter.

The A-DRIVE, B-DRIVE, and C-DRIVE resources are the server's A:, B:, and C: disk drives. If your server has more than one logical hard disk, you may see additional network drives; there will be one for each partition on your hard disk.

Again, you can add, modify, and delete shared disk resources with the Network Manager's Shared Resources Management menu item. When you select this item from the main Network Manager menu, you'll see a list of available resources like the one that appeared in Figure 6.4.

Adding New Disk Resources

To add a new disk resource, press INS from the resource display screen. You'll be asked to enter a name for the new resource. It's helpful to give your network disks meaningful names, but resource names are limited to the standard "eight-by-three" DOS file name format. Some example resource names might be XTALK.NET, WORDPERF, ACCT.DAT, and LOTUS123.

Once you've named the new disk resource, the Network Manager will ask you to enter its pathname. Remember that you can specify a single subdirectory as a network disk resource. If you want other users to access the entire C: drive, enter C:\ as the pathname. If you want to make a single subdirectory available for network use, enter the subdirectory name. For example, to make only your WordPerfect subdirectory available for network use, you'd enter C:\WP51 as the pathname, but to make multiple directories available, you'd have to create a separate disk resource for each subdirectory.

After you've entered the pathname, the shared resources list reappears on the screen. Your new resource should be at the bottom of the list. Figure 6.6 shows the resource list on our example server after we added a new resource named GAMES.

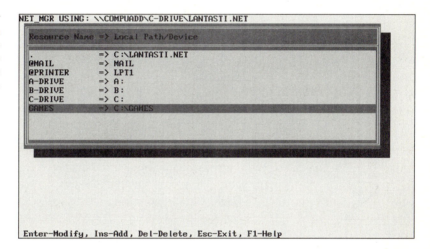

Figure 6.6

The Network Manager resource list display. In this example, we've added a new resource named *GAMES* to the default resources installed by LANtastic.

When you create a new resource, LANtastic automatically creates a new access control list for it and grants all access rights except I and P to the * group, which effectively grants all access rights to all network users.

Modifying a Disk Resource

You can use the Network Manager to modify any existing disk resource. Select Shared Resources Management from the main Network Manager menu, choose a resource to modify from the list that appears, and then press Enter. You'll see a detailed resource description like the one in Figure 6.7.

The resource description screen works like most other LANtastic screens: To change an item, you move the highlight bar with the arrow keys and press Enter.

When you create a new disk resource, LANtastic prompts you for the resource name and path. As you can see in our example, LANtastic has filled in the name and path in the detailed information screen.

You may find it helpful to fill in the Description field because this field appears next to the resource name in the Connection Manager when users are selecting a resource. The description can be up to 64 characters long.

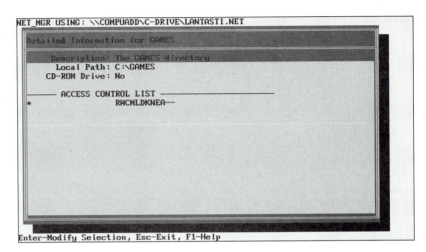

Figure 6.7

The disk resource detailed information screen. In this example, we're working on the GAMES resource. You can see that the disk resource is contained in the subdirectory *C:*\GAMES, and that the * group has all access rights except I and P.

The Local Path field contains the path information you supplied when you created the resource. Normally, you'd change this field only if you were moving the shared files to another subdirectory.

The CD-ROM Drive field tells LANtastic whether this disk is a CD-ROM drive. If it is, this field must be set to Yes.

The bottom half of the detailed information screen shows the access control list entries for this resource. There is only one entry in our example—the one for the * group. Later, we'll modify this entry and add another one.

When you move the cursor to the access control list, the menu at the bottom of the screen changes to show the keys you can use to manage the ACL. Table 6.2 lists these editing keys.

To add a new ACL entry, press INS. LANtastic will ask you to enter the user or group name for the new ACL. Remember that you can use the * character to match any name. For example, if you create a new entry for the group WRITERS_*, any username beginning with WRITERS_ will receive the rights permitted by that entry.

To change an existing ACL entry, move the highlight bar to the desired entry, and use the keys in Table 6.2 to set or remove the desired rights. When you're finished adding and removing rights, press the F9 key to store the edited entry.

When you're editing ACL entries, it's important to remember that LANtastic checks a user's file rights by starting at the top of the ACL list and working down until it finds a match. The * (match any user) entry is always the last item in the ACL list, and cannot be deleted. Remember, the * ACL entry contains the default rights for all users not explicitly named in the ACL. You can use this feature in two ways:

- If the * ACL entry has all rights (the default condition), you can use the preceding ACL entries to *deny* certain rights to certain users. To do this, create an ACL entry for each user or group you wish to deny access. Make sure you remove the desired rights from each ACL entry, but leave the * entry with all rights. When LANtastic scans the ACL, it will find a match for the users who are denied access, but will fall through to the default rights for all other users.

Table 6.2

The Access Control List Editing Keys

KEY	PURPOSE
INS	Adds a new ACL entry before the highlighted entry
DEL	Deletes the highlighted ACL entry
F3	Sets all rights except I and P for the selected entry
F4	Removes all rights from the selected entry
F9	Stores the changed ACL entry
F10	Restores the last saved state for the current entry
R	Adds/Removes the read access right
W	Adds/Removes the write access right
C	Adds/Removes the create file right
M	Adds/Removes the create directory right
L	Adds/Removes the file lookup right
D	Adds/Removes the delete file right
K	Adds/Removes the delete directory right
N	Adds/Removes the rename files right
E	Adds/Removes the execute program right
A	Adds/Removes the change file attributes right
I	Adds/Removes the indirect file right
P	Adds/Removes the physical access right

- If the * ACL entry has no rights, you can add ACL entries to grant specific rights to specific users. To do this, remove all rights from the * entry, and then create an ACL entry for each group or user who should have access. When LANtastic checks the ACL list, it will find a match only for users specifically named in the ACL; all others will receive the default rights—in this case, none—for the resource.

Figure 6.8 shows our example ACL again. This time, we've modified the ACL so the * group has no rights to the GAMES directory, but users FRANK and LES have all rights, so they can use the files in the directory.

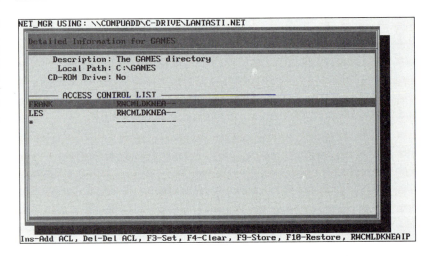

Figure 6.8

A modified ACL entry for the GAMES directory. In this example, users FRANK and LES have all rights to the files in C:\GAMES, but other users have no rights to these files.

Note that users can see a resource in the Connection Manager only if they have some rights to the resource. If a user has no rights to a resource, the resource won't appear as a possible connection in the Connection Manager drive-mapping screen.

Deleting Shared Disk Resources

To delete an existing shared disk resource, select the resource from the resource list screen, and press DEL. The Network Manager will ask you to confirm the deletion. Note that resources cannot be recovered once they are deleted.

Shared Printer Resources

LANtastic allows any printer attached to any server to be shared by other users on the network. Like access to network disks, access to network printer resources is controlled by an access control list. Before network users can use a shared printer, you must create a shared resource to describe it. Printer resource names must begin with @.

Like network disks, any single printer can have multiple resources associated with it. This is most useful with printers that can print in more than one mode. For example, the Okidata 390 dot-matrix printer can print in either normal (10 characters per inch) or compressed (16.7 characters per inch) mode; you could create two resources named @OKINORM and @OKICOMP to access this printer in normal and compressed modes respectively. When you set up the printer resources, you would enter the codes to put the printer in normal and compressed modes. After that, LANtastic would take care of putting the printer in the proper mode before each print job.

You can also create multiple resources for a single printer that accepts different types of paper. For example, you might have a dot-matrix printer that you use with plain white paper, green bar paper, and checks. You could create three resources for that printer named @PLAIN, @GREENBAR, and @CHECKS. Then you could use the Queue Manager's Printer Streams feature to separate print jobs so that each one prints on the proper type of paper. By restricting the ACL for the @CHECKS print device, you could also keep unauthorized people from printing checks. We'll look at printer streams in detail later in this chapter.

You manage network printer resources with the same Shared Resources Management screen that you use for shared network disks.

Adding a New Printer Resource

To add a new printer resource, press INS from the shared resources list screen. LANtastic will ask you to enter a name for the new printer resource. Printer names are subject to the same eight-by-three restrictions as DOS file names, and must begin with @. Try to choose a name that describes each printer to its users; @*PRINTER* (the default printer name) doesn't tell users anything about the printer. Some good names might be @DESKJET, @HP_LASER, @OKI.390, or @LW2NTX.

After you've entered a printer name, The Network Manager asks you to select a printer port. LANtastic supports parallel printer ports LPT1 through LPT3, and serial ports COM1 and COM2. If your printer supports both parallel and serial, use the parallel connection.

When you type the printer name and press Enter, the Network Manager creates the printer resource, and LANtastic assigns default settings and access rights to it.

Modifying Printer Resources

Once you've created a printer resource, you may want to change the default settings and rights for that printer. Select the desired printer resource from the Shared Resources Management resource list screen and press Enter. LANtastic will display the settings and ACL for the specified printer resource, as shown in Figure 6.9.

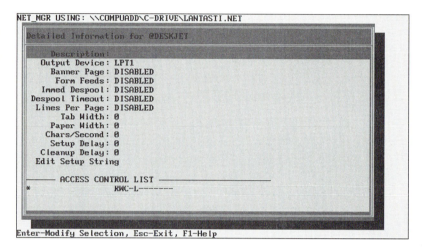

Figure 6.9

Editing a parallel printer resource. This screen shows the default settings assigned to a newly created printer resource. Note that the * group has R, W, C, and L rights to the resource.

As you can see, there's quite a bit of information on this screen. Some of these settings (like Output Device) serve an obvious purpose; others require some explanation. If you create a serial printer resource, the resource display will contain additional items to control the serial communication settings. Table 6.3 describes each setting for our example printer resource.

To change any of these settings, move the highlight bar to the setting and press Enter.

Deleting Printer Resources

To delete an existing printer resource, select the resource from the resource list screen, and press DEL. The Network Manager will ask you to confirm the deletion. Note that resources cannot be recovered once they are deleted.

Printer Access Control Lists

Shared printer resources have an access control list, just as shared disks do, and you edit a printer ACL in exactly the same way you edit one for a shared disk. LANtastic follows the same rules for matching user names with ACL lists as it does for shared disk resources.

Only four rights apply to printers: read, write, create, and lookup. To allow access to a printer, grant all four of these rights; to deny access, revoke all four.

Table 6.3

The Printer Resource Settings

SETTING	DEFAULT VALUE	PURPOSE
Description	Blank	An optional field used to describe the printer to users. The description may be up to 16 characters long, and appears in the Connection Manager when users are choosing a printer.
Output Device	None	Tells LANtastic which printer port to use for the resource. Valid choices are LPT1 through LPT3 and COM1 or COM2.
Banner Page	Disabled	When this feature is enabled, LANtastic prints a banner page before each print job showing the user name, machine name, date and time printed, number of copies, and optional user comments. This is most useful when several users share an unattended printer.
Form Feeds	Disabled	When this feature is enabled, LANtastic sends a form feed character (ASCII value 12 decimal) to the printer after each print job. On most line printers and many non-PostScript laser printers, the Form Feed character advances the paper to the top of the next page, insuring that the next print job will begin on a new sheet of paper.
Immed Despool	Disabled	When activated, the immediate despooling feature tells LANtastic to begin printing jobs before the workstation issues an "end-of-job" indicator. Typically, you use this option when printing very large files so the printer can get started as soon as possible. It is very useful when printing from Windows, because Windows sends most printer output as large graphic images.
Despool Timeout	Disabled	Valid only if immediate despooling (above) is enabled, this option sets the time in seconds that a currently printing job can leave the printer idle. The timeout can be from 0 to 3,600 seconds. If a job leaves the printer idle for more than the allotted timeout period, LANtastic assumes the user is finished with the printer and begins printing the next job in the print queue. A setting of 0 seconds disables the timeout feature.

Table 6.3

(continued)

SETTING	DEFAULT VALUE	PURPOSE
Lines Per Page	Disabled	Sends a form feed (ASCII 12 decimal) to the printer after the specified number of lines, which can be in the range of 0 to 255. A setting of 0 disables the option.
Tab Width	0	Controls automatic tab expansion. Some application programs use the ASCII tab character (ASCII 8 decimal). Most printers understand the tab to mean "move the printhead to the next column," usually in multiples of eight spaces; however, some printers do not support tab characters. Setting this option to a value other than 0 causes LANtastic to send the specified number of spaces to the printer each time a tab character is received. Note that tab expansion can have undesirable effects on word processor and graphics files.
Paper Width	0	Tells LANtastic how many columns your printer can print. This setting is used to determine the allowable width of the banner page. If you are using 8 $\frac{1}{2}$-by-11-inch paper, leave this setting at 0; if you're using a wide-carriage dot-matrix printer, set it to your printer's maximum width (in columns).
Chars/ Second	0	Tells LANtastic how fast to send data to the printer in characters per second. With this option you can direct LANtastic to take time from other tasks (like handling file requests) in order to achieve the desired printing speed. You would typically use this feature to maintain maximum print speed at the possible expense of network performance.
Setup Delay	0	Controls the amount of time LANtastic pauses after sending a setup string (described below) to the printer. This setting is normally used only on older printers that require a pause between mode changes.
Cleanup Delay	0	Controls the amount of time LANtastic pauses after sending a cleanup file to the printer. This setting is normally used only on older printers that require a pause between mode changes.

Table 6.3

(continued)

SETTING	DEFAULT VALUE	PURPOSE
Edit Setup String	None	Pops up a menu that allows you to enter setup and cleanup codes for your printer. See the section on "Printer Setup Strings" for more details.
If you selected a serial communications port for your printer, the printer resource screen will contain these additional settings:		
Baud Rate	9,600	Selects the communication speed between the serial port and your printer. Both the port and the printer must be set to the same speed. LANtastic supports all standard speeds between 110 and 115,200 bits per second.
Word Length	8	Defines the number of data bits to be sent to the printer. Most printers accept 8-bit data, but some older daisy-wheel printers accept only 7-bit data.
Stop Bits	1	Selects the number of stop bits to be added to the printer data stream. Normally, you use 1 stop bit with 8-bit data or 7-bit data with parity, and 2 stop bits for 7-bit data without parity.
Parity	None	Sets the parity-checking used in the printer data stream. For printers that can accept 8-bit data, set this to none. If your printer uses 7-bit data, use the same parity setting at both ends. The possible choices are odd, even, mark, and none.
Flow Control	Hardware	Selects the flow-control method used between your printer and the server. Hardware handshaking is the best choice, but some older printers cannot perform hardware flow control. With those machines, you can probably use XON/OFF (also known as DC1/DC3) flow control.
To change any of these settings, move the highlight bar to the setting and press Enter.		

Printer Setup Strings

As mentioned earlier, you can create several shared printer devices for the same physical printer, and each shared device can put the printer into a particular print mode.

To use this feature, you must know the printer control codes for the various print modes you want to use. Virtually all printers use special sequences of characters to control different aspects of their operation. These sequences almost always begin with the ASCII escape character (decimal 27), so they are known as *escape sequences*.

It's important to note that many application programs, particularly word processors, can control the printer modes themselves. If you're using an application program that knows how to change printer modes, you don't need setup strings. The setup strings feature is most often used in conjunction with applications that can't control the printer modes directly.

As an example, let's look at a typical dot-matrix printer, the Okidata 390. This printer can print several type styles in a variety of sizes. For our example, we'll create two shared print devices named @OKINORM and @OKICOMP. The @OKINORM print device will print at the normal 10 characters per inch, and @OKICOMP will print in compressed print mode at 16.7 characters per inch.

The escape sequence to put the Okidata printer in compressed print mode is Escape, followed by Ctrl-O. To reset the printer to normal printing, you send the printer Escape-@.

We'll begin by creating the @OKINORM and @OKICOMP print devices, using the procedure described earlier in this chapter, under "Adding a New Printer Resource." Then we'll edit the @OKINORM device to add the printer reset codes to it. When you move the highlight bar to the Edit Setup String item and press Enter, the Network Manager displays the pop-up menu shown in Figure 6.10.

There are two ways to use printer setup strings: If your printer requires a brief setup string before the print job, you can use the Setup String option, which sends a user-defined string of characters before each print job. If your printer requires setup strings before *and* after each print job, you can use the Setup File option. To use this option, you put the setup and cleanup strings in disk files and tell LANtastic to send the contents of the files to the printer before and after each print job.

If you choose the second method, you must prepare one or two text files that contain the necessary printer control codes. If your printer uses the ASCII escape character as the command prefix character (most do), you'll need to use a text editor program that allows you to insert control characters into the file (many text editors don't). For our example, we only need to send a brief string before each print job, so we'll use the Setup String method.

Managing Shared Resources

Figure 6.10

Editing the printer setup strings. The pop-up menu allows you to define a string of characters to send to the printer before each job, or a file to send to the printer before and after each job.

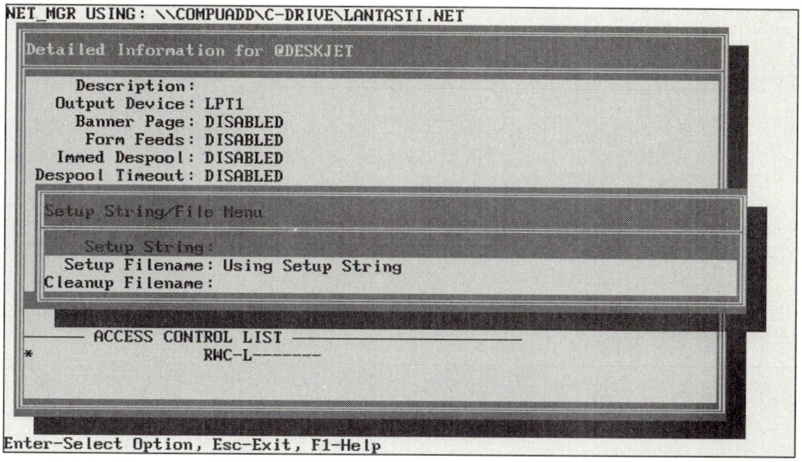

To add our printer reset code to the printer resource, select Setup String and press Enter. Another pop-up window appears on the screen, showing a blank setup string. To insert the first character (escape), press INS. A third pop-up window appears, asking for the first character of the string, as shown in Figure 6.11.

Figure 6.11

Entering a printer setup string. In this example, we're entering the ASCII escape character, which has a hexadecimal value of 1B.

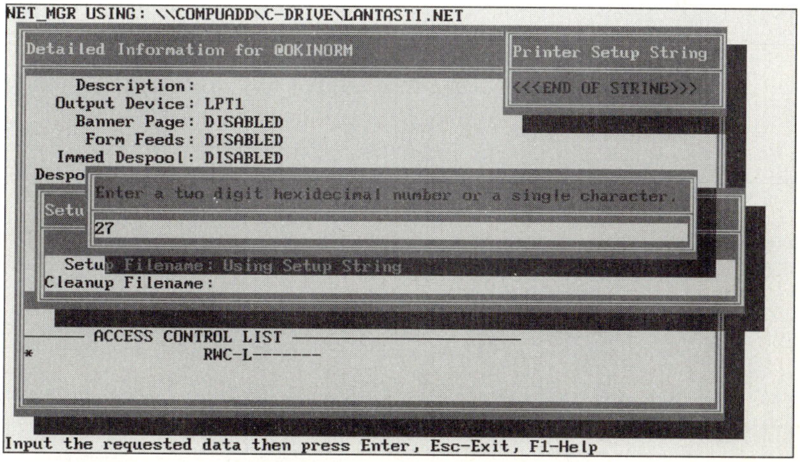

To add the second character (@) of the escape sequence, we repeat the process, this time entering @ as the second character of the string. Note that printer control codes are case sensitive, so you must enter them exactly as they are shown in your printer manual.

Next, we repeat the process for the @OKICOMP printer device, this time using the characters Escape, Ctrl-O to put the printer into compressed mode. Now, when users print to @OKICOMP, LANtastic will send Escape, Ctrl-O to the printer, and when they print to @OKINORM, LANtastic will send the Escape-@ printer reset sequence to the printer before each job.

■ Managing Servers

In many cases, you can simply install LANtastic with the INSTALL program and begin using your network. LANtastic will deliver perfectly acceptable server performance, and you may never need to deal with the technical end of server maintenance.

There are some situations, though, where "tweaking" the server a little will go a long way toward improving your network's performance. In this section, we'll show you how to adjust LANtastic's server settings and how to use the program's server auditing features.

Server Startup Parameters

Artisoft's engineers designed LANtastic as a peer-to-peer networking system. In real terms, this means many network users will have to run the SERVER.EXE program on their PC so that other users can share its resources. SERVER.EXE needs memory, and every byte of memory it uses is one less byte available to the user.

When SERVER.EXE starts up, it has to set several operating parameters which are then stored in the control directory on each server. The startup parameters control how much RAM the SERVER.EXE program can use, and also determine how SERVER.EXE uses the server PC's available RAM and CPU resources.

Many of the default server settings were chosen to provide the best possible server performance with minimal RAM usage. If you'll be running memory-hungry applications on a server machine, you'll appreciate LANtastic's relatively low RAM consumption.

On dedicated servers or servers that will receive only light use as workstations, RAM usage isn't a major consideration. By adjusting some of the server parameters, you can dramatically increase the server's performance.

To adjust these settings select Server Startup Parameters on the main Network Manager menu. Figure 6.12 shows a typical startup parameters display.

Table 6.4 lists the server parameters in the order in which they appear on the screen. We've marked the performance-related settings with a 👍 symbol. You may have to do some good old fashioned trial-and-error experimentation to find the best combination of settings for your needs.

Managing Servers

Figure 6.12

Editing the server startup parameters.

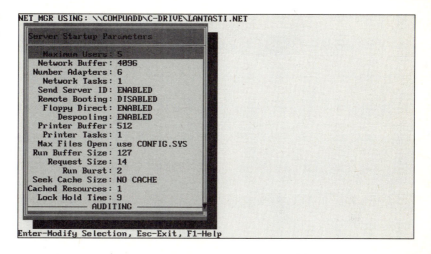

Table 6.4

LANtastic's Server Parameters

SERVER SETTING	DEFAULT VALUE/ POSSIBLE SETTINGS	PURPOSE
Maximum Users	5/2 to 300	Sets the maximum number of users that can be logged into the server at one time.
Network Buffer	4,096/2,048 to 57,344 bytes	Sets the size of the communication buffer on the server. Larger buffers enhance network performance because the server can send more data at one time; however, they also use more memory. If you change this setting, you should also change the buffer size setting on every workstation that will connect to this server.
Number Adapters	6/1 to 6	Sets the maximum number of network adapter cards that can be installed in this server. You can leave this setting at the maximum value of 6 even if you have only one adapter card in the server.
Network Tasks	1/1 to 32	Sets the number of tasks the server can manage at one time. You should allocate at least one task for each adapter card installed in the server. Each task requires one network buffer (see above).

Table 6.4
(continued)

SERVER SETTING	DEFAULT VALUE/ POSSIBLE SETTINGS	PURPOSE
Send Server ID	Enabled	When this option is enabled, the server's name appears in the Connection Manager login dialog. If it is disabled, the server's name does not appear, and the user must know the name in order to connect to the server. You can use this as a security tool to hide a server from users—only those who know the server's name will be able to connect to it.
Remote Booting	Disabled	Enabling this option allows diskless workstations to boot from this server using a boot image file. See Chapter 8 for more information on diskless workstations.
Floppy Direct	Enabled	Allows direct disk operations to floppy drives. If this setting is disabled, users cannot format floppy disks or run the DOS CHKDSK utility on the server's floppy drives.
Despooling	Enabled	Allows queued print jobs to print to the attached printer(s).
Printer Buffer 👍	512/512 to 32,768 bytes	Sets the size of the print queue buffer. A larger buffer increases printing performance, but uses more server memory. Even a small increase in buffer size (2,048 bytes, for example) will speed network printing considerably.
Printer Tasks	1/0 to 5	Selects the number of tasks assigned to network printers. Set this option to the number of printers connected to this server, up to the maximum of 5. A setting of 0 disables network printing on this server.
Max Files Open 👍	Use DOS CONFIG.SYS setting/0 to 5,100	Sets the maximum number of files that can be open at once. Normally, LANtastic gets this information from the DOS CONFIG.SYS file, but DOS allows a maximum of only 255 open files. If you have a large number of users on the server, you may need to increase this setting.
Run Buffer Size	127/0 to 1,024	Sets the size (in bytes) of the command buffer reserved for NET RUN commands. Setting the buffer size to 0 disables NET RUN commands.

Table 6.4

(continued)

SERVER SETTING	DEFAULT VALUE/ POSSIBLE SETTINGS	PURPOSE
Request Size 👍	14/14 to 2,048	Sets the size of the server's user request buffer. One request buffer is created for each of the Maximum Users defined above. Increasing this buffer can improve server response time, but uses additional server memory, especially if Maximum Users is set to a large number.
Run Burst 👍	2/1 to 255	Specifies how long (in $1/18$ second intervals) the server can use the CPU before returning control to DOS. Increasing this number to the maximum drastically increases server performance at the expense of any other programs running on the server.
Seek Cache Size 👍	No Cache/0 to 64k	Specifies the size of the memory cache reserved for disk seeks. A larger cache provides faster network disk operation. Even a small cache (2 to 4k) will improve server disk performance.
Cached Resources 👍	1/1 to 50	Sets the number of resources that can be stored in the cache at one time. On dedicated servers, increase this setting by 1 for each shared disk on the server.
Lock Hold Time	9 seconds/0 to 182	Sets the amount of time (in $1/18$ second intervals) the server will wait for a locked record before informing the user that the disk request has failed. Increase this setting to a longer interval (up to 10 seconds at maximum setting) if many users regularly access the same file at the same time.

Auditing Network Activity

LANtastic includes a comprehensive set of auditing tools. Each server can keep an optional audit log file in the control directory that can track server, user, and shared resource activity. You can view the audit log from the Network Manager's Audit Trail Maintenance menu.

Log entries are displayed in the format:

Type Date Time Username Machine Reason {data}

The Type code indicates the type of log entry. The audit log type codes are

Code	Meaning
!	Server shut down
*	Server started
A	User access allowed to resource
D	User access denied to resource
I	User logged in
O	User logged out or server connection broken
Q	User placed an entry on the queue
S	User queue entry sent to network printer
U	User manually placed an entry in the audit log

The Date and Time fields indicate the date and time the audit entry was added to the log. Username and Machine indicate the name of the user involved and the machine the user logged in from. The Reason field indicates the reason the audit entry was made. For shared device (printers and disks) auditing, the Reason field will contain a letter representing the ACL right (RWCD, and so on) that triggered the audit entry. Other reason codes are

DISCON	Server disconnected.
NORMAL	User logged off normally.
SHUTDOWN	User was logged out because server was shut down.
TIMEOUT	User's time-of-day login privileges expired; user was logged out by server.
UPS	User was logged out because server switched to battery back-up power.

The data field contains the name of the file, disk, or printer resource that triggered the audit entry. Figure 6.13 shows a typical audit log.

You can use audit logs to watch for potential security problems, or just to keep track of user activity on the network. Keep in mind that the audit log file expands continually, consuming an increasing amount of disk space on the server. As you can see from our example, the log file can grow very quickly!

Server auditing is controlled through the Server Startup Parameters screen. When you first select this screen, the server startup parameters you saw in Figure 6.12 appear. To see the auditing parameters, press the PgDn key. Figure 6.14 shows the server audit parameters display.

Figure 6.13

A typical server audit log. For this example, we turned on all server auditing features. As a result, the log shows log in, drive mapping, and individual file access activities. Note that this log covers only the few minutes from 4:05 to 4:08 p.m., with only one user on the server.

```
* 92.07.18 16:05:16
I 92.07.18 16:05:26 LES ALR486
A 92.07.18 16:05:27 LES ALR486 L   \????????.???
A 92.07.18 16:05:29 LES ALR486 L   SYDOS
A 92.07.18 16:05:30 LES ALR486 L   \????????.???
A 92.07.18 16:05:33 LES ALR486 L   \C-DRIVE
A 92.07.18 16:05:37 LES ALR486 L   \@???????.???
A 92.07.18 16:05:38 LES ALR486 L   \@DESKJET
A 92.07.18 16:06:06 LES ALR486 L   \SYDOS\????????.???
A 92.07.18 16:06:06 LES ALR486 L   \SYDOS\
A 92.07.18 16:06:11 LES ALR486 L   \SYDOS\TEST
A 92.07.18 16:06:11 LES ALR486 D   \SYDOS\TEST
A 92.07.18 16:06:11 LES ALR486 L   \SYDOS
A 92.07.18 16:07:57 LES ALR486 L   \C-DRIVE\????????.???
A 92.07.18 16:07:57 LES ALR486 L   \C-DRIVE\????????
A 92.07.18 16:07:57 LES ALR486 L   \C-DRIVE\????????.???
A 92.07.18 16:07:57 LES ALR486 L   \C-DRIVE\
A 92.07.18 16:08:20 LES ALR486 L   \C-DRIVE\NET_MGR.???
A 92.07.18 16:08:20 LES ALR486 L   \C-DRIVE\LANTASTI.NET
A 92.07.18 16:08:20 LES ALR486 L   \C-DRIVE\LANTASTI.NET
```

Figure 6.14

The server audit parameters. These settings determine which events cause an entry to appear in the server audit log.

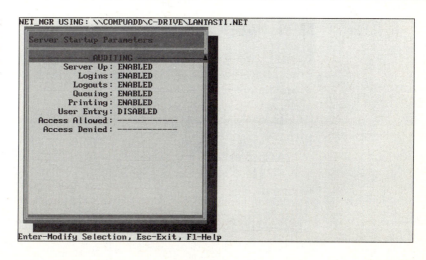

As you can see, there are eight audit parameters. Table 6.5 explains each of them.

Table 6.5

LANtastic's Audit Parameters

AUDIT SETTING	POSSIBLE VALUES	ADDS AN ENTRY TO THE SERVER AUDIT LOG WHEN...
Server Up	Enabled/Disabled	The server starts up
Logins	Enabled/Disabled	A user logs into the server
Logouts	Enabled/Disabled	A user logs out of the server
Queuing	Enabled/Disabled	A job is placed in the server's print or mail queue
Printing	Enabled/Disabled	A job is printed on the server's printer
User Entry	Enabled/Disabled	A user adds a comment via the NET AUDIT command
Access Allowed	Any combination of RWCMLDKNEAIP	Access to a resource is granted via the specified right(s)
Access Denied	Any combination of RWCMLDKNEAIP	Access to a resource is denied via the specified right(s)

■ Network Printing

In many organizations, the initial motivation for installing a network comes from the need to share a few printers among many users. It's not difficult to share printers with LANtastic, but there are a few tricks that can preclude problems and increase your network's flexibility. Network printing requires close cooperation between application programs and the network software. It also requires a degree of coordination among network users.

In Chapter 5, we mentioned some pitfalls of network printing. In this section, we'll look at the entire printing process, and show you how to avoid those pitfalls.

LANtastic Printing Facilities

Every LANtastic network has at least one file server. A file server can also act as a print server. A *print server* takes print jobs from workstations, stores the data in a disk file on the server, and then sends the data to the correct printer. A server can have up to five printers attached to it. LANtastic also supports external print servers that run on Artisoft's Central Station processor, and each Central Station print server can have several printers attached.

Every server has a *printer queue* associated with it, which is simply a storage area for print jobs. Each queue feeds one or more printers. As you know if you've read Chapter 5, you use the Connection Manager's Network Disks and Printers menu to redirect data from your PC's printer port to a network print queue. Once the data is in a print queue, LANtastic makes sure it goes to the correct printer.

Queue, Stream, and Printer Management

In Chapter 5, we explained how to use the Connection Manager's Printer Queue Management screen to manage your own print jobs. Briefly, you use the Printer Queue Management screen to add, delete, and modify jobs in the print queue. Users designated as queue managers (those with the Q privilege) may use the same screen and keystroke commands to manage other users' print jobs. See Chapter 5 for details on managing print queues.

In addition to their expanded queue management privileges, queue managers also have direct control over printers and printer streams on the server. In this section, we'll focus on printer device and stream management.

Printer Streams

LANtastic allows you to create multiple shared print devices for any shared printer. Earlier in this chapter, we showed you how to use the Setup String feature to print in several operating modes on the same printer.

If you have created several print devices, LANtastic's printer streams feature allows you to determine which devices, or *streams*, may print to the printer. The printer streams feature is very flexible; you can use it to separate print jobs by paper type, ink or toner cartridge type, user or group name, or any other way you want.

As an example, we've used the Network Manager to create two print devices for the same HP Deskjet printer. The printer is attached to port LPT1 on our example server. The first device, @HPPLAIN, is for plain paper print jobs. The second device, @HPLTR, is for jobs that need to print on company letterhead. To manage output to these two print devices, we'll use the Printer Queue Management screen.

Figure 6.15 shows a typical Printer Queue Management screen. As you can see, there are no jobs in the queue. At the lower-left corner, notice that the printer stream named "???????.???" is enabled. This is the default printer stream, which is automatically enabled each time the server starts up. The question mark means "match any character in the stream name," so the ???????.??? stream allows any print device to print.

Figure 6.15

The Printer Queue Management screen. At the lower left, you can see that the default printer stream of @???????.??? is enabled, allowing all queued jobs to print.

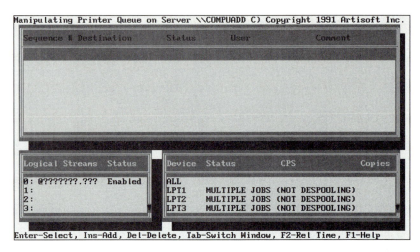

We want to restrict printing to our specific @HPPLAIN and @HPLTR devices, so we'll disable the default printer stream. To do this, press the Tab key until the highlight bar moves to the Logical Streams display. Then use the arrow keys to move the highlight bar to stream number 0 and press the F5 key. The stream display will indicate Disabled, and the default stream will not send jobs to the printer.

Next, move the highlight bar to stream number 1 and press Enter. When LANtastic asks for a stream name, enter @HPPLAIN. This allows jobs for the @HPPLAIN print device to print. Now move the highlight bar to stream number 2 and create a stream for @HPLTR. Since our printer has plain paper in it, we'll immediately disable the @HPLTR print stream by pressing the F5 key. Figure 6.16 shows our new print setup with @HPPLAIN enabled and @HPLTR disabled.

LANtastic allows you to define up to 20 streams at one time. Unfortunately, LANtastic cannot store the stream settings, so you must re-create your streams setup each time you restart the server. The best way to do this is to place the desired NET STREAM commands in a DOS batch file. The syntax for NET STREAM is

```
NET STREAM(/ENABLE /DISABLE) \\server [[index] [name]]
```

Index is a number that indicates which of the 20 printer streams to control, and *name* provides a name for the specified printer stream. /ENABLE enables the printer stream, and /DISABLE disables it. Note that there is no space between STREAM and /ENABLE or /DISABLE. This is how you would reproduce our example streams using NET STREAM commands:

```
NET STREAM/DISABLE \\mainserver 0 @???????.???
NET STREAM/ENABLE \\mainserver 1 @HPPLAIN
NET STREAM/DISABLE \\mainserver 2 @HPLTR
```

Figure 6.16

Using printer streams to control printing. In this example, @HPPLAIN can send data to the printer, but @HPLTR is disabled. Note that several jobs are waiting for the @HPLTR device. These jobs will remain on hold until we change the paper and enable the @HPLTR stream.

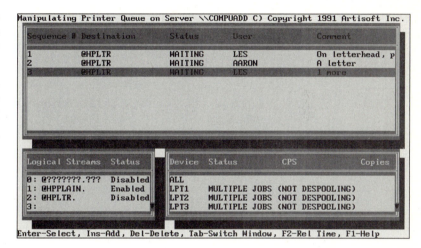

Here again, you've disabled the default stream and created two new streams. Stream number 1 (HPPLAIN) will be allowed to print, but stream number 2 (@HPLTR) will not.

If you will be using the same NET STREAM commands every day, you can add them to the end of your STARTNET.BAT network startup batch file.

Controlling Print Devices

LANtastic lets you attach up to five printers to each server. There may be times when you want to stop one of the network printers temporarily, perhaps to change a ribbon or toner cartridge, or to add paper.

If you are a queue manager, you can control each printer individually from the Network Manager's Printer Queue Management screen. The printer control window is at the bottom-right corner of the screen. To control a printer, press the Tab key until the highlight bar is on one of the items in the printer control window. Use the arrow keys to select the desired printer and press Enter. Note that selecting All controls all printers at once. When you select a printer and press Enter, a pop-up printer control window will appear as shown in Figure 6.17.

140 Chapter 6: Network Management and Security

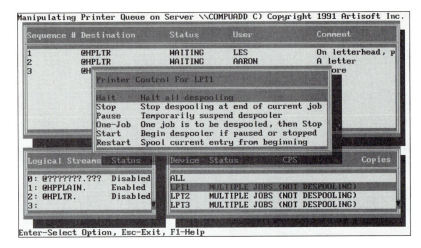

Figure 6.17

Controlling a shared printer with the Network Manager. In this example, we are working with the printer on port LPT1.

As you can see, there are six possible actions you can take for the selected printer. Here's what each of them does.

Action	Effect
Halt	Immediately stops all printing. The printer will remain unavailable until a Start or Restart command is issued.
Stop	Allows the currently printing job to complete, and then stops printing.
Pause	Stops printing temporarily. To resume, select Start from the printer control menu.
One-Job	Allows one print job to print, and then stops printing.
Start	Begins printing after a Pause or Stop.
Restart	Same as Start, but restarts the currently printing job from the beginning.

Printing to a File

Many application programs provide a way to print to a disk file. There are several reasons you might want to do this:

- You may be working on a PC that is not on the network, and has no printer of its own.

- You may be printing from an application that takes a long time to print, and may know that you'll want to print more copies of this document.

- The target printer for your job may be down or unavailable.

If your application program does not provide a way to print to a disk file, you can use the NET USE command to capture your print data into a disk file on the network. Once the data is captured to a file, you can use the NET PRINT command to send that file to a printer. To capture to a file, you use the command

```
NET USE LPTx \\server\pathname
```

Pathname must be a valid file name that already exists. Any data already in the file with that name will be overwritten with the new print data. The print job will continue to be captured to the file until you issue a NET UNUSE command to stop the printer redirection.

Printing Multiple Copies of a Document

There are several ways to make more than one copy of a document. The most obvious (and often the best) way is to print the document on your printer and then make additional copies on a copying machine. This is the best approach to take when you need a large number of copies, and don't mind a "photocopied" look.

If you want all your copies to be "originals," you'll want to print them all rather than copying them. Many application programs, especially word processors, include a feature that allows you to specify more than one copy for your printed output. This approach works fine, except that the program usually sends the print data to the server more than once. If you're making seven copies, the data is sent to the server seven times. This can take a considerable length of time, especially if the document contains graphics.

You can avoid this delay, but it takes a little work on your part. To print multiple copies of a document, follow these steps:

1. Redirect your printer output to a file as described in the previous section. The command

   ```
   NET USE LPT1 \\server\pathname
   ```

   reroutes your LPT1 printer to a file named *pathname*.

2. Run your application program and print your document.

3. Use the NET UNUSE command to stop redirecting your printer output. This will close the print file.

4. Use the NET PRINT command to print multiple copies of your file. For example, the command

```
NET PRINT print.doc @hplaser "annual report" 10
```
will print 10 copies of the data contained in print.doc on the printer @hplaser with the comment "annual report."

When you use this method, your application sends the print job to the file only one time; then NET PRINT sends your job to the printer as many times as you specified. Since NET PRINT sends the same file to the printer repeatedly, your job comes out collated; no hand-sorting is required.

Network Printing Tips and Tricks

This section offers some tips and tricks to help you make the most of your networked printers.

Tip #1: Print to the Right Place!

As pointed out in Chapter 5, it is important that you send your print data to the correct queue. This is especially vital on networks with several types of printers.

To illustrate the potential for problems, we'll take a look at a typical network with one HP laser printer, one NEC PostScript printer, and one Epson dot-matrix printer.

Problem scenario #1: You are running WordPerfect on your workstation, and you have installed WordPerfect for the HP laser printer. If you send the print job to the print queue that feeds the HP printer, everything will come out fine. But if you accidentally send the print job to the queue for the Epson line printer, your text will be interspersed with gibberish. This happens because the Epson printer doesn't understand HP's printer language, and vice-versa.

Problem scenario #2: You are running Microsoft Word installed for a PostScript printer, but you send the print job to the HP laser printer queue. When you pick up your print job, you find dozens of pages of semi-intelligible text, with your document's text mixed in. HP printers don't normally speak PostScript, so the HP printer dutifully prints PostScript commands on the paper. Again, this happens because the HP printer doesn't understand PostScript commands. So you'll know it when you see it, we have included a small portion of a PostScript printout in Figure 6.18.

Problem scenario #3: This time, your WP program is installed for an HP printer, but you send the print job to the PostScript printer. After a lengthy wait, nothing has printed at all. This happens because PostScript printers ignore any data that is not PostScript. If you send a non-PostScript job to a PostScript printer, the printer simply ignores the data.

You and the people using your network can avoid all three of these scenarios by making sure you use the proper print queue.

Figure 6.18

Non-PostScript printers don't know how to process PostScript commands, so they simply print the commands on the page.

```
%!PS-Adobe-2.0 ExitServer
%%Title: Microsoft Word Driver Prolog
%%Creator: Microsoft
%%CreationDate: Fri Aug 18 1988
%%BeginDocument: Microsoft Word 5.0 0
%%msinifile: PSNEW
%%EndComments
%%BeginExitServer: 0
 userdict /msinifile known
 {msinifile (PSNEW) eq {stop} if} if
 serverdict begin 0 exitserver
 userdict /msorigstate known {msorigstate restore} if
 save /msorigstate exch def
```

Tip #2: Use Descriptive Queue Names

When you create a new shared printer device, it's wise to give the printer a meaningful name. If a user sees seven network print queues named @PRINTER, he or she has no idea what type of printers are available. Names like @DESKJET, @HPLASER, and @OKI390 help tell users what type of printer each queue represents.

Tip #3: Use Streams to Separate Print Jobs

If you have one printer that uses several types of paper, you probably spend a good bit of time changing paper. We've also found that users tend to assume a particular type of paper is loaded in the printer—even when it isn't.

To avoid changing paper several times a day, you can create a queue for each paper type. For example, if you have a dot-matrix printer that you use for plain paper, green-bar paper, and 3-by-5 cards, create queues named @PLAIN, @GREENBAR, and @3X5CARDS.

You can keep the most commonly used paper (probably plain white) in the printer most of the day, leaving the @GREENBAR and @3X5CARDS print streams disabled. When several jobs have piled up in the @GREENBAR queue, disable the @PLAIN queue, change the paper, and start the @GREENBAR stream to print all your green-bar paper jobs. Repeat the process as necessary for the 3-by-5 cards.

Tip #4: Know How to Manage Downloadable Printer Fonts

Most laser printers contain several built-in typefaces, or *fonts*. In addition to the built-in fonts, virtually all laser printers allow you to send additional fonts to the printer. The process of sending a new font to a printer is called *downloading*.

Downloadable fonts are a wonderful tool; they allow you to use a wide range of typefaces with your printer. Unfortunately, they can create some problems for you and other users, but with a little caution, these problems can usually be avoided.

The first problem with downloadable fonts is space; font files take up a lot of room on the disk. Since most people on the network will use the same fonts, we suggest you place downloadable font files in a shared directory on the network. Keeping the font files on the network ensures that all users have access to all fonts. This arrangement also saves disk space on individual workstations. But this approach has one drawback: It increases the amount of traffic on the network. Every time a user needs a font file, the file must be retrieved from the file server.

The second problem is also related to the size of the font files. If your application program calls for a downloadable font, the font data is sent to the printer before your print data. If you are using several downloadable fonts, the print data file can get very large. Most application programs do not know which fonts are already loaded in the printer, so they download all the fonts every time you print.

A solution to this problem is to have frequently used downloadable fonts "pre-downloaded" to the printer. If you know, for example, that the Times Roman and Avant Garde fonts are already present in your printer, you can usually tell your application program not to download those font files.

A printer can store only a certain number of fonts; this number varies according to the make and model of the printer. Obviously, you cannot store more fonts than the printer can hold in memory. The system administrator should check with the other network users to determine which fonts should be preloaded to the printer.

The actual method used to download the fonts also varies according to the type of printer you use. Most printer fonts come with a font downloader program and some programs (like Microsoft Windows) can download their own fonts to a printer.

Whatever method you use to download fonts, remember that fonts disappear from the printer's memory when the printer is turned off. If your printers are turned off overnight, or if there is a power failure, you will have to download the fonts to the printer again. This is a good argument for protecting laser printers with an uninterruptable power supply (UPS) system. However, UPS devices for PCs often don't provide the pure sine wave power recommended for efficient operation of printers, so be careful to select UPS products designed for laser printers.

Some PostScript printers (like the Apple LaserWriter II NTX, IIf, and IIg) can store fonts on a hard disk built into the printer itself. These printers do not lose their font files when the power is turned off because the files are written on the hard-disk drive.

■ Networking Your Applications

In most companies, networks are used as a central repository for shared files, and as a connecting point for shared resources like printers and CD-ROM drives. Since all network users can access any group of files on a server, it makes good sense to use the network as a storehouse for application programs as well. There are two major advantages to keeping your application software on the network.

First, networking reduces the need to store a copy of each application on every PC in the office. With a network, all users have access to all the applications they need, while using little or no local storage space.

Second, networking ensures that everyone is using the same version of each application. In large organizations, it is not uncommon to have one or more people assigned the chore of keeping users "up-to-date." In a networked environment, users get access to the latest version of new software virtually overnight.

There are, of course, problems and legal issues associated with sharing application programs on a network. In the next section, we'll point out the problem areas and show you how to keep your network both productive and legal.

Networking and the Law

Virtually all PC software is supplied in a shrink-wrapped box. Usually, the outside of the box contains a legal document called a *license agreement*. When you "buy" software, you are actually buying a license to use the software; the ownership of the product remains with the developer or publisher. The license agreement grants you or your organization the right to use the software, usually on a single computer.

Typically, installing an application program on a network gives many people the technical ability to use the application at the same time. This raises some sticky moral and legal questions. Different software companies have different policies regarding networks; some even have different policies for different products in their own line.

Marketing a networked application is a challenging task. The technology of file sharing isn't a problem anymore; any competent programmer knows how to write applications that allow simultaneous multiple accesses to the same data file. But LAN software piracy is a real threat to the survival of many software producers.

Some companies try to ignore networks and have no network licensing agreements. If you want to use their package at multiple PCs legally, you need multiple copies of the program. This approach leads to closets full of shrink-wrapped packages—one for each potential user—while one copy of the program is shared on the network. Although this arrangement is completely legal, since each user of the software "owns" a copy of the software package, it is also wasteful.

Other vendors take a more sensible approach. For example, Microsoft's Word 5.5 can be installed on a network. As you add users to the network, you purchase additional network "License Packs." The License Pack is just a piece of paper; it does not include any additional disks or manuals. This approach works on the honor system; as you add users, you should purchase additional licenses. WordPerfect Corp. uses a similar plan for WordPerfect. You install one copy on the network, and purchase additional licenses for each user that will be using the program.

Other vendors aren't quite so trusting. Symantec's Q&A program knows when it is running on a network, and will allow only one user to use the program at a time. To allow more than one user to use Q&A at once, you must purchase a network upgrade kit from Symantec. Borland International uses a similar approach with Paradox. Any Paradox package can be installed on a network, but you must purchase a network upgrade kit to enable more than one user at a time to access the program files.

Many vendors also have site licensing agreements available. The most common site licensing agreement is on a "per server" basis. You pay a fixed fee for the program, and all the users on the network are allowed to use it. Per-server site licenses are usually expensive for small LANs and many network administrators find that buying enough single-copy versions of the program to meet peak demand is still the most economical alternative.

LAN Metering Software

LAN administrators have a moral and legal responsibility to audit or meter the use of all licensed applications. Software companies lose money when people violate their software licenses by letting more than the allowed number of users access a program.

Experienced network managers also know that it usually isn't economical to have a separate copy of an application program for each person on the network. Seldom does everyone need to use any one particular application at the same time. Smart network planners and administrators attempt to buy enough copies of an application to meet peak demand, but demands have a way of changing.

LAN metering programs are tools for metering your network activity; they give you important information on how the network and network applications are used. Metering programs have the unique ability to regulate the number of simultaneous users for each application on your network, and they can establish better security on your LAN at the same time.

Metering products vary in price from $100 to $800 and up, according to the applications and nodes on your network. You can choose from simple packages that reports LAN usage, menuing programs that control applications from behind customized screens, and auditing packages that create extensive reports on every type of network activity.

Because metering programs give you a full picture of who uses what resource when, they provide great support for budget requests and operations reports. You can produce professional-looking reports from most of these programs. Add a few month-to-month statistics, put them on an overhead chart, and you'll never again have to worry about justifying your budget requests.

Some LAN metering packages have additional capabilities. For example, Brightwork Development's SiteLock and Certus International's Certus LAN can identify corrupt executable programs that may indicate viruses on your network.

Installing Networked Applications

On a stand-alone PC, each application program is typically installed in its own subdirectory. For example, you might have your WordPerfect files in a directory named C:\WP51, and your Paradox files in a directory named C:\PARADOX. This approach works fine on individual PCs, but installing a program on a network adds a few complications.

When you install an application, you generally have to select a screen driver, printer driver, mouse driver, and other options. On a network, each user may have a different combination of printers, video boards, and mice.

Most application programs consist of several modules contained in several files. For example, a typical word processing program might have a program file (the .EXE file), several overlay files, a spelling checker dictionary, a thesaurus file, a user-defined dictionary, a preferences file, and a collection of printer drivers. On a stand-alone PC, these files are usually installed into one subdirectory. Some of them are static; others are not. Typically, the program .EXE file and any overlay files are static, but the user dictionary, style sheets, and preference files may need to be changed.

Before you install any application program on the network, it is important to understand how the program uses its various files. Most applications that can be installed on a LAN include specific instructions for network installations. Usually, these programs require that certain files be located in specific subdirectories.

As networks become the rule rather than the exception, more application software vendors are adding network-specific features to their products. Many application programs automatically sense that they are running on a network and provide extra features for network users. For example, WordPerfect for Windows allows each user to specify the subdirectories to use for program files, data files, and spelling dictionaries. This allows each user to keep his or her data files separate from other people's files.

- *The Command-Line Interface*
- *Using DOS Batch Files with LANtastic*
- *LANtastic String Macros*

CHAPTER

7

Using LANtastic from the DOS Command Prompt

So far, we've shown you how to run LANtastic from the Connection Manager and Network Manager menu systems. Both the Connection Manager and the Network Manager can also accept commands directly from the DOS command line. In this chapter, we'll discuss the Connection Manager and Network Manager command-line commands.

■ The Command-Line Interface

Both the LANtastic Connection Manager (NET.EXE) and the Network Manager (NET_MGR.EXE) can accept direct commands from the DOS command line or from a DOS batch file. The command-line interface provides an extra degree of flexibility, and speeds network operations. To connect a network disk with the Connection Manager takes six or seven steps:

1. Start the Connection Manager (NET.EXE).
2. Select the Network Drives and Printers screen.
3. Select the drive letter to use for the network drive.
4. Select a server from the list of servers.
5. Enter your user name and password if you aren't already logged in.
6. Respond to the Set Your Clock dialog.
7. Select a network disk to use and press Enter.

To perform the same task with the NET.EXE command line, you'd enter

```
NET USE  D: \\MAINSERVER\@C-DRIVE
```

This command redirects drive D: to the shared disk C-DRIVE on the server MAINSERVER, replacing the six steps required to use the Connection Manager with a single line.

Another advantage of the command-line interface is that you can use the NET.EXE and NET_MGR.EXE command lines to create batch files. By combining the appropriate NET and NET_MGR commands in a DOS batch file, you can log in, attach printers, and connect to network disk drives by typing a single command. The following batch file, named LOGIN.BAT, prompts the user for a user name and password, logs in to two servers, attaches two network drives and a printer, and shows the status of the user's network connection.

```
@REM LOGIN.BAT - Log in and attach net drives and printer
@echo off
net user ?"User Name:" ^"Password:"
net login \\lte386
net login \\alr486
net use lpt1 \\alr486\@DESKJET
net use F: \\lte386\c-drive
net use G: \\lte386\d-drive
net echo "Hello,",!"user".
net echo "It's",!"day",!"date"
net show
```

Some operations can only be performed from the NET and NET_MGR command lines. In the following sections, we'll explain each of the NET and NET_MGR command line options. Then, in the last section, we'll show you how to create a DOS batch file using the command line options.

NET.EXE Command-Line Options

This section lists the NET command-line options in alphabetical order. Where appropriate, we include an example of the command in use. Items in brackets [ ] are optional; those in parentheses ( ) are required, but may be one of several options. All other items must be entered in the order shown.

ATTACH

Syntax: `NET ATTACH[/VERBOSE] \\server-name`

Usage: Connects all available local drives to every available shared resource on the target server.

Options: /VERBOSE displays all drives and their corresponding network resource.

Examples: `NET ATTACH \\bigserver`
`NET ATTACH/VERBOSE \\myserver`

AUDIT

Syntax: `NET AUDIT \\server-name reason "audit-text"`

Usage: Creates an audit entry in a server's audit log. LANtastic maintains an optional audit log for each server; *server-name* indicates which audit log to use. *Reason* can be any text up to 8 characters long. *Audit-text* can be any text up to 64 characters long. If you want to include spaces, quotation marks or commas in *audit-text*, you must enclose the entire string in quotation marks.

Notes: Server auditing must be enabled, and you must have the U privilege to use this command.

Examples: `NET AUDIT \\mainserver note "Added 2Mb memory"`
`NET AUDIT \\alr486 @printer new_toner_cart`

CHAT

Syntax: `NET CHAT`

Usage: Enters Chat mode, exactly as if you had selected Chat with Another User from the Connection Manager menu.

Example: `NET CHAT`

CHANGEPW

Syntax: `NET CHANGEPW \\`*`server-name old-pword new-pword`*

Usage: Changes the password for your user account on the target server. *Server-name* indicates the name of the server to use. *Old-pword* should be your old password and *new-pword* indicates the new password you want to use.

Notes: Use this command with caution. If you mistype your new password, your account will be "stuck" with an unknown password. Use the Change Password choice on the Connection Manager User Account Management screen instead.

Example: `NET CHANGEPW \\mainserver apples oranges`

See also: Connection Manager User Account Management menu

CLOCK

Syntax: `NET CLOCK\\`*`server-name`*

Usage: Sets your workstation's clock to the server's clock. *Server-name* indicates the name of the server to use.

Example: `NET CLOCK \\mainserver`

COPY

Syntax: `NET COPY[/VERBOSE]` *`from-path to-path`*

Usage: Copies files on a server. Use this instead of the DOS COPY command when you're copying files on the same server. *From-path* is the complete pathname of the file(s) to copy, and *to-path* is the name of the target directory. Both must reside on the same server.

Options: /VERBOSE shows the contents of from-path before it is copied.

Notes: You can use the DOS COPY command to copy files on a server, but DOS will send the data from the server to your workstation and then back to the server again. NET COPY copies the files directly on the server, thus decreasing network traffic.

Examples:
```
NET COPY F:\docfiles\*.doc \backups
NET COPY/VERBOSE F:\backups \archive
```

DETACH

Syntax: `NET DETACH \\server-name`

Usage: Discontinues redirection of all drives on *server-name*. If you want to remove only one drive mapping on a server, use the NET UNUSE command instead.

Example: `NET DETACH \\mainserver`

See also: NET UNUSE

DIR

Syntax: `NET DIR[/ALL] [pathname]`

Usage: Displays network directory and file information, including file attributes.

Options: /ALL Displays all files including system and hidden files.

Notes: NET DIR is similar to the DOS DIR command, but NET DIR understands LANtastic pathnames. NET DIR also shows each file's attributes; DOS's DIR command doesn't. *Pathname* is the pathname or file name to show, and may be a complete network pathname like \\mainserver\D-DRIVE. The pathname may also specify a wildcard file name like *.EXE.
The NET DIR display is slightly different from the DOS DIR command. NET DIR shows each entry on a separate line. The directory information is in the form

```
FILENAME   ATTRIBUTES   SIZE   DATE   TIME
```

The *Filename* column contains the name of the file. The *Attributes* column displays each file's attributes, which may be

Attribute	Meaning
A (Archive flag)	This file has not been backed up.
D (Directory flag)	This item is a directory.
H (Hidden file)	This file is marked as hidden.
I (Indirect file)	This entry is an alias for another file.
R (Read only file)	This file may be read but not written.
S (System file)	This file contains part of the DOS system software.
V (Volume label)	This entry is a disk volume label.

Size indicates the size of each file. *Date* shows each file's creation date, and *Time* shows each file's creation time. The following example is a typical NET DIR display.

Example:
```
C:\LANTASTI>net dir \\alr486\c-drive\lantasti\A*.exe
        Directory of \\ALR486\C-DRIVE\LANTASTI\
AE2.EXE          -A-----      10437  15-Feb-1992  16:10:00
AEX.EXE          -A-----      10437  15-Feb-1992  16:10:00
AILANBIO.FXF     -A-----      16985  15-Feb-1992  16:10:00
ALONE.EXE        -A-----      20549  15-Feb-1992  16:10:00
```

DISABLEA

Syntax: NET DISABLEA *server-name password*

Usage: Disables your user account.

Notes: If you plan to be away from your office for some time, you can use NET DISABLEA to disable your user account temporarily. This prevents others from using your account, even if they know your account name and password. Once disabled, your account must be reenabled from the Network Manager menu or with the NET_MGR command line. *Server-name* specifies the server on which to disable the account; *password* is your password on the server. This command is only effective if your concurrent logins setting is set to 1.

Example: NET DISABLEA \\mainserver apples

ECHO

Syntax: NET ECHO *string*

Usage: Displays a string of characters on the screen. NET ECHO is similar to the DOS ECHO command, but NET ECHO allows you to use LANtastic's special string macros.

Notes: See "LANtastic String Macros" at the end of this chapter for more information on string variables.

Example: `NET ECHO "The time is",!"TIME"`

EXPAND

Syntax: `NET EXPAND[/PHYSICAL][/RECURSE] pathname`

Usage: Expands a network pathname to show its actual physical location. This can be useful when you want to know the exact physical location of a shared file.

Options: /PHYSICAL shows the server's physical pathname (like C:\) for the file given in *pathname*.

/RECURSE shows the true pathname for indirect files.

Notes: Do not insert a space between EXPAND and /PHYSICAL or /RECURSE.

Examples: `C:\LANTASTI>NET EXPAND F:\wina20.386`

Returns:
`\\ALR486\C-DRIVE\WINA20.386`

`C:\LANTASTI>NET EXPAND/PHYSICAL F:\wina20.386`
Returns:
`C:\WINA20.386`

See also: NET INDIRECT

FLUSH

Syntax: `NET FLUSH \\server-name`

Usage: Closes and resets all caches on the server specified in *server-name*. Use this command when you have modified a resource with NET_MGR and want the update to take effect immediately.

Example: `NET FLUSH \\mainserver`

See also: Network Manager, NET_MGR command line

HELP

Syntax: NET HELP

or

NET HELP `command-name`

Usage: By itself, NET HELP displays a list of all the NET.EXE command-line commands. This is helpful when you want to use a NET command but can't remember its name.

NET HELP *command-name* displays specific information about the command given in *command-name*.

Examples: NET HELP
NET HELP ATTACH

INDIRECT

Syntax: NET INDIRECT `pathname actual-name`

Usage: Creates an alias named *pathname* for the file named in *actual-name*. The aliased file appears in the specified directory; any actions performed on the indirect file actually affect the file named in *actual-name*.

Notes: The indirect attribute must be set on the shared resource which will contain the indirect file.

Example: `NET indirect example.doc \d-drive\doc original.doc`

See also: NET EXPAND

LOGIN

Syntax: `NET LOGIN[/WAIT] \\server-name user password [#]`

Usage: Establishes a connection to a server, but does not create any network disk drive or printer connections. This command is most commonly used in a batch file where it is usually followed by one or more NET USE statements. *Server-name* is the name of the server to log in to; *user* and *password* are the user name and password to use. The optional parameter # specifies the number of the network adapter board to use; this option is valid only if you have multiple network adapters installed in your PC.

Options: /WAIT pauses LOGIN until the specified server becomes available.

Notes: NET LOGIN will not replace an existing login. If you are already logged in to the server under one user name, you must log out before you can log in under another name.

Examples: `NET LOGIN \\mainserver Les apples`
`NET LOGIN \\mainserver frank oranges 1`

See also: NET LOGOUT

LOGOUT

Syntax: `NET LOGOUT \\server-name`

Usage: Logs out of the server specified in *server-name* and cancels all network drive and printer redirections on that server.

Example: `NET LOGOUT \\mainserver`

LPT

Syntax:
```
NET LPT COMBINE
NET LPT FLUSH
NET LPT SEPARATE
NET LPT[/ENABLE][/DISABLE] NOTIFY
NET LPT TIMEOUT time
```

Usage: Controls the way LANtastic handles your printer output.

Combining Print Jobs

The first three forms of the NET LPT command (NET LPT COMBINE, NET LPT FLUSH, and NET LPT SEPARATE) are used together to combine multiple print jobs into a single job. NET LPT COMBINE combines printer output from several print jobs so that they are handled as a single job. NET LPT FLUSH tells LANtastic to close out your combined print jobs and send them to the printer. NET LPT SEPARATE indicates that you wish to split the combined print jobs into separate jobs again. These three commands can be used only in batch files. You can use this feature to force several print jobs to print together. The following batch file sets combined printing, starts Microsoft Word, and then releases any print jobs to the print queue:

```
NET LPT COMBINE
CD \WORD5
WORD
NET LPT FLUSH
```

When a user runs this batch file and prints from Microsoft Word, any print jobs generated by Word will be printed together *after* the user exits from Word.

Print Job Notification

LANtastic can send you a message when your print job has finished printing. The command NET LPT /ENABLE NOTIFY tells LANtastic to display a pop-up message on the screen when your job is ready.

Setting the Printer Timeout

Normally, LANtastic clears the printer buffer and sends your job to the print queue each time an application program ends. If you stay in a particular application program (a word processor, for example), your documents may not print until you exit to DOS. The NET LPT TIMEOUT command sets the amount of time (specified by *time*) LANtastic waits before it closes out a print job.

MAIL

Syntax: `NET MAIL[/VERBOSE][/VOICE] filename \\server-name recipient [comment]`

Usage: Sends a mail message contained in *filename* to user *recipient* on server *server-name*. The file can be a plain ASCII text file, or a voice data file created with an ArtiSound board. *Comment* is an optional comment that appears in the message header on the recipient's PC.

Options: /VERBOSE displays the text file name as the message is sent. /VOICE indicates that the file contains voice information.

Examples: `NET MAIL message.txt \\mainserver Les`
`NET MAIL/voice urgent.voc \\mainserver Frank`

See also: NET POSTBOX

MESSAGE

Syntax: `NET MESSAGE(/ENABLE /DISABLE) (BEEP POP)`

Usage: Enables and disables the pop-up messages that LANtastic occasionally sends to your screen. LANtastic normally beeps and sends a pop-up message

- When you receive new mail

- When another user asks you to chat
- When you have used the NET LPT/NOTIFY command

Options: The command NET MESSAGE/DISABLE POP disables network messages; NET MESSAGE/ENABLE POP reenables network messages. Similarly, NET MESSAGE/DISABLE BEEP turns off the beep sound that accompanies a network message and NET MESSAGE/ENABLE BEEP turns the beep back on again. Both of these options are on by default.

Examples:
```
NET MESSAGE/DISABLE BEEP
NET MESSAGE/ENABLE POP
```

See also: NET SEND, NET RECEIVE

PAUSE

Syntax: `NET PAUSE[/NEWLINE] message [time]`

Usage: NET PAUSE is normally used in batch files. As its name indicates, it pauses execution of the batch file and waits for a keypress from the user. An optional *message* string may be displayed. If your message contains blanks, commas, or tab characters, you must enclose it in quotation marks. If you specify a timeout in *time*, NET PAUSE waits *time* seconds for a keypress. The *time* setting may be 0 to 999 seconds; a setting of 0 causes NET PAUSE to wait indefinitely.

Options: /NEWLINE prints a blank line after the message.

Examples:
```
NET PAUSE "Please press a key when ready:"
NET PAUSE "Waiting 10 seconds" 10
```

POSTBOX

Syntax: `NET POSTBOX [\\server-name]`

Usage: Checks for new mail messages on the server specified in *server-name*. If no server is specified, NET POSTBOX checks for mail on all attached servers.

Examples:
```
NET POSTBOX
NET POSTBOX \\mainserver
```

See also: NET MAIL

PRINT

Syntax: NET PRINT [options] file device [comment [copies]]

Usage: Prints a file through a network print queue. The file named in *file* is printed on the device specified by *device*. You can print multiple files by specifying a wildcard file name like *.DOC. You can also add an optional comment field and specify the number of *copies* to print.

Options: /BINARY prints the file in binary mode.
/DELETE deletes the file after printing. This option works only in conjunction with /DIRECT.
/DIRECT instructs LANtastic to print the file directly to the printer. When you print a file, LANtastic normally makes a copy of the file and then prints the copy. This option tells LANtastic to use the original file rather than a copy.
/NOTIFY notifies you when the print job is complete. This option overrides the NET LPT/DISABLE NOTIFY setting.
/NONOTIFY is the opposite of /NOTIFY; it overrides the NET LPT/ENABLE NOTIFY setting.
/VERBOSE displays file names as they are sent to the queue.

Examples: NET PRINT LANWIN.DOC @PRINTER1
NET PRINT\VERBOSE *.DOC @HPLASER

See also: NET USE, NET QUEUE

QUEUE

Syntax: NET QUEUE command \\server-name [[LPTn COMn ALL]]

Usage: Controls the printer queues on the server specified in *server-name*. LPT*n*, COM*n*, or ALL specifies which printer port to control. *Command* can be any of the commands in the following table.

Command	Action
HALT	Stops all despooling immediately. If a job is currently printing, it is rewound and placed back in the print queue when printing is resumed. This option allows you to interrupt a job to correct a printing problem (out of toner, stuck paper, etc.), and then restart the job from the beginning.

The Command-Line Interface

	PAUSE	Pauses despooling immediately. Any currently printing job pauses and resumes printing when you restart the spooler. This option is most useful when you need to replace a ribbon or realign the paper in a dot-matrix printer.
	RESTART	Restarts despooling from the start of the file; equivalent to HALT followed by START.
	SINGLE	Despools a single print job.
	START	Resumes despooling after a HALT, PAUSE, or STOP command.
	STATUS	Displays status of physical printer on server.
	STOP	Stops despooling after the current job is complete.

Examples: NET QUEUE HALT LPT1
NET QUEUE STOP ALL

RECEIVE

Syntax: NET RECEIVE [*position delay*]

Usage: Recalls the last network message received. *Position* is an optional line number from 0 to 23 indicating where to position the message on the screen. *Delay* is an optional delay time indicating how long to display the message.

Examples: NET RECEIVE
NET RECEIVE 10 10

RUN

Syntax: NET RUN[/NOCR] *server-name* "*command*"

Usage: Sends a command to the server specified in *server-name*. The command runs on the server as if it were typed on the server's keyboard. The command given in *command* can be any valid DOS command or a LANtastic NET command.

Options: /NOCR omits the carriage return from the command string.

Notes: The screen output from the program being run is not redirected to the machine that issued the NET RUN command. If you want to control another PC remotely, use Artisoft's Network Eye or another network remote control program. Do not send NET RUN commands to a server that is running the ALONE command.

Example: `NET RUN \\mainserver "NET SHOW"`

SEND

Syntax: `NET SEND machine "message" [[server] [username]]`

Usage: Sends a pop-up message to one or more users on the network. The recipient(s) must have pop-up messages enabled to receive the message.

Machine specifies the name of the machine to send the message to. If no machine name is given, the message is sent to all machines. *Message* is the text of the message to send, enclosed in quotation marks. *Server* specifies an optional server name; if one is specified, a user must be logged in to the named server to receive the message. Similarly, *username* specifies an optional user name. If a user name is given, only the user(s) with names matching *username* receive the message. If you use the *username* option, you must also specify a server name. You can use the asterisk (*) character to match any user or machine name.

Examples: `NET SEND * "The Pizza is here" \\ENGR *`

(Sends message to all users on all machines logged into \\ENGR)

`NET SEND \\FRANK "Call me at extension 4040"`

(Sends message only to machine named \\FRANK)

See also: NET MESSAGE

SHOW

Syntax: `NET SHOW[/BATCH]`

Usage: Shows the status of your LANtastic settings. Here is a typical NET SHOW report:

The Command-Line Interface 165

```
LANtastic (R) Connection Manager V4.10 - (C)
Copyright 1991 ARTISOFT Inc.
Machine ALR486 is being used as a Redirector and
a Server
File and record locking is currently ENABLED
Unsolicited messages will BEEP and POP-UP
LPT notification is DISABLED
LPT timeout in seconds:0
Autologin is ENABLED with username LES
Logged into \\ALR486 as LES on adapter 0
Logged into \\LTE386 as LES on adapter 0
Disk F: is redirected to \\LTE386\C-DRIVE
Disk G: is redirected to \\LTE386\D-DRIVE
```

Options: The /BATCH option reports your current settings in batch-file format. By redirecting this information to a file, you can easily create a DOS batch file that will re-create your current network settings. The following example shows the /BATCH output created for the same settings as the previous example:

```
NET MESSAGE/ENABLE BEEP
NET MESSAGE/ENABLE POP
NET LPT/DISABLE NOTIFY
NET LPT TIMEOUT 0
NET USER LES ^"Enter password: "
NET LOGIN \\ALR486 LES ^"Enter password: " 0
NET LOGIN \\LTE386 LES ^"Enter password: " 0
NET USE F: \\LTE386\C-DRIVE
NET USE G: \\LTE386\D-DRIVE
```

To create a batch file from your current settings, use the command

```
NET SHOW > FILE.BAT
```

where FILE.BAT is the name of the batch file to create. You won't see anything on the screen when you do this; the > tells DOS to copy the output from NET SHOW into FILE.BAT. To check your batch file, use the command

```
TYPE FILE.BAT
```

Examples:
```
NET SHOW
NET SHOW > MYSTART.BAT
```

See also: "Using DOS Batch Files with LANtastic" at the end of this chapter.

SHUTDOWN

Syntax: `NET SHUTDOWN[/REBOOT][/CANCEL][/HALT][/SILENT] \\server [[minutes] "message"]`

Usage: Performs a shutdown on the server specified in *server*. All open files on the server are closed, all users are involuntarily logged out, and the server is no longer available for use. *Minutes* specifies an optional delay time to wait before the server shuts down. If no time given, the server shuts down immediately.
Message is an optional message to send to all users logged in to the server. You can include the special characters # and $ in your message text: The # expands to indicate the number of minutes remaining before shutdown, and the $ expands to an *s* if *minutes* is greater than 1.

Options: /REBOOT reboots the target machine after shutdown.
/CANCEL cancels a shutdown already in progress.
/HALT halts all processing on the server after shutdown.
/SILENT prevents notification of network users before shutdown.

Notes: You must have the S privilege on the target server to use the SHUTDOWN command. Because a server shutdown can cause other users to lose their work in progress, you should use this command with caution and provide plenty of warning time.

Examples: `NET SHUTDOWN \\MAIN 15 "Going down in # minute$"`
`NET SHUTDOWN/REBOOT \\MAIN`

SLOGINS

Syntax: `NET SLOGINS(/ENABLE][/DISABLE) \\server`

Usage: Enables or disables logins on the server specified in *server*. When logins are disabled, no additional users can log in to the server.

Options: /ENABLE reenables logins after a /DISABLE.
/DISABLE disables logins for the specified server.

Notes: You must have the S privilege to use this command.

Example: `NET SLOGINS/DISABLE \\MAIN`

STREAM

Syntax: NET STREAM(/ENABLE /DISABLE) \\server [[stream-index] [stream-value]]

Usage: Manages printer streams on the server specified in *server*. *Stream-Index* indicates which of the 20 printer streams to control, and *stream-value* specifies a new value for the specified printer stream.

Options: /ENABLE enables a printer stream.
/DISABLE disables the specified printer stream.

Examples: NET STREAM/DISABLE \\MAIN11

(Disables stream 11)

NET STREAM/ENABLE \\MAIN10 @HPLASER

(Enables stream 10 as @HPLASER)

See also: "Printer Streams" in Chapter 6

STRING

Syntax: NET STRING[/LEFT=x][/RIGHT=y] var [str1 [str2]]

Usage: Sets the DOS environment variable specified in *var* to the string of characters specified by *str1* and *str2*. The strings can be plain text or a LANtastic string macro. (See the section "LANtastic String Macros" later in this chapter for detailed information on string macros.) When two strings are specified they are concatenated before any characters are extracted.

Options: /LEFT=x where x specifies the character position to begin extraction.
/RIGHT=y where y specifies the character position to end extraction.

Notes: The DOS environment variable specified in *var* must already exist; LANtastic cannot create new environment variables. (See your DOS manual for more information on environment variables.)

Examples: `NET STRING TEMP G:\SWAP`

(Sets TEMP to G:\SWAP)

`NET STRING UNAME !"USER"`

(Sets UNAME to current user name)

`NET STRING/LEFT=4 /RIGHT=5 MINS !"TIME"`

(Sets the DOS environment variable MINS to the number of minutes past the hour)

`NET STRING NETDIR !"PROGRAM"`

(Sets NETDIR to location of NET.EXE)

See also: "LANtastic String Macros" later in this chapter

TERMINATE

Syntax: `NET TERMINATE \\server user [machine] [time]`

Usage: Logs users out from a server. This command is typically used to make sure all users are logged out from a server before taking the server down or performing a server backup. *Server* specifies the server to log the users out from, and *user* specifies the name of the user(s) to log out. You can specify the * user name to log out all users.
Machine specifies an optional machine name; if a machine name is specified, NET TERMINATE logs out only users who logged in from the specified machine.
Time is an optional warning period, specified in minutes. When you use this option, a pop-up message warns users that they must log out.

Notes: You must have the S (system manager) privilege to use this command, and you cannot terminate your own login with it. Because TERMINATE can cause other users to lose their work in progress, you should use this command with caution.

Examples: `NET TERMINATE \\mainserver *`

(Logs all users out from mainserver)

`NET TERMINATE \\mainserver BOB BOBS_PC 10`

(Logs user BOB out after 10 minutes, but only if he logged in from machine BOBS_PC)

UNLINK

Syntax: NET UNLINK

Usage: Restores drives A: and B: to their local, physical drives.

Notes: This command is only used after a remote boot from a diskless workstation.

Example: NET UNLINK

UNUSE

Syntax: NET UNUSE (*drive* LPT*n* COM*n*)

Usage: Cancels a network disk or printer redirection. This command is the opposite of NET USE.

Examples: NET UNUSE F:

(Cancels redirection for drive F:)

NET UNUSE LPT2

(Restores LPT2 to local connection)

See also: NET USE

USE

Syntax:
```
NET USE drive \\server [\path...]
NET USE (LPTn COMn) \\server [[\path... @device]]
```

Usage: One of the key LANtastic commands, NET USE redirects a local drive or printer port to a shared network device. There are two forms of this command: one for network drives and one for printers.

The first form connects a local drive letter specified by *drive* to a network drive resource contained in *path* on server *server*.

The second form connects the local printer port specified by LPT*n* or COM*n* to the printer device named @*device* on server *server*.

To remove a network drive or printer assignment, use NET UNUSE.

Examples: `NET USE F: \\mainserver\C-DRIVE`

(Connects drive F: to C-DRIVE on \\mainserver)

`NET USE LPT2 \\mainserver\@NEC_LASER`

(Connects printer port LPT2 to printer @NEC_LASER)

See also: NET UNUSE

USER

Syntax: `NET USER[/DISABLE] user-name [password] [adapter#]`

Usage: Sets the user name, password, and adapter number to be used for subsequent network logins. Normally, LANtastic requires a valid user name and password each time you create a new connection to a server. The NET USER command tells LANtastic to activate the autologin feature, and LANtastic then uses the supplied account name, password, and optional network adapter number for any subsequent login attempts. Note that NET USER does not override LANtastic's security; you must provide a valid user name and password to use the autologin feature.

Options: The /DISABLE option turns the autologin feature off if it has been enabled.

Examples: `NET USER FRANK NACLTK9`
`NET USER/DISABLE`

NET_MGR Command-Line Options

The Network Manager command-line options are quite similar to those for NET.EXE. The only difference is that the Network Manager commands are preceded by the command NET_MGR instead of NET.

    This section lists the Network Manager command-line options in alphabetical order. Where appropriate, we show you an example of the command in use. Items in brackets [ ] are optional; those in parentheses ( ) are required, but may be one of several options. All other items must be entered in the order shown.

BACKUP

Syntax: `NET_MGR {/P=pw} BACKUP path target-file`

The Command-Line Interface

Usage: Makes a backup copy of the LANtastic control directory. The control directory contains information essential to the operation of LANtastic, including user names, passwords, access control lists, printer and disk names, and other shared-device information.
If you have chosen to password protect the NET_MGR program, you must use the /P= option to specify your manager password.
Path specifies the location of the LANtastic control directory, and is usually C:\LANTASTI.NET. *Target-file* specifies the name of the file to receive the backup copy of the control directory information.

Note: We recommend that you keep the backup file on a different drive than the control directory. Then, if you lose the contents of the hard disk containing the control directory, you'll still have a copy on a different disk.

Examples: `NET_MGR BACKUP C:\LANTASTI.NET A:CONTROL.NET`

(Backs up the control directory to CONTROL.NET on floppy drive A:)

`NET_MGR BACKUP /P=xyzzy C:\LAN.NET D:\BACKUP.NET`

(Copies control directory information from LAN.NET to BACKUP.NET on drive D:)

COPY

Syntax: `NET_MGR {options} COPY USER user1 {user2}`

Usage: Allows you to copy a user account to a different user name or to another control directory. This command is most often used to add a new user to the network.
To copy a user account within the same control directory, you must specify *user1* as the user to copy from, and *user2* as the new account name to which the user information should be copied.
To copy an account into a different control directory, you must specify the location of the target control directory.

Options: /C=*path1* Defines the location of the control directory as *path1*. The default value is C:\LANTASTI.NET.
/P=*pw1* specifies the password for the control directory.
/DC=*path2* specifies the location of a second control directory to receive the copied information. If none is specified, LANtastic assumes you want to use the default control directory.
/DP=*pw2* Specifies the password for the second control directory.

Examples: `NET_MGR COPY USER Mike Susan`

(Creates new account SUSAN based on existing account MIKE)

`NET_MGR /c=lan.net /p=weasel /dc=lan2.net COPY USER\ARNIE`

(Copies account ARNIE from control directory LAN.NET to directory LAN2.NET)

CREATE

Syntax: `NET_MGR {/C=path}{/P=pw} CREATE USER name`

Usage: Creates a new user account with the name given in *name*.

Options: /C=*path* specifies the pathname of the control directory where the new account will be created. The default value is \LANTASTI.NET.
/P=*pw* specifies the password for the control directory.

Example: `NET_MGR CREATE USER BERT`

DELETE

Syntax: `NET_MGR {/C=path}{/P=pw} DELETE [USER GROUP] name`

Usage: Deletes a user or a group account. DELETE USER *name* deletes the user given by *name*; DELETE GROUP *name* deletes the group specified in *name*.

Options: /C=*path* specifies *path* as the control directory containing the account to delete.
/P=*pw* specifies the password for the control directory.

Examples: `NET_MGR DELETE USER Ernie`
`NET_MGR DELETE GROUP MANAGERS`

RESTORE

Syntax: NET_MGR {/P=*pw*} RESTORE *file path*

Usage: Restores a control directory that has been backed up with NET_MGR BACKUP. *File* specifies the name of the backup file to use. *Path* indicates the name of the control directory to restore.

Options: /P=*pw* specifies the password for the control directory.

Example: NET_MGR RESTORE backup.net c:\lantasti.net

(Restores LANTASTI.NET from backup copy BACKUP.NET)

SET

Syntax: NET_MGR{/C=*path*}{/P=*pw*} SET [USER GROUP] *name* {*setting*=*value*}

Usage: Controls account settings for individual user and group accounts. The account name to modify is determined by the name provided in *name*. *Setting=* defines the attribute(s) to change. The settings are

USERNAME=*name*	Sets the user or group account name to *name*
PASSWORD=*pword*	Sets the account password to *pword*
DESCRIPTION=*text*	Sets the account description to the text given in *text*
LOGINS=*n*	Sets the number of concurrent logins allowed for this account to *n*
PRIVILEGES=*x*	Sets the privileges for this account to *x*, which may be any or all of A (ACL manager), Q (queue manager), M (mail manager), U (user audit privilege), or S (system manager)
ACCT_EXP=*date*	Sets the account expiration date to *date*; the date must be in the format *dd-mm-yyyy* or *month-date-year*

	PW_EXP=*date*	Sets the password expiration date to *date*; the date must be in the format *dd-mm-yyyy*, or *month-date-year* Sets the user's account name.

Options: /C=*path* specifies *path* as the control directory containing the account to change.
/P=*pw* specifies the *password* for the control directory.

Examples: `NET_MGR SET GROUP MANAGERS Privileges=AQMS`

(Grants ACL manager, queue manager, mail manager, and system manager privileges to members of the group MANAGERS)

`NET_MGR SET USER MARIA Logins=10`

(Sets user MARIA's maximum logins to 10)

`NET_MGR SET GROUP AARON PW_EXP=040/1993`

(Sets user AARON's account to expire on July 4, 1993)

SHOW

Syntax: `NET_MGR {/C=path}{/P=pw} SHOW [USER GROUP] name`

Usage: Displays information about a user or group account. *Name* specifies the name of the user or group to display, and may contain wildcard characters like * and ?. Here is a typical NET_MGR SHOW command for a single user:

```
C:\NET_MGR SHOW USER MARIA
             USER NAME: MARIA
   ACCOUNT DESCRIPTION: Maria Forrest
    ACCOUNT PRIVILEGES: Q
     CONCURRENT LOGINS: 4
ACCOUNT EXPIRATION DATE: 29-Jun-1993
PASSWORD EXPIRATION DATE: NONE
       LAST LOGIN DATE: NONE
```

Options: /C=*path* specifies *path* as the control directory containing the account to show.
/P=*pw* specifies the password for the control directory.

Examples: `NET_MGR SHOW USER LES`
`NET_MGR SHOW /C=LAN.NET /P=WEASEL GROUP MANAGERS`

■ Using DOS Batch Files with LANtastic

DOS batch files are files that contain DOS commands. Any program name is a DOS command, so you can use a batch file to load and run virtually any program on your system.

A DOS batch file must have the file type .BAT. Batch file commands are entered one command per line. You can use any plain text editor to create batch files; the EDIT.EXE text editor supplied with DOS 5.0 is ideal.

When you run a batch file, DOS reads the command lines from the batch file one at a time, and passes each line to the DOS command processor.

The STARTNET.BAT file created by the LANtastic installer program is a good example of a simple batch file; it loads the pieces of the LANtastic system software.

At the beginning of this chapter, we showed you an example batch file, LOGIN.BAT. Now that you've seen how the LANtastic command-line options work, you'll probably have a better understanding of what each line does. Let's take another look at LOGIN.BAT the way DOS sees it—a line at a time. (We've added line numbers to LOGIN.BAT for this example.)

```
[1]   @REM LOGIN.BAT-Log in and attach net drives and printer
[2]   @echo off
[3]   net user ?"User Name:" ^"Password:"
[4]   net login \\lte386
[5]   net login \\alr486
[6]   net use lpt1 \\alr486\@DESKJET
[7]   net use F: \\lte386\c-drive
[8]   net use G: \\lte386\d-drive
[9]   net echo "Hello,",!"user".
[10]  net echo "It's",!"day",!"date"
[11]  net show
```

Line 1 starts the batch file with a REM statement. Like the REM statement in most computer languages, the DOS REM statement doesn't cause an action; it contains a remark. The @ at the beginning of the line tells DOS not to echo the REM statement to the screen. Line 2 turns off the DOS ECHO parameter. When ECHO is on, DOS echoes each batch file line to the screen as the file runs. We overrode the ECHO setting in the first and second lines by using the @ command prefix.

Line 3 contains the first LANtastic NET command. Here NET USER sets the default user name and password for all subsequent logins. This line also contains two command-line macros. The *?"User Name:"* macro causes LANtastic to print the prompt

```
User Name:
```

176 Chapter 7: Using LANtastic from the DOS Command Prompt

and wait for the user to type a name. Similarly, the ^"*Password:*" macro tells LANtastic to print the prompt:

    Password:

and wait for the user to type a password. We'll examine command-line macros more thoroughly in the next section.

Lines 4 and 5 log in to two servers, \\LTE386 and \\ALR486, using the default user name and password entered by the user in line 3.

Line 6 connects printer LPT1 to the print queue @DESKJET on server \\ALR486. Similarly, lines 7 and 8 connect logical drives F: and G: to the shared disks c-drive and d-drive on server \\LTE386.

Lines 9 and 10 use the LANtastic NET ECHO command to print a greeting message on the screen. Line 11 wraps up our batch file by using the NET SHOW command to display the network status. The result of our batch file appears in Figure 7.1.

Figure 7.1

The LOGIN.BAT batch file in action

```
C:\LANTASTI>login
User Name:les
Password:
Hello, LES.
It's Monday  6-Jul-1992
LANtastic (R) Connection Manager V4.10-(C) Copyright 1991
ARTISOFT Inc.
Machine ALR486 is being used as a Redirector and a Server
File and record locking is currently ENABLED
Unsolicited messages will BEEP and POP-UP
LPT notification is DISABLED
LPT timeout in seconds: 0
Autologin is ENABLED with username LES
Logged into \\ALR486 as LES on adapter 0
Logged into \\LTE386 as LES on adapter 0
Disk F: is redirected to \\LTE386\C-DRIVE
Disk G: is redirected to \\LTE386\D-DRIVE
Printer PRN is redirected to \\ALR486\@DESKJET
```

■ LANtastic String Macros

NET.EXE and NET_MGR.EXE both support the use of special command-line string macros. A *macro* is a sequence of characters that has a special meaning for LANtastic. All macros begin with an exclamation point (!), a caret (^), or a question mark (?). For example, the macro !"TIME" returns the current time. Thus, the NET command

```
NET ECHO !"TIME"
```

causes NET.EXE to print the current time on the screen.

You can use a macro string to replace any argument to any LANtastic command line. For example, the NET LOGIN command requires three parameters: the server name, your user name, and your password. The command

```
NET LOGIN \\MAINSERVER !"USER" ^"Enter Your Password:"
```

would log you into the server \\MAINSERVER using your default account name (from !"USER"), but only after you had typed your password as requested by the macro.

Here are all the LANtastic command-line macros in alphabetical order:

Macro Name	Comments
!"DATE"	Returns the current date in the form 1-Jan-1993.
!"DAY"	Returns the current day of the week as text (e.g., Monday).
!"DIRECTORY"	Returns the current drive and directory (e.g., C:\LANTASTI).
!"ETEXT=*n*"	Returns the error message associated with error number *n*.
!"FILE=*pathname*"	Returns the first line of text contained in the file specified by *pathname*.

!"INSTALLED"	Returns characters corresponding to installed LANtastic programs:
	
	`N=NETBIOS  P=LANPUP R=REDIR  S=SERVER`
	`=Not installed`

!"LOGIN=*server*"	Returns TRUE if you are logged into *server*, FALSE if you are not.
!"MACHINEID"	Returns the machine name (e.g., ALR486).
!"NODEID"	Returns the 12-digit NETBIOS address of your PC.
!"PROGRAM"	Returns the full pathname of the NET.EXE program.

?"*prompt*"	Prints the message contained in "*prompt*" on the screen, waits for the user to type a string on the keyboard, and returns the string. The user input is echoed to the screen.
^"*prompt*"	Same as ?"*prompt*", but echoes ← for each character typed.
!"TIME"	Returns the current time.
!"USER"	Returns the default autologin user name, or a blank if none is defined.

- *Diskless Workstations*
- *The Sounding Board*
- *Sharing Modems on the Network*
- *Sharing CD-ROM Drives*
- *Artisoft's Central Station*

CHAPTER

8

Expanding Your Network

Now that we've covered the essentials of LANtastic, we'll look at ways to expand and improve your network. This chapter provides an overview of the expansion capabilities built into LANtastic.

■ Diskless Workstations

Diskless workstations—PCs without local floppy or hard drives—have become a hot topic among network managers. Since they have no disk drives, these workstations must load their operating system software from a special "boot image file" on a file server.

When diskless workstations first appeared on the market, they were touted as a cure for every LAN administrator's headaches: They were cheaper and smaller than other PCs, and left little room for variation among workstations.

In fact, though, most of these advantages are illusory. Recent price decreases on desktop PCs have eliminated the small price advantage diskless workstations once enjoyed, even when you add the cost of a network adapter card. Moreover, the new "pizza box" style PCs are as small as their diskless counterparts. That leaves the issue of consistency. If every workstation is identical, the administrator can set up the first one, and all the others will work exactly the same, right?

Not quite. One vital component is missing from the equation: Every workstation may be the same, but every user will have different needs. Because all diskless workstations boot from the same boot image file, they all share a common CONFIG.SYS and AUTOEXEC.BAT file.

Still, diskless workstations are popular in some organizations because of the extra level of security they provide. Without local disk drives, users can't copy files to or from the network. This may be an important consideration if your organization works with sensitive data, or if you're concerned about computer viruses making their way onto the network.

In the following section, we'll show you how to set up a boot file to start diskless workstations from the network, and how to tailor the network boot process to meet the individual user's needs.

The Network Boot File

If a workstation doesn't have a drive, how does it start up? Normal PCs go through a startup process that includes searching the A: and C: drives (if they are available) for a track of data that contains a special program called the boot loader. The boot loader's sole function is to load DOS from the boot disk. This process is coded into the ROM chip built into every PC. Diskless workstations don't, by definition, have disk drives, so where do they find the boot loader? As mentioned earlier, they get it from a special boot image file located on a network file server. Once the workstation has booted, it works just like any other PC, except it has no local disk drives.

Diskless workstations must use network adapters able to hold programmable read-only memory (PROM) that gets the startup information for the PC. All Artisoft network adapters can be equipped with a remote boot PROM. Note however, that the PROM is specific to the adapter and the network operating system. You must have the right PROM for the specific type of adapter card you use.

The network boot PROM replaces some of the information contained in the standard PC ROMs, and tells the PC to treat the network boot file as if it were an additional disk drive.

When you start a workstation equipped with a network boot ROM, the workstation attempts to locate a boot server. If one is found, the workstation loads the boot image file from it. If no boot server can be located, the workstation waits for one to appear on the network.

Even PCs that have a full array of floppy- and hard-disk drives can use the remote booting process. If a workstation is equipped with a local floppy or hard disk, you can boot from the local drive by pressing the F1 key during the network boot process. This capability is handy for people who want their PCs configured with specific DEVICE, FILES, LASTDRIVE, or BUFFER statements for network operation and with different parameters when they're operating without a network connection.

Preparing Your Network for Remote Booting

Before any diskless workstations can boot from the network, you must take three steps:

1. Install the boot ROM chips in your remote booting workstations.

2. Prepare a bootable floppy disk containing DOS, CONFIG.SYS, AUTOEXEC.BAT, and the LANtastic workstation software.

3. Prepare the boot image file with the Network Manager program.

Installing the Boot ROMs

To install the network boot ROMs, you must remove the network adapter cards from the workstations. Follow the installation instructions provided with the boot ROM, taking care to insert the chip correctly.

While you have the network adapters out of the machines, check the I/O address and IRQ settings for the boards. If you're using Artisoft network adapters, all the remote booting workstations must use the standard I/O address of 300h, and interrupt request line IRQ3 or IRQ15. For other brands of network adapters, check the boot ROM manufacturer's specifications. Don't forget to reconnect the network cable after you put the adapter back in the PC!

Preparing a Bootable Floppy Disk

In this step, you'll prepare a bootable floppy containing the DOS system files, the COMMAND.COM DOS command processor, and the necessary LANtastic workstation files. In the next step, you'll use the LANtastic Network Manager to make a "boot image" of this entire floppy disk, which will then be stored on a server's hard disk. DOS and LANtastic require less than 300k of disk space. If you use a high-density 5 ¼-inch 1.2Mb floppy or 3 ½-inch 1.44Mb floppy for this step, the Network Manager will copy the entire floppy-disk image to the boot file, even though most of the file will be empty. To save disk space on the file server(s), we recommend you use a 360k 5 ¼-inch disk for this step.

To prepare the bootable disk, follow these steps:

1. Insert a blank floppy disk in your system's A: or B: drive.

2. Type

    ```
    FORMAT A: /F:360 /S
    ```

    for 5 ¼-inch disks, or

    ```
    FORMAT A: /F:720 /S
    ```

    for 3 ½-inch disks. Note that these example commands assume drive A:, and are for DOS version 5.0. Change the A: to B: if you're using the B: drive. Earlier versions of DOS use different FORMAT options—see your DOS manual for details.

3. Copy the DOS command processor onto the floppy disk with the command

    ```
    COPY C:\COMMAND.COM A:\
    ```

You now have a bootable floppy disk. To make sure your disk has all the necessary files on it, leave it in the A: drive, and reboot your PC with the floppy disk in the drive. The PC should boot from it.

The floppy disk now has the necessary DOS files on it, but it still doesn't have the LANtastic workstation software installed. Follow these steps to install the LANtastic software:

1. If you booted your PC from the floppy disk as described above, remove the floppy, reboot your PC from the hard disk, and reinsert the floppy disk.

2. Switch to the LANtastic directory (usually C:\LANTASTI), and run INSTALL. INSTALL will ask you to enter a machine name. The machine name you enter at this point is meaningless, but you have to enter one anyway.

3. Select A:\ as the installation directory, and A:\STARTNET.BAT as the network startup file. Tell INSTALL not to modify your CONFIG.SYS file. When you've set these options, your screen should look like the one in Figure 8.1.

Figure 8.1

Using the INSTALL.EXE program to copy the LANtastic workstation software to the bootable floppy disk. Note that the installation directory is A:\, and we've told INSTALL not to modify CONFIG.SYS.

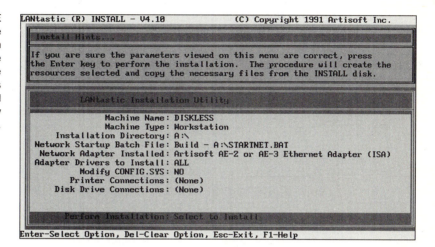

4. Move the highlight bar to select Install on the INSTALL menu, and press Enter. The INSTALL program will copy the necessary LANtastic files onto the floppy disk.

The final step you must take to prepare your bootable floppy is creating the CONFIG.SYS and AUTOEXEC.BAT files for the boot disk. Keep in mind that these files will be used for all remote booting machines. If you want to load any device drivers (like ANSI.SYS or QEMM) on the diskless workstations, you must include those commands in the CONFIG.SYS on the boot disk, and the device drivers themselves must also be copied to the boot disk.

Artisoft recommends the following CONFIG.SYS file. (We've added a line that loads ANSI.SYS to show you how to load device drivers from the boot image file.)

```
BUFFERS=16
FILES=20
LASTDRIVE=Z
FCBS=16,8
DEVICE=ANSI.SYS
```

The boot disk AUTOEXEC.BAT file is a little more complicated than you might expect. Here is a modified version of the AUTOEXEC.BAT file recommended by Artisoft for diskless workstations:

```
REDIR # buffers=2 size=2048
NET LOGIN/WAIT \\(server name) ?"Username:" ^"Password:"
NET USE C: \\(server name)\(resource)
...(more NET USE commands as necessary)
C:
PATH C:\;C:\DOS;C:\LANTASTI
SET COMSPEC=C:\COMMAND.COM
PROMPT $P$G
SET NAME=AAAAAAAA
NET STRING/LEFT=-8/RIGHT=-1 NAME !"NODEID"
CALL C:\%NAME%.BAT
```

This AUTOEXEC.BAT file uses the network string variables described in Chapter 7 to execute a unique login batch file for each remote booting machine.

The DOS environment variable NAME contains the last eight digits of the workstation's Ethernet address, and the last line of the file calls a batch file of the same name. Let's examine this file one line at a time to see exactly what happens when it runs.

When we ran INSTALL earlier, you supplied a machine name, and we told you the name didn't matter. It doesn't matter because all remote booting machines get their machine name from their Ethernet address. The first line of our example AUTOEXEC file, which begins REDIR #, loads the LANtastic REDIR.EXE redirector program. The # after REDIR tells REDIR to use the last eight digits of the machine's Ethernet address as the machine name. Since many users will be using this AUTOEXEC.BAT file, you can't put a specific machine name in it. The options BUFFERS=2 and SIZE=2048 tell REDIR to create two buffers of 2k each, which allows LANtastic to use some of your RAM as a network read/write buffer. The 2k size allows the server to send and receive more data at one time.

The next line, beginning NET LOGIN/WAIT, logs you into the server named in *server name*. Replace *server name* with the name of a server on your network. The ?"Username:" and ^"Password:" options prompt the user to enter a user name and password.

The NET USE C: command creates network drive mapping using the specified *server name* and *resource*. As our example indicates, you can add additional NET USE commands as necessary to utilize additional network drives and/or printers.

Diskless Workstations

The next line, C:, sets drive C: as the working drive. This line must come after the NET USE command, because the C: drive won't exist before the NET USE command executes.

The line PATH C:\;C:\DOS;C:\LANTASTI sets the DOS PATH environment variable. This command assumes there are directories named \DOS and \LANTASTI on the server. The PATH environment variable tells DOS where to look for program files. Setting the path to \DOS and \LANTASTI allows remote workstation users to access the DOS and LANtastic utility programs.

The next line, SET COMPEC=C:\COMMAND.COM, tells DOS where to locate the COMMAND.COM file. COMMAND.COM is the DOS command processor, the program that takes commands from the DOS prompt. At times, DOS may unload the command processor from memory to make room for large application programs. When the application program exits back to DOS, DOS must be able to reload the command processor. The file specified in COMSPEC must be the same version of COMMAND.COM that you used to create the bootable floppy disk.

The PROMPT PG command sets the DOS prompt to indicate the current pathname, followed by a > symbol, so the DOS prompt will be C:\> after logging in.

The next line, SET NAME=AAAAAAAA, creates a DOS environment variable called NAME that is eight characters long. This variable is used by the next command, NET STRING/LEFT=-8/RIGHT=-1 NAME !"NODEID", which extracts the last eight characters of the LANtastic NODEID network node identifier, and copies them into the DOS NAME environment variable. As a result, after this command executes, NAME will contain a unique eight-character name based on each workstation's unique Ethernet address.

The final line, CALL C:\%NAME%.BAT, executes a DOS batch file with the same name as the last eight digits of the Ethernet address, cleverly allowing each user to execute a unique batch file at login time. Our example assumes that the batch file is in the C:\ directory, but you may want to create a special \BATCH directory for login batch files. Remember that this feature is based on the machine name, not the user name.

Creating the Boot Image File

Once you've prepared the bootable floppy disk, you're ready to create the actual boot image file. Place the floppy disk in the A: drive, and run the Network Manager program. Select Boot Image Maintenance from the Network Manager menu, and press Enter. Choose Build Boot Image from the next menu. If your PC has more than one floppy disk, you'll be asked to select the floppy drive containing the boot disk. Select the correct drive, and press Enter.

The Network Manager will read the contents of your floppy disk and copy them into the boot image file, which is stored in a file that is named C:\LANTASTI.NET\SYSTEM.NET\BOOT.IMG.

Your network is now ready for remote booting. If you change DOS versions or need to update the CONFIG.SYS or AUTOEXEC.BAT boot files, you must repeat the entire process. To disable remote booting, just select Delete Boot Image from the Boot Image Maintenance menu.

■ The Sounding Board

As you'll recall from Chapter 2, the Sounding Board is an add-on expansion board that adds sound capability to your PC. You can use it to send and receive voice mail messages via the LANtastic network mail facility. The Sounding Board includes drivers that allow you to use the product with Windows 3.1. Under Windows, you can use the Sounding Board as the standard Windows Multimedia sound device.

The Sounding Board Hardware

The Sounding Board kit includes a printed circuit board, a handset, and an installation disk. Because the board doesn't use any I/O ports or memory addresses, installation is usually a matter of plugging the card into an available slot.

The Sounding Board normally uses two DMA channels, DMA1 and DMA3. One channel is for playback and one is for recording. Many CD-ROM drives and removable cartridge hard drives also require a DMA channel, so these devices can conflict with the Sounding Board. By changing jumper settings on the board, you can use a single DMA channel for both operations, but if you need to record and playback simultaneously, both DMA channels must be enabled.

The supplied telephone-style handset contains a microphone for making recordings and an earphone for listening to them. Two RCA-style jacks on the rear edge of the board provide audio input and output connections that allow you to connect the Sounding Board to external amplifiers, tape recorders, and anything else that uses line-level (600 millivolt) audio inputs and outputs.

The Sounding Board's audio output isn't strong enough to drive a speaker by itself. If you want to use an external speaker, we suggest any of the self-contained amplified ones available from most computer and software stores. These speakers contain a built-in amplifier, and most provide a convenient volume control.

Similarly, the Sounding Board takes "line level" audio input. If you want to record audio onto your PC, you'll need to provide a line-level input to the

Sounding Board. Virtually all CD players, tape recorders, and portable radios have an "audio out" jack that provides this signal. Most turntables and external microphones produce "mike-level" audio, which is a much lower-level signal. You'll need a preamplifier to boost such signals to line level. Note, too, that the handset microphone is always active. If you want to record audio from a tape recorder or CD player through the Sounding Board, unplug the handset to avoid picking up room noise (and your computer's fan) through the microphone.

The Sounding Board Software

The Sounding Board kit includes a floppy disk with drivers for DOS and Windows. The DOS driver provides a software interface between the Sounding Board hardware and the LANtastic electronic mail system. If you have a Sounding Board and the DOS driver installed, you can use the Sounding Board to send voice mail messages through the LANtastic mail facility.

The Sounding Board Windows driver allows you to use the Sounding Board with any Windows application that supports sound. LANtastic for Windows can use the Sounding Board or any other Windows-compatible sound board to send voice mail messages through the LANtastic mail system. We'll take a closer look at LANtastic for Windows in Chapter 9.

■ Sharing Modems on the Network

One of the main incentives for installing a network is to allow several users to share expensive equipment such as large hard disks, laser printers, and plotters.

At first glance, it may not seem sensible to share modems, since you can buy a decent-quality 2,400 BPS modem for less than $100. But business phone lines are not cheap, and 9,600 BPS modems still command price tags of $500 or more.

Aside from the cost of the modems and phone lines, there's another barrier to putting a modem on every PC: Many office telephone systems are not designed to accept modems. In some buildings, running the phone wires themselves is a major problem.

That's where a communication server comes into play. Since you already have an installed LAN, you can add a communication server for relatively little money. An asynchronous communication server, or ACS, runs on a PC attached to the LAN. The machine running the ACS contains a number of serial ports or modems that are available to all users on the LAN. Workstations on the network can use the modems and serial ports on the server through normal communication software such as CrossTalk or Procomm.

This arrangement, shown in Figure 8.2, gives each user access to a modem and phone line without having to install a modem and run a line to every PC on the LAN.

Figure 8.2

An asynchronous communications server (ACS) can make a shared pool of modems available to people using the network. Each client PC must use communications software with special capabilities to address the ACS.

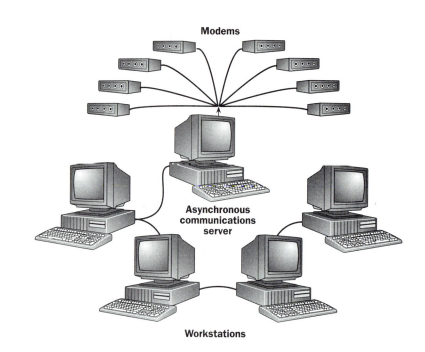

An ACS can also be used to share ports to a mainframe or minicomputer. Connecting the mainframe or mini to serial ports on the ACS gives each user access to a port on the big computer. Again, this saves the expense of providing a host computer port for each user and running RS-232 lines to every PC that needs access to the mainframe.

Artisoft's ACS: ArtiCom

Most ACS products are expensive, difficult to set up, and require a dedicated PC to act as a modem server. Artisoft's ArtiCom software is a simple but effective ACS package that can run on any network server or workstation. The ArtiCom server program uses only 6k of memory, and doesn't even need a hard disk to operate. The ArtiCom package also includes a capable general-purpose communication program.

The ArtiCom software has four major components:

- *The ArtiCom server* (A-SERVER.EXE), which loads as a TSR program on the machine acting as the modem server, can control up to four COM ports, each with an attached modem or mainframe/minicomputer link.

- *The ArtiCom redirector* (A-REDIR.EXE) also loads as a TSR program, but resides on the workstations that need access to the shared modems. A-REDIR provides a software interface (INT14) that most communication programs understand. When you want to use a networked modem, you first run A-REDIR, and then ACOM.EXE (described below) to "claim" a port on the server. After that, you can use ACOM.EXE as a terminal program or run your own communication program. Your communication software talks to the shared modem via the INT 14 software interface provided by A-REDIR.

- *The ArtiCom application program* (ACOM.EXE) serves two purposes: First, it establishes a connection between the A-REDIR program on the workstation and the A-SERVER program running on the modem server. Once the connection is established, you can use any INT14-compatible communication program to talk to the networked modem. Second, ACOM itself serves as a simple communication program, providing terminal emulation, file transfer, and a dialing directory of frequently called numbers.

- *The ArtiCom utility programs* (AINSTALL.EXE and ACOM-MGR.EXE) are used to install and configure the ArtiCom software.

In the following sections, we'll show you how to install and operate the ArtiCom software, and how to use the ArtiCom server with third-party communications programs.

What Is INT14?

To understand the use of interrupt 14, you should first know that there are a number of different, incompatible ways for communications software to "talk" to a port on the LAN communication server.

Unlike those for ordinary modems and serial ports, the methods for communicating with a modem server are relatively new. When IBM's engineers first designed the PC, they chose the Western Digital 8250 serial controller chip for the serial port. The programmers who wrote the PC's ROM BIOS routines provided a set of software routines that programmers could and still can use to communicate with the serial ports. These routines are known as software interrupt 14, or INT14.

Unfortunately, the INT14 routines built into the PC's ROM BIOS aren't of much use to communication software designers; they don't provide fast, interrupt-driven input and output, and they appear to have been designed with serial printers, not modems, in mind.

Early on, the designers of PC communications software realized that the only way to get acceptable performance from the PC's serial interface was to bypass the INT14 routines and talk directly to the 8250 chip itself. Virtually all communication programs on the market today talk directly to the 8250 chip or to its replacement, the 16550A.

The situation is analogous to the way most application programs write data to the PC's screen. Although IBM provided a video interface (INT10) in the system ROM for programmers to use, many application developers found the original INT10 too slow. PC users expect blindingly fast screen updates, and INT10 just couldn't deliver the performance required. Consequently, most programs written today print data directly to the video hardware, bypassing INT10 entirely.

When IBM introduced its asynchronous communications server, it also released a new specification to define the method a communication program should use to talk to the server; however, several other servers have come on the market since the IBM offering, and most of them use a different set of rules for talking to the server.

Ironically, the standard adopted by most server vendors is an extension of the old INT14 interface. Because most programmers are at least passingly familiar with INT14, it provided a logical basis for a new, extended standard that programmers can use to talk to servers.

ArtiCom uses the INT14 interface to pass data between the A-REDIR program and the communication program running on the workstation. In turn, A-REDIR converts the INT14 information into NETBIOS messages that travel over the network cable to connect A-REDIR to the A-SERVER program running on the server.

Because ArtiCom uses the standard NETBIOS and INT14 interfaces, it can operate over any NETBIOS-compatible network and work with any communication program that supports INT14.

Installing the ArtiCom Software

To install the ArtiCom software, you use the AINSTALL.EXE program provided on the ArtiCom distribution disk. The program is very similar to the INSTALL.EXE program that you use to install LANtastic. You can install ArtiCom as either a server, a workstation, or both.

The ArtiCom server program (A-SERVER.EXE) can be installed on virtually any network workstation or server. The program doesn't require a hard disk, so you can even run it on a floppy-only system. The ArtiCom redirector

(A-REDIR.EXE) and application (ACOM.EXE) should be installed on all workstations that will need access to the ArtiCom server.

Unless you're very tight on disk space, we recommend you install the workstation software on all communication servers. If you ever need to test or adjust the server software, it's helpful to have the workstation software available.

Like the LANtastic INSTALL program, the ArtiCom installer allows you to specify a destination directory for the ArtiCom files. If you're installing the ArtiCom server, you must also name the server. Figure 8.3 shows the ArtiCom AINSTALL program.

Figure 8.3

Preparing to install the ArtiCom server and workstation.

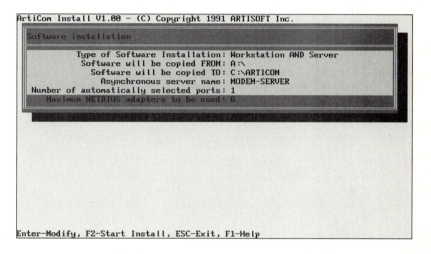

During installation, the ArtiCom installer program checks to see how many serial ports are installed in the server. If you're installing the ArtiCom server, the installer assumes that you want to share all of your installed serial ports. If you don't want to share all of your ports, select Number of Automatically Selected Ports from the installer screen and press Enter. Move the highlight bar to the port you don't want to share, and press DEL to delete it.

The installer program stores detailed information for each shared port. In most cases, you can simply accept the default information generated by the program. To see the detailed information, select the port as described above, but press Enter instead of DEL. You'll see detailed port information similar to that shown in Figure 8.4.

Table 8.1 explains each item on the detailed port information screen. Note that in most cases, you can use the default settings provided by ArtiCom.

Figure 8.4

The detailed port information screen, from which you can view and change any of the settings for the selected serial port.

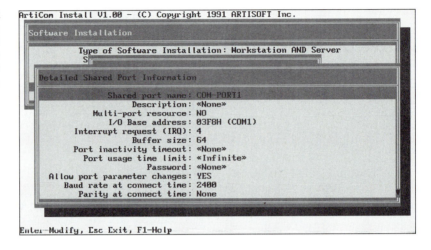

Table 8.1

The ArtiCom Server Detailed Port Information Settings

ITEM	DEFAULT SETTING	PURPOSE
Shared port name	COM-PORTx	Sets the name users will see when presented with a list of available network ports. You may want to change this to a more descriptive name like HAYES_9600.
Description	None	Contains up to 64 characters of descriptive information about the port. Like the port name, the description appears on screen when users are selecting a network modem port.
Multi-port resource	NO	Tells ArtiCom what type of serial port board your system has. If you are using a supported multiport serial board, set this field to YES. If you're using the standard PC serial ports or an internal modem board, choose NO.
I/O base address	Varies	Sets the I/O base address for the serial port. Some systems use nonstandard serial port addresses, particularly for ports COM3 and COM4. To use one of these ports, the installer must know the correct I/O address and IRQ line.
Interrupt request	Varies	See *I/O base address*, above.

Table 8.1

(continued)

ITEM	DEFAULT SETTING	PURPOSE
Buffer size	64 bytes	The ArtiCom server maintains two first-in, first-out (FIFO) buffers, one each for transmitted and received data. On a heavily loaded server, you may need to increase the buffer size to prevent the server from losing incoming and outgoing characters, especially if the modem server is running on a machine that is also acting as a file server. If you experience this problem, increase the buffer size until the problem clears.
Inactivity timeout	None	Tells ArtiCom how long a user can keep an idle port open. If no characters are sent or received for the specified amount of time, the server automatically disconnects the user from the shared port.
Port usage time limit	None	Specifies how long a user can use the shared port. This setting is similar to the Inactivity timeout, but applies even if the port is in use.
Password	None	Unlike other shared resources, server ports do not have an access control list. This field sets an optional password that users may be required to enter before they can use the serial port. Each port can have its own password.
Allow port parameter changes	YES	Determines whether the port user will be able to change the speed and data format of the port. If set to NO, the user's communication software settings must agree exactly with the serial port settings defined in the next entries.
Baud rate at connect time	2,400 BPS	Sets the default baud rate for the port. When a user first connects to a shared port, it will be set for this speed.
Parity at connect time	None	Sets the default parity for the port.
Word length at connect time	8 bits	Sets the default word length for the port.

Table 8.1

(continued)

ITEM	DEFAULT SETTING	PURPOSE
Stop bits at connect time	1 bit	Sets the default stop bit for the port. Use 1 stop bit with 8 data bits or with 7 bits and parity. Use 2 stop bits for 7 data bits and no parity.
Raise DTR/RTS on connect	YES	Tells ArtiCom whether to turn on the RTS and DTR handshaking lines to the modem when a user connects to a shared port. If your communication software controls RTS and DTR by itself, you can set this to NO.
Drop DTR/RTS on disconnect	YES	Similar to the previous setting, this one tells ArtiCom whether to drop the DTR and RTS lines when a port is released.
Flow control	None	Tells ArtiCom how to control the flow of data between the modem and the serial port. The three possible settings are None, Hardware, and XON/XOFF. Most high-speed modems (above 2,400 BPS) don't require flow control. Modems with speeds above 2,400 BPS typically use hardware (also called RTS/CTS) flow control. Consult your modem's manual for the best setting. In many cases, the default setting of None will work.
Hardware FIFO control	Disabled	Many newer PCs are equipped with an NS16550A serial communications chip, which has a hardware first-in, first-out (FIFO) buffer that allows it to receive and store data even while the CPU is busy with another task. If your PC has this chip, ArtiCom can use the buffer to ensure that no incoming or outgoing characters are lost.
Default initialization string	ATZ<CR><W1.5>	Contains the default reset string for the modem. The command ATZ resets virtually all Hayes-compatible modems, and should work for 99 percent of the modems in use today. If your modem requires a different reset string, you can enter it here. The <CR> represents a carriage return, and the <W1.5> instructs ArtiCom to wait 1.5 seconds after the ATZ is sent.

Table 8.1

(continued)

ITEM	DEFAULT SETTING	PURPOSE
Default dialing string	ATDT<P> <CR>	Contains the string sent to the modem instructing it to dial a phone number. The default setting is for tone dialing; if your phone system requires rotary (pulse) dialing, change ATDT to ATDP. The <P> represents the phone number to be dialed.
Default hangup string	<W1.5> +++ <W1.5>ATH <CR>	Tells ArtiCom how to disconnect a call in progress. Hayes and compatible modems use the string +++ to return the modem to the command state, and it must be preceded and followed by a one second pause. The ATH command hangs up the phone line.
Time of day port available	Always	Determines what times of day the shared port will be available.

Once you've made any necessary changes to the port configurations, you're ready to install the ArtiCom software. Press the F2 key, and the installer will copy the files to your hard disk.

If you need to change your shared modem settings after you've installed A-SERVER, use the ACOM-MGR program, which allows you to add, delete, or change any of the shared port settings.

Using Shared Modems

After you've installed the ArtiCom server, you can use the shared modems from any workstation on your network. As mentioned earlier, you can use the ACOM.EXE communication program supplied with ArtiCom or any INT14-compatible communication program.

To use a shared modem, follow these steps:

On the server,

1. Load LANtastic, or at least the AEx and AILANBIO programs. The ArtiCom server does not have to be logged into the network.

2. Run the A-SERVER.EXE program.

On the workstation,

1. Load LANtastic, or AEx and AILANBIO. You need not be connected to a file server to use an ArtiCom server.

2. Load the A-REDIR.EXE serial port redirector program.

3. Load the ACOM application program and select a modem port to use, or use ACOM's command-line option to select a shared port.

4. Use ACOM's built-in communication program, or exit ACOM and load another communication program.

5. After completing your communication session, run ACOM again and remove the shared port.

In the next section, we'll take a closer look at ACOM. Then we'll show you how to use the ArtiCom software with a third-party communication program.

The ArtiCom Application Program

The ACOM.EXE program provided with ArtiCom serves two purposes: First, it controls the logical connection between the shared ports on the modem servers and the communication ports on the workstations. Before you can use a shared modem, you must create a connection between one of the workstation's communication ports and one of the server's shared modem ports.

Second, ACOM serves as a basic, but very functional, communication program. While not as flexible as third-party packages like CrossTalk or Procomm, ACOM does provide basic terminal emulation and file transfer features.

Because ACOM uses the same menu structure as the Connection Manager and Network Manager programs, you'll feel comfortable with it right away. Figure 8.5 shows the main ACOM menu.

The first item on the menu, Terminal Emulator, activates ArtiCom's terminal emulation mode. In this mode, ACOM.EXE mimics a terminal; it displays received characters on the screen, and sends characters typed on the keyboard to the modem.

The second menu item, COM Port Servers and Resources, displays a list of available shared modem ports.

The third item, Network COM Ports, lets you select a network modem port to use. This screen works very much like the Network Manager's Network Drives and Printers screen. To connect a local port to a network modem port, you must choose a local port, a modem server, and a shared modem. Figure 8.6 shows a local port being connected to a shared modem.

The Detailed Redirector Information menu item shows the version number, buffer size, and other information about the A-REDIR.EXE program's settings. This screen is read-only; you can view the settings but you can't change them.

Figure 8.5

The main ACOM menu

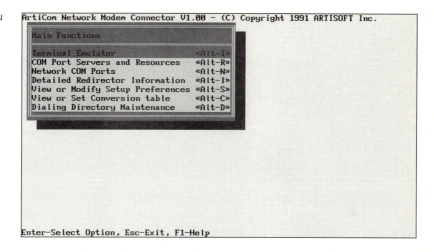

Figure 8.6

Connecting a local COM port to a shared modem port. In this example, port COM2 is being connected to a modem named WORLDPORT on the server named 9600MODEMS.

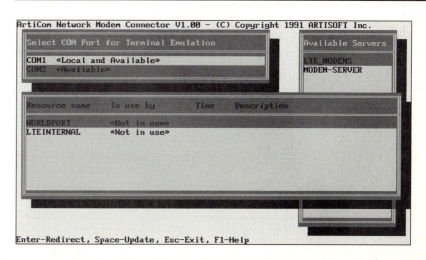

The View or Modify Setup Preferences item, in Figure 8.5, allows you to view and change the communication, file transfer, and terminal emulation settings used by the terminal emulator.

The next menu choice, View or Set Conversion Table, lets you select, edit, and create character conversion tables. ArtiCom comes preconfigured with character conversion tables for most European languages, including English (American and UK), Danish, French, German, Italian, Norwegian, Spanish, and Swedish.

The final menu item, Dialing Directory Maintenance, maintains ArtiCom's telephone directory list, which contains the name, phone number, and communication settings for frequently called systems.

Using ArtiCom with Third-Party Software

You can use the ArtiCom software with any communication programs that support INT14 modem servers. Most popular communication programs support INT14 directly or are available in special INT14-compatible versions.

You must load the A-REDIR port redirector program, which provides the necessary software interface between your communications program and the modem server, before you can use one of the shared ports on the modem server.

After you've loaded A-REDIR, you must run the ACOM program and select a shared modem port to use. There are two ways to do this: You can select a port from the Network COM Ports menu in ACOM, or you can tell ACOM which server and port to use from the DOS command line.

To select a port using the menus, follow these steps:

1. Start the ACOM.EXE program.

2. Select Network COM Ports from the menu that appears. You'll see a display of the available COM ports. Select a port and press Enter.

3. A list of available modem servers will appear. Select the server you want to use and press Enter.

4. You'll see a list of the modems available on the chosen modem server that also shows which modems are available. Select a modem and press Enter.

5. Press ESC twice to exit from the ACOM program.

6. Start your communication program, and set the software to use the port you selected in step 2.

7. After using your communication program, run ACOM again, select Network COM Ports, and press DEL to release the modem so others can use it.

If you'll be using a shared port frequently, you may want to create a batch file to automate this process. The following example batch file loads A-REDIR, selects a port using ACOM's command-line options, starts CrossTalk Mark 4, and then runs ACOM again to release the network modem.

```
@ECHO OFF
CD \LANTASTI\ARTICOM
A-REDIR
ACOM USE COM2 \\MODEMSERVER\COURIER
```

```
CD \XTALK4
XTALK
CD \LANTASTI\ARTICOM
ACOM UNUSE COM2
```

■ Sharing CD-ROM Drives

If you have a CD-ROM drive installed on a file server, you can create a shared resource for the CD-ROM drive. If you've used a CD-ROM drive with MS-DOS, you know that you must load the MSCDEX.EXE CD-ROM extensions program before you can use the CD-ROM drive. This is true for shared CD-ROM drives as well, but instead of loading MSCDEX.EXE on each individual workstation, you load it on the server.

To create a shared resource for a CD-ROM drive, follow these steps:

1. Make sure the CD-ROM driver software is loaded from the CONFIG-.SYS file on the server. For most CD-ROM drives, you'll need a command like

   ```
   DEVICE=CDROM.SYS /D:MSCD001
   ```

   in your CONFIG.SYS file. Consult your CD-ROM software manual to determine the exact command for your system.

2. Edit the STARTNET.BAT file on the server to include the MSCDEX command for your CD-ROM drive. The MSCDEX program must load after the LANtastic REDIR.EXE program, but *before* SERVER.EXE, as shown in this example:

   ```
   @echo off
   PATH %PATH%;C:\LANTASTI
   SHARE /L:200
   AEX IRQ=15 IOBASE=300 VERBOSE
   AILANBIO
   REDIR MAIN LOGINS=5
   MSCDEX.EXE /D:MSCD005 /M:8 /E /L:E
   SERVER
   ```

   Of course, the individual settings in your STARTNET.BAT file may be different from those shown here.

3. Start the Network Manager program, and select Shared Resources from the main menu.

4. Press INS to create a new shared resource for the shared CD-ROM drive. Enter a resource named for the shared drive.

5. Select the newly created drive resource, and press Enter. Move the highlight bar to the CD-ROM Drive field, and press Enter to change the selection from NO to YES.

Your CD-ROM drive is now available for use on the network. The individual workstations do not need to have the MSCDEX program loaded to use the CD-ROM drive. LANtastic provides the necessary DOS CD-ROM extensions for all stations on the network.

■ Artisoft's Central Station

In Chapter 2, we introduced Artisoft's Central Station connectivity processor. Physically, the Central Station is an external box with its own CPU and memory. In essence, it's an Artisoft AE-3t Ethernet adapter with a dedicated CPU, RAM, and ROM—sort of a mini-PC in a box the size of a modem that you can use as an external "zero-slot" LAN adapter for laptop and notebook computers.

The Central Station attaches to the PC's parallel port, so the client PC's LAN throughput is limited by that port to well under a megabit per second, depending on the type and speed of the CPU in the client PC. However, the Central Station doesn't block the PC's ability to print, as most external LAN adapters do, because it has its own parallel port for a printer connection. The Central Station will work with any computer, even the oldest PC, to carry the burden of network and other I/O tasks.

Artisoft has announced plans to develop a full suite of connectivity applications called StationWare for the Central Station. Several StationWare applications are already available, including printer servers and Dial-in access servers for LANtastic and NetWare.

In the following section, we'll explain how to use the Central Station to connect a laptop PC; then we'll look at some StationWare applications.

Connecting with the Central Station

The Central Station comes with a power transformer, a special parallel port cable, and a driver disk. Installation is simple: Just connect the cable to the LPT1 or LPT2 parallel port on your PC and plug the power transformer into an outlet. Then connect the transformer and your network cable to the Central Station. If your PC has a local printer attached, you can plug it into the port marked LPT1 on the back of the Central Station (see Figure 2.9).

PCs attached via a Central Station run the same version of LANtastic as the other PCs on your network, but the Central Station units require a different Ethernet driver program. Instead of the normal AEX.EXE Ethernet driver, the Central Station PCs use a driver named CSPPORT.EXE, which is supplied on the Central Station driver disk.

If you're installing a new copy of LANtastic on a machine attached via a Central Station, you won't see the Central Station listed in the INSTALL program's list of drivers. To install LANtastic for a Central Station, follow these steps:

1. Install LANtastic using the INSTALL program.

2. Copy the CSPPORT.EXE driver from the Central Station disk.

3. Edit the STARTNET.BAT file created by INSTALL. Remove the line that begins with *AEX*, and replace it with *CSPPORT*.

4. If your Central Station is attached via the LPT2 port, add PORT=LPT2 after the CSPPORT command. If your computer's parallel port uses a nonstandard address or interrupt request line, you can specify the address and IRQ line on the CSPPORT command line. The option IOBASE= sets the I/O base address, and the option IRQ= sets the IRQ request line.

5. Save the modified STARTNET.BAT file and exit from your text editor.

That's all there is to it. Here is a typical STARTNET.BAT file configured for a Central Station:

```
@ECHO OFF
PATH C:\LANTASTI;%PATH%
SHARE /L:200
CSPPORT
AILANBIO
REDIR LTE386 LOGINS=3
SERVER
```

As you can see, this STARTNET file is virtually identical to the one described back in Chapter 5. The only difference is the substitution of CSPPORT for AEX.EXE.

Once you've modified the STARTNET.BAT file, you're ready to run LANtastic. At the DOS command line, type STARTNET to start LANtastic.

The StationWare Applications

As mentioned earlier, there are currently four StationWare applications available for the Central Station:

- LANtastic Printer Server

- NetWare Printer Server

- LANtastic Dial-Up Connection
- NetWare Dial-Up Connection

The two printer servers and the two dial-up connection products are functionally identical, except that one supports LANtastic and the other supports NetWare.

When running any of the StationWare products, the Central Station operates as a stand-alone unit; however, you'll need to connect a PC to the Central Station to install and configure the StationWare applications. Once the applications are installed and configured, the Central Station will operate with or without a PC attached. You can use the Central Station as an external LAN adapter while the StationWare applications are running.

Several StationWare applications can run on one Central Station, but the applications may not share a port. For example, you could run the NetWare Printer Server using a serial printer on port COM2, and also run the LANtastic Printer Server using the parallel port and serial port COM1.

The Central Station stores its program code in an EEPROM (Electrically Erasable Programmable Read-Only Memory). EEPROMs are like ROMs, except they can be reprogrammed. Like conventional ROMs, EEPROMs keep the contents of their memory even when the power is off. Once you load your StationWare applications into a Central Station, they will remain in the EEPROM until you reprogram the Central Station.

The LANtastic Printer Server

The first StationWare application developed for the Central Station was the LANtastic Printer Server. The Printer Server lets you attach up to three printers (one parallel and two serial) to a Central Station. The Central Station and its attached printers can be located anywhere on your network. Once you've installed the Central Station Printer Server, you can send print jobs to the Central Station printers just as you would to any other network printer. Figure 8.7 shows a typical LANtastic installation with a file server, several workstations, and a Central Station Printer Server.

Print jobs bound for a Central Station must first pass through a print queue on a server. A driver program on the server reroutes one or more of the server's printer ports to the Central Station Printer Server.

The LANtastic Dial-Up Connection

Networks are for sharing. But people often want to share the network's resources from somewhere other than an office with a LAN installation. The LANtastic Dial-Up Connection provides a way for people to access network resources from anywhere, via a modem.

Figure 8.7

A LANtastic network showing two printers connected to a Central Station. The Central Station is running the LANtastic Printer Server application.

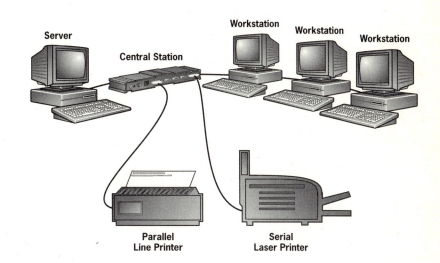

The Dial-Up Connection installs on the Central Station like other StationWare products. There's one caveat, however: You can use the Dial-Up Connection simultaneously with any of the other StationWare applications, but you can't use the Central Station as an external LAN adapter when the Dial-Up Connection is in use.

To use the Dial-Up Connection, you simply attach a modem to one of the Central Station's serial ports. When a remote user calls in, the modem answers the line and connects the user to the LAN.

At the calling end, you need a modem as well as a specially configured version of LANtastic. Remote workstations use a special modem port driver in place of the usual Ethernet driver. The remote client PC treats the modem like a (very slow) network interface adapter and routes all the networking activity through the serial port. The advantage of this technique is that it gives remote PCs a full set of redirected drives, just as though they were connected locally. The very big negative aspect of this setup is slow response time. Pushing and pulling lots of small, low-level messages across a relatively slow modem link is a very inefficient process. Fast modems are a must here—the faster the better.

- *Windows's Requirements*
- *Installing Windows with LANtastic*
- *Running Windows with LANtastic*
- *LANtastic for Windows*

CHAPTER 9

LANtastic and Windows

Microsoft's Windows 3.*x* operating environment contains several features that let Windows and your network software work as a team. Windows 3.0 was the first version to provide direct support for networked devices like drives and printers. The level of network support improved with version 3.1, and future versions will be even more tightly integrated into the world of network computing.

As it comes out of the box, Windows provides access to basic networking services like shared disks and printers. To make LANtastic easier to use with Windows, Artisoft has developed a special Windows-based version of LANtastic called LANtastic for Windows. In this chapter, we'll show you how to use LANtastic and Windows together, and then we'll look at the LANtastic for Windows product.

■ Windows's Requirements

Before you can run Windows with LANtastic, you need to make sure your system meets Windows's requirements. Windows likes memory: To run the program with LANtastic, you need at least 2Mb of memory as a practical minimum, and whenever you have more than 1Mb, you also need memory management software compatible with Microsoft's XMS standard, or with the LIM EMS 4.0 standard. Microsoft provides an XMS-compatible memory manager, HIMEM.SYS, with Windows.

In addition, you need a Windows network driver for LANtastic. There are three ways to obtain this driver: from the Windows installation disks, from the LANtastic installation disks, or from the LANtastic for Windows package.

■ Installing Windows with LANtastic

Windows can run from your local hard disk, from a combination of your disk and the network, or entirely from the network. Before we discuss the specifics of the installation process, you need to decide which of these three methods is best for your installation.

If you have a local hard disk, you can and probably should run Windows entirely from that disk. Windows performs best running from a locally attached hard disk. The downside is that a minimum Windows installation takes about 10 to 12Mb of local disk space.

If you have a local hard disk but don't want to give up the disk space required by Windows, you can install Windows to load from the network. With this method, Windows installs a minimal amount of data on your local hard disk; the rest of the program is loaded from a shared directory on the network. Installed this way, Windows performs nearly as well as it does running entirely from the hard disk. The disadvantage is that you can't run Windows unless you're connected to the network.

If you are using a diskless workstation and don't have a local hard disk, you must run Windows entirely from the network. There are several drawbacks to this approach. First, all of the Windows program code must load from the server. Since Windows is very disk-intensive, this greatly increases the amount of traffic on the network.

Second, on 386 and 486 systems, Windows creates a large (typically 3 to 4Mb) workspace swap file that's deleted when you exit from the program. This process takes a noticeable amount of time, even with a fast 386 system on a lightly loaded network.

The third and biggest drawback is that this method creates a great deal of network traffic. Unnecessary network traffic is every system administrator's number one enemy, and several diskless workstations running Windows from the network can create a serious traffic jam. If you have a diskless 386 or 486 workstation, we strongly suggest you set up a large RAM drive to contain your swap file.

Installing Windows on Your Local Hard Disk

There are no special tricks to installing Windows on your local hard disk. If you're installing Windows for the first time, load LANtastic before you run the Windows SETUP program. If LANtastic is loaded when you run SETUP, the SETUP program will recognize the LANtastic software and automatically configure Windows for LANtastic.

If you install Windows without LANtastic loaded, several necessary files won't be installed. To correct this, change to your Windows directory (usually C:\WINDOWS), and run SETUP again. You don't have to reinstall Windows; just select Change Options, and change the Network setting to LANtastic version 4.10 and above. SETUP will copy the LANtastic support files onto your hard disk.

Installing Windows from a File Server

If you need to install Windows on several network workstations, you may prefer to install from the network. This method allows you to keep a master copy of Windows on a server and install individual workstations from the master copy. To create the master copy, you run SETUP with the /A (administrative) option. SETUP prompts you to insert each Windows disk, and as you do so, it copies the files onto the server's hard disk.

There are two ways to use the master copy of Windows. First, you can use it instead of the original disks to perform a complete local installation of Windows on any workstation on the network. This method is very convenient because you don't have to insert and remove the six Windows diskettes over and over again. To use this option, follow these steps:

1. Install the master Windows files onto a server with the SETUP/A command.

2. Go to the workstation where you want to install Windows and map a drive to the server that contains the master Windows files.

3. Run SETUP from the shared Windows directory.

After SETUP is finished, you'll have a complete copy of Windows on the workstation, just as if you had installed it from the floppy disks.

The second method allows you to create a Windows installation where most or all of the program loads from the network. The SETUP program copies a few essential files to the workstation hard disk or to a private directory on a server, but the bulk of the Windows program files load from the shared directory on the server. This solution works well if your workstations don't have enough free disk space (about 11Mb) for the full Windows installation. To use this option, follow these steps:

1. Install the master Windows files onto a server with the SETUP/A command.

2. Go to the workstation where you want to install Windows and map a drive to the server that contains the master Windows files. If you're using a diskless workstation, create another drive mapping to contain your personal Windows files.

3. Run SETUP/N from the shared Windows directory. SETUP will copy only the necessary Windows files to your local hard disk or network directory.

When you run Windows, it will start from your personal directory or local hard disk, and will load the bulk of its program code from the shared network installation directory. Table 9.1 lists the files SETUP copies to your personal directory.

Table 9.1

Files Copied to Your Personal Directory by the Windows SETUP Program with the /N (Network) Option

FILE	PURPOSE
_DEFAULT.PIF	Default program information file for DOS programs
ACCESSOR.GRP	The accessories group file; contains the icons and program names of the Windows accessory programs
AUTOEXEC.WIN	Suggested replacement for AUTOEXEC.BAT
CONFIG.WIN	Suggested replacement for CONFIG.SYS
CONTROL.INI	The Windows control panel configuration information file

Table 9.1

(continued)

FILE	PURPOSE
EMM386.SYS	Microsoft's EMS manager for 386 and 486 systems (not copied on 286 systems)
GAMES.GRP	Group file for the games group
HIMEM.SYS	Microsoft's XMS memory manager device driver
MAIN.GRP	Group file for the main Windows programs
PROGMAN.INI	The Windows Program Manager configuration file; contains information about your Program Manager display screen
RAMDRIVE.SYS	Microsoft's RAM disk device driver
SMARTDRV.EXE	Microsoft's Smart Drive disk cache program
SYSTEM.INI	The Windows system configuration file; a plain text file containing information about your system's hardware
WIN.COM	The Windows program loader; run to start Windows
WIN.INI	The Windows initialization File
WINVER.EXE	Windows version program; used internally by Windows and SETUP

Windows, CONFIG.SYS, and AUTOEXEC.BAT

During the installation process, Windows will ask if it can modify your CONFIG.SYS and AUTOEXEC.BAT files. *Do not* allow SETUP to make the requested changes. Instead, select Make modifications later. SETUP will place the suggested modifications in two files named CONFIG.WIN and AUTOEXEC.WIN. You can then review these files to see whether you want to make the suggested changes. If you do, copy the files to CONFIG.SYS and AUTOEXEC.BAT on your boot disk.

In most cases, SETUP changes CONFIG.SYS to install the HIMEM.SYS memory manager. If you're using another memory manager (like QEMM or 386MAX), you do not need or want to install HIMEM. If SETUP thinks you need more DOS file handles or disk buffers, it will change the FILES and BUFFERS statements in your CONFIG.SYS file. If you're using a third-party memory manager program like QEMM, NetRoom, or 386MAX, it's possible those programs have already increased your files and buffers.

The SETUP program also makes some changes to AUTOEXEC.BAT: It adds the locations of the Windows installation directory and your personal Windows directory to the DOS PATH statement. We don't consider this a good idea on systems with local hard disks; if you put the two Windows directories into your DOS path in AUTOEXEC.BAT, your system will look for program files in those directories *even if you aren't logged into the network*. Instead, add the two Windows directories as additional paths in your STARTNET.BAT file. The Windows installation directory should come first, followed by your personal Windows directory.

Note that on systems equipped with a hard disk, SETUP places HIMEM.SYS in the root directory of your boot drive (usually drive C:). If you don't need HIMEM.SYS, you can delete this file.

If you are using a diskless workstation, you may need to create a new boot image file to incorporate the changes required for Windows. See Chapter 8 for more information on boot image files.

SETUP and Printer Assignments

During the installation process, the Windows SETUP program asks you to select a printer from a list. This procedure can be confusing for first-time users, because the SETUP program assumes you already know how to set up a network printer!

There are actually three steps to the setup procedure. First, you select a printer type from a long list of printers. Then you select the printer port and pick a local LPT port for the printer. Finally, you tell Windows which ports belong to which printer queues. To select a queue, click on the Network button in the Printer Control panel. Then pick an LPT port and type the name of a shared printer queue to go with that port. Repeat this process for each printer if you have more than one.

■ Running Windows with LANtastic

If you are running Windows from a local hard disk, you must load the LANtastic workstation software (usually AEX and REDIR) before you start Windows, but you don't have to log into a server before you start the program. If you're running Windows from the network, you should load LANtastic and log into the server containing the Windows files before you start Windows.

Controlling LANtastic from Windows

Windows running with LANtastic doesn't look any different than Windows on a stand-alone PC. There is a difference, however: With LANtastic installed, you have access to network drives and printers. Windows includes several features that allow you to control network drives and printers directly from the program. These features are roughly equivalent to the Connection Manager's Network Drives and Printers screen, but they are built into Windows itself.

Using Network Drives with Windows

When you start Windows, any existing network disk assignments will be in place, just as they were under DOS. For example, if you have network drives mapped to drives F: and G:, those mappings will still exist after you start Windows.

You can use the Windows File Manager program to add, change, or delete LANtastic drive mappings while Windows is running. To do so, select Network Connections from the File Manager's Drive menu. Figure 9.1 shows the File Manager adding a new drive mapping.

Figure 9.1

Using the File Manager to add a new drive mapping

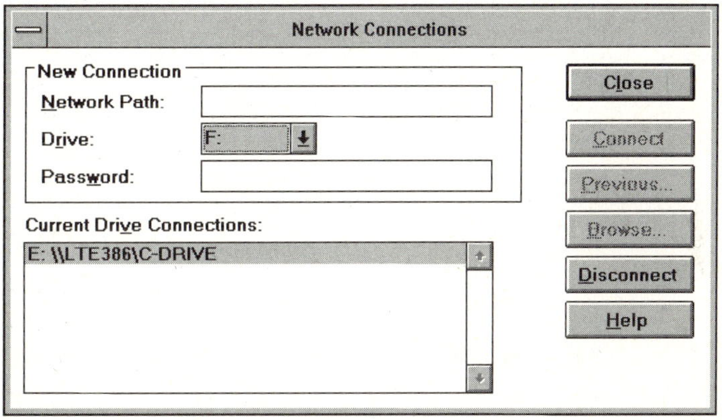

To add a drive mapping from the File Manager, type the full path name of the server and drive resource in the Network Path box; then select a drive from the Drives pull-down menu. Click on the Connect button, and your new drive mapping will appear in the Current Drive Connections list box. To delete a network drive mapping, select the mapping from the Current Drive Connections list box, and then click on the Disconnect button.

Using Network Printers with Windows

When you install Windows with the SETUP program, it asks you to choose your printer or printers from a long list of printer types. SETUP automatically copies the necessary printer drivers to your Windows installation directory. Although the program allows you to select more than one printer, only one at a time may be active. If you're using a network that has several printers, you'll need to make sure your selected printer is connected to the correct network printer queue.

Windows printer assignments are controlled via the Printers icon in the Windows control panel. To open the control panel, double-click Control Panel from the Windows desktop. To see or change the printer assignments, double-click on the Printers icon.

On a stand-alone PC, the Printers icon selects the type of printer you have and tells Windows which printer port to use. In a network environment, the Printers icon also tells Windows which network printer queues to use. The printer selection process can be somewhat confusing, because Windows will let you assign any printer type to any printer queue. The good news is that Windows remembers your printer settings between sessions.

To select a printer, choose the printer from the list box and click on the Connect button. Select a local printer port (it really doesn't matter which one), and click on the Network button. You'll see a display like the one in Figure 9.2.

Figure 9.2

Connecting a printer to a network printer queue

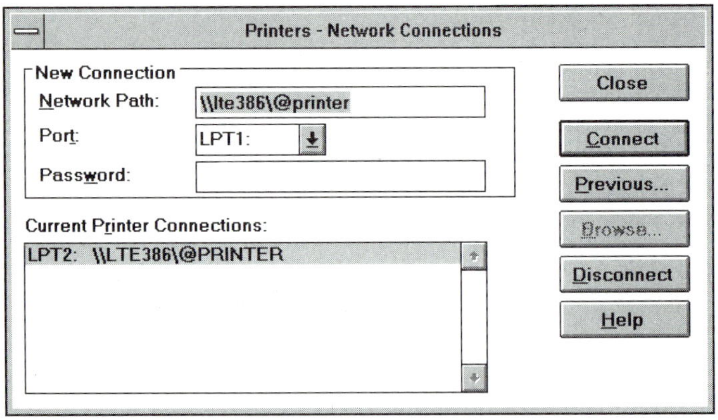

To connect the printer port to a network printer queue, type the full name of the shared printer resource in the box marked Network Path, and then click on Connect. The new printer connection should appear in the list of network printer connections. To delete a network printer connection, select the desired connection and click on Disconnect.

Because Windows remembers your printer selections between sessions, the next time you start the program, the printer settings will be reactivated.

Although the printer control panel allows you to install several printers, remember that only one at a time can actually be used for printing. If you look at the bottom of the printer selection menu, you'll notice that one printer is designated the default. Windows always uses the default printer; to select a specific printer for a print job you must go to the control panel and make that printer the default. To select a new default printer, move the mouse pointer to the desired printer and double-click on it. The new default printer setting should appear at the bottom of the printer selection box.

Using Windows Applications on the Network

One nice feature of Windows is that each user can customize the Program Manager display. As you add new software to your system, you can add those programs to the display. When you first install Windows, SETUP creates three Program Manager groups: MAIN, WINDOWS, and GAMES. You add new programs to one of these groups by selecting New from the File menu, and then New Program from the dialog box that appears. The programs you add can be on a local or a network drive.

To add a network program to a program group, select New from the File menu; then click New Program in the dialog box. Windows will display another dialog box, asking you to fill in the name and path name of the program. To add a program from a file server, you can type the entire path name (if you know it), or select Browse. The Browse box displays a list of all available files and drives. Once you've selected a program, Windows displays the warning message shown in Figure 9.3 to inform you that the file you've selected may not be available the next time you run Windows. Since network drives can come and go, Windows wants to be certain it can find this program in the future. This is another reason to make sure your drive mappings remain consistent each time you start Windows.

Figure 9.3

Windows displays this warning message when you add a network program to the Program Manager.

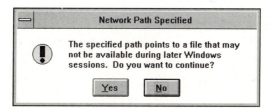

■ LANtastic for Windows

So far, we've talked about running Windows with the standard LANtastic software. As you've seen, Windows and LANtastic work very well together, but if you'll be using them together frequently, you may want to add the LANtastic for Windows product to your network. The package includes

- A Windows version of the Connection Manager
- A Windows version of the Network Manager
- The Windows LANtastic network drivers
- An installation program

The LANtastic for Windows package increases your network's flexibility, adding all the functions of the Connection Manager and Network Manager programs to the Windows environment.

Installing LANtastic for Windows

Before you can install LANtastic for Windows, you should install LANtastic, Windows, and your network hardware. Make sure your network software is operating properly; if it doesn't work under DOS, it won't work with Windows. Similarly, start Windows and make sure it is installed and operating properly.

Once you're sure Windows and LANtastic are installed correctly, you're ready to install the LANtastic for Windows package. Follow these steps to install LANtastic for Windows:

1. Boot your system and load LANtastic. If you're running Windows from the network, create a drive mapping to your network Windows directory.

2. Place the LANtastic for Windows diskette in a floppy drive, either A: or B:.

3. Start Windows by typing **WIN** from the DOS prompt.

4. Select File from the main Program Manager menu, and Run from the File menu.

5. Type **A:\WINSTALL** (or **B:\WINSTALL**) and press Enter. The LANtastic for Windows installer program will appear, as shown in Figure 9.4.

6. In the Install From box, type the drive letter of your LANtastic for Windows installation disk, either A: or B:.

7. In the Install To box, type the name of the directory where you want to install the files. In most cases, this will be C:\LANTASTI.

8. Make sure the Copy Files box is checked; this box tells WINSTALL to copy the LANtastic for Windows files to your local disk.

9. Click the Install button. WINSTALL will copy the LANtastic for Windows files to your hard disk and modify your Windows setup files to contain the new LANtastic drivers.

Figure 9.4

The LANtastic for Windows installer program. This program copies the LANtastic for Windows files to your hard disk and automatically modifies your Windows setup files.

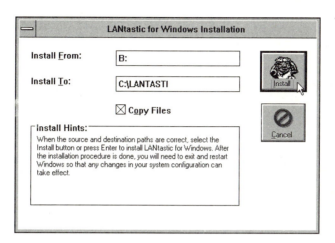

After the installer program copies the files to your disk, you must exit from and restart Windows. Select the Exit Windows button on the installer menu and restart Windows by typing **WIN**.

Using LANtastic for Windows

After you've run the LANtastic for Windows installer program, you'll see a few changes on your Windows desktop. The installer program adds a new program group named LANTASTIC that includes two programs: Network Manager and Connection Manager. If you start Windows with LANtastic loaded, the Connection Manager program starts automatically.

The Windows Connection Manager and Network Manager programs contain all the functionality of their DOS counterparts. For the remainder of this section, we'll assume you're familiar with the DOS versions of these programs and with LANtastic network concepts in general. If you're not, you should read Chapters 5 and 6 for detailed background information on these topics.

The Windows Connection Manager

When you start Windows with LANtastic loaded, Windows automatically loads the LANtastic for Windows Connection Manager program. The Connection Manager loads as an icon, and should be visible at the bottom of your Windows desktop.

To see the main Connection Manager menu, move the mouse pointer to the Connection Manager icon and click twice. The main Connection Manager menu will appear, as shown in Figure 9.5.

Figure 9.5

The main LANtastic for Windows Connection Manager menu, which offers the same choices as the DOS Connection Manager program.

As you can see, the Windows Connection Manager display is a graphical version of the NET.EXE Connection Manager program. If you're familiar with NET.EXE, you'll understand the icons immediately; however, note that there are eight icons in this menu, while the DOS Connection Manager has only seven choices. That's because the Windows Connection Manager has separate menus for network drives and printers, which are on one menu in the DOS version.

Here are the eight menu choices, along with a brief explanation of each one:

- *Drives* adds and removes network drives.

- *Printers* adds and removes network printer connections.

- *Mail* takes you to the mail menu, where you can exchange electronic mail messages with other users on the network.

- *Chat* allows you to conduct a real-time, back-and-forth keyboard conversation with another user on the network.

- *Queues* controls network printer queues.

- *Login/Out* lets you make or break connections with the servers on your network.

- *Account* lets you change your network password, check your network access privileges, and monitor the status of your network account.

- *Server Mgt* lets you monitor and control access to servers.

To use any item on the Connection Manager menu, move the mouse pointer to the desired item and click the mouse button. If you'd rather use the keyboard, you can press the first letter of the item. For example, pressing *L* takes you to the Login/Out menu.

In addition to the eight icons, there are two pull-down menus on the Connection Manager display. The Net pull-down menu lets you check and set several network-related configuration items, and the Help menu starts the Windows help system. The Net pull-down menu contains these seven entries:

- *Pop-up Messages...* sends messages to or responds to messages from other network users.

- *Printer Timeout...* sets the printer timeout interval.

- *Login Defaults...* sets the default user name, password, and network adapter for subsequent logins.

- *Pop-up Enabled* enables or disables network pop-up messages.

- *Print Notification* tells LANtastic to send you a pop-up message when your pending print job is complete. Note that Pop-up Messages must also be enabled for you to receive print notification messages.

- *Auto Save/Restore* automatically saves your network configuration each time you leave Windows (or when you close the Connection Manager program), and restores the configuration when you restart Windows and the Connection Manager. The saved information includes all network logins and all shared resources.

- *Exit* exits from the Connection Manager program.

While the concepts behind each Connection Manager icon are the same as those behind each DOS menu entry, the two kinds of menus are completely different in appearance and operation. In the following sections, we'll examine each item on the Connection Manager screen.

Managing Network Disk Drives

The Drives button lets you view, add, and delete network drive assignments. When you select Drives, you'll see a screen like the one in Figure 9.6.

As you can, the Drive Connections display features two large, side-by-side windows. The left window displays available network drive resources, and the right one shows your current disk drive connections. Note that you must be logged into a server to see that server's resources.

If you look closely at Figure 9.6, you'll notice that each icon shows what type of drive it represents. Drives A: through D: are local drives; A: is a $3^{1}/_{2}$-inch floppy, and B: is a $5^{1}/_{4}$-inch floppy, while C: and D: are hard disks.

Figure 9.6

The Connection Manager Drive Connections display, which is used to view, add, or delete network drives

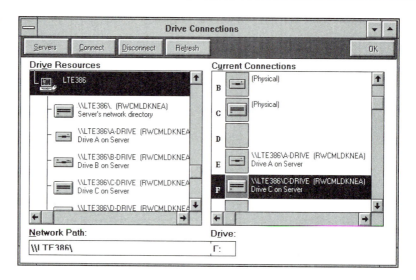

To create a network drive connection, select the desired network resource with the mouse, hold down the left mouse button, and drag the resource icon onto the desired drive letter. If there are too many resources or drive letters to fit in the windows, you can use the scroll bars at the side of each window to scroll through the drives or resources list.

If you wish, you can connect all of any server's drive resources at one time. To do so, select the server's icon and drag it to the next available drive letter. LANtastic will connect each of the server's shared resources to the next available drive letter.

There are five buttons at the top of the drives display. The Servers button allows you to log into additional file servers. If you don't see the server you want on the list of available resources, click on the Servers button, and a login box will appear, as shown in Figure 9.7.

To log into an additional server, select the desired server from the list of available servers, and click the Login button.

The Connect button on the Drive Connections screen lets you connect additional drives without the mouse. This is most useful on a laptop or notebook computer that doesn't have a mouse attached. To connect a drive without using the mouse, follow these steps:

1. Use the Tab key to move the highlight bar into the Drive Resources list; then use the Up Arrow and Down Arrow keys to select the server resource you want to use.

To use any item on the Connection Manager menu, move the mouse pointer to the desired item and click the mouse button. If you'd rather use the keyboard, you can press the first letter of the item. For example, pressing *L* takes you to the Login/Out menu.

In addition to the eight icons, there are two pull-down menus on the Connection Manager display. The Net pull-down menu lets you check and set several network-related configuration items, and the Help menu starts the Windows help system. The Net pull-down menu contains these seven entries:

- *Pop-up Messages...* sends messages to or responds to messages from other network users.

- *Printer Timeout...* sets the printer timeout interval.

- *Login Defaults...* sets the default user name, password, and network adapter for subsequent logins.

- *Pop-up Enabled* enables or disables network pop-up messages.

- *Print Notification* tells LANtastic to send you a pop-up message when your pending print job is complete. Note that Pop-up Messages must also be enabled for you to receive print notification messages.

- *Auto Save/Restore* automatically saves your network configuration each time you leave Windows (or when you close the Connection Manager program), and restores the configuration when you restart Windows and the Connection Manager. The saved information includes all network logins and all shared resources.

- *Exit* exits from the Connection Manager program.

While the concepts behind each Connection Manager icon are the same as those behind each DOS menu entry, the two kinds of menus are completely different in appearance and operation. In the following sections, we'll examine each item on the Connection Manager screen.

Managing Network Disk Drives

The Drives button lets you view, add, and delete network drive assignments. When you select Drives, you'll see a screen like the one in Figure 9.6.

As you can, the Drive Connections display features two large, side-by-side windows. The left window displays available network drive resources, and the right one shows your current disk drive connections. Note that you must be logged into a server to see that server's resources.

If you look closely at Figure 9.6, you'll notice that each icon shows what type of drive it represents. Drives A: through D: are local drives; A: is a $3^{1}/_{2}$- inch floppy, and B: is a $5^{1}/_{4}$-inch floppy, while C: and D: are hard disks.

Figure 9.6

The Connection Manager Drive Connections display, which is used to view, add, or delete network drives

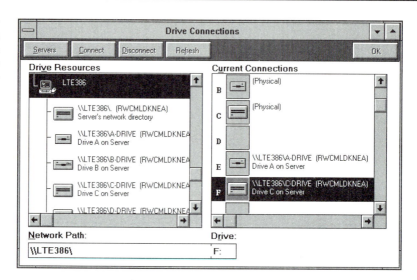

To create a network drive connection, select the desired network resource with the mouse, hold down the left mouse button, and drag the resource icon onto the desired drive letter. If there are too many resources or drive letters to fit in the windows, you can use the scroll bars at the side of each window to scroll through the drives or resources list.

If you wish, you can connect all of any server's drive resources at one time. To do so, select the server's icon and drag it to the next available drive letter. LANtastic will connect each of the server's shared resources to the next available drive letter.

There are five buttons at the top of the drives display. The Servers button allows you to log into additional file servers. If you don't see the server you want on the list of available resources, click on the Servers button, and a login box will appear, as shown in Figure 9.7.

To log into an additional server, select the desired server from the list of available servers, and click the Login button.

The Connect button on the Drive Connections screen lets you connect additional drives without the mouse. This is most useful on a laptop or notebook computer that doesn't have a mouse attached. To connect a drive without using the mouse, follow these steps:

1. Use the Tab key to move the highlight bar into the Drive Resources list; then use the Up Arrow and Down Arrow keys to select the server resource you want to use.

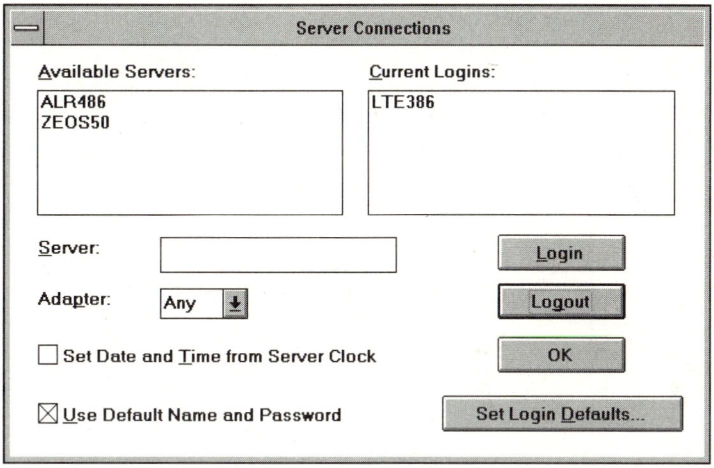

Figure 9.7

Logging into an additional server from the Drive Connections screen

2. Press Tab again to move the highlight bar into the Current Connections drive list; then use the arrow keys to select an unused local drive letter.

3. Press Alt-C (Connect) to connect the resource to the local drive letter.

The Disconnect button removes network drive connections. To delete a network drive, select the drive with the mouse or the keyboard, and then click the Disconnect button or press Alt-D to disconnect the drive.

The Refresh button redraws the list of available resources. Pressing this button causes the Connection Manager to recheck the available resources on the network.

The OK button saves your drive assignments and closes the Drive Connections window.

Managing Network Printers

The Printers button displays, connects, and disconnects network printer assignments. When you select this button, you'll see a display like the one in Figure 9.8.

The Printer Connections screen works just like the Drive Connections screen. To connect a network printer, you select a printer resource and drag the resource to one of the five available printer ports.

To connect all of a server's shared printers, select the server's icon and drag it to the desired printer port. LANtastic will connect all of that server's shared printers to your local printer ports, beginning with the port you've selected.

Figure 9.8

The Connection Manager Printer Connections display, from which you can add, delete, and view your network printer assignments

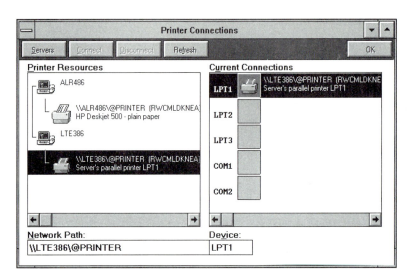

The five buttons at the top of the Printer Connections screen operate exactly like those in the Drive Connections screen.

Network Electronic Mail

You use the Mail button to send and receive network mail messages. If you have a Sounding Board or other Windows-compatible sound board installed in your system, you can also send and receive voice mail messages through the LANtastic mail system.

When you select the Mail button from the Connection Manager menu, you'll be prompted to select a server from a list of available servers. Once you select a server, you'll see the Mail display screen, shown in Figure 9.9.

The Mail display screen consists of two windows, one for incoming and one for outgoing mail. The incoming mail display shows messages addressed to you; the outgoing display shows messages you have sent to other users. An icon next to each mail item indicates the type of mail it is: An envelope icon designates a text-based mail message; a cassette tape icon indicates a voice mail message.

The message icons change color to show how long they've been waiting in the mail queue. Darker icons indicate older messages.

The nine buttons at the top of the screen are used to create, read, save, and delete mail messages. In addition to the buttons, the Mail screen offers the two pull-down menus Mail and Options. Since most of the choices on the pull-down menus are duplicated on the buttons, we'll examine the buttons first.

Figure 9.11

Choosing a file to send via LANtastic mail. You can send any type of file through the mail system.

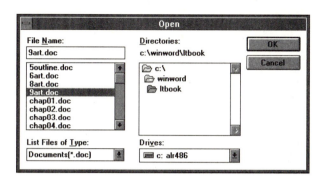

To record an outgoing mail message, click the Voice button on the Mail screen. The voice mail recorder display will appear, as shown in Figure 9.12.

Figure 9.12

Recording an outgoing voice mail message

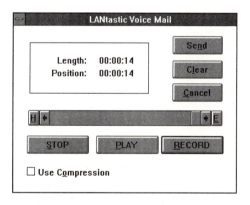

To send a voice mail message, follow these steps:

1. Click on the RECORD button and record your message.
2. When you've finished recording, click on STOP.
3. If you want to play back your message, click PLAY. If you want to rerecord your message, click Clear, and then click RECORD again.
4. To send your message, click Send; then pick one or more users from the list of users.

The Use Compression box in the recorder display tells LANtastic to reduce the size of a voice mail file by compressing the data in it. Using compression slightly reduces the sound quality of the message.

You can add a comment to a voice mail message; however, the comment will appear in the recipient's Incoming Mail display.

Chatting with Other Users

Like the DOS version, LANtastic for Windows allows you to carry on a keyboard-to-keyboard conversation with any other network user. To call another user, you use the Chat button on the main Connection Manager menu.

When you select the Chat button, you'll see the network Chat window. To call another network station, select the Call button and type the name of the machine you wish to call. LANtastic will send a pop-up message to the user on the called machine. When the other user responds, you'll see a <<Connect>> message in the lower window on your screen. Figure 9.13 shows a network Chat session in progress.

Figure 9.13

Using the network Chat facility

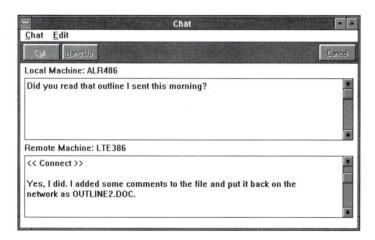

To end a Chat session, select the Cancel or Hang Up button.

Managing Printer Queues

As mentioned, LANtastic for Windows users can employ the same shared printer queues as DOS users. To help you manipulate printer queues, the Connection Manager includes a queue management screen, which operates very much like the DOS printer queue manager; you can use it to add, delete, and modify entries in the printer queue. As in the DOS version, you must have the Q queue manager privilege to see or modify other users' printer queue entries.

To see the queue management screen, select the Queues button from the main Connection Manager menu. You'll be prompted to select from a list of

Figure 9.9

The Mail display screen. This example shows one message waiting to be read and several outbound messages to other users. Icons next to each mail item indicate that the message is voice or text.

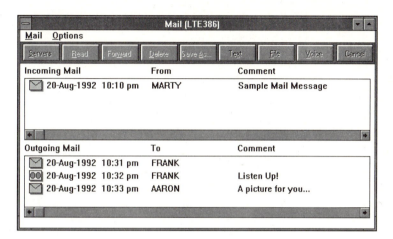

Changing Servers   The Servers button is just like the Servers button on the Drive Connections and Printer Connections screens; it allows you to log into and out of additional servers. If you have mail on more than one server, you can use the Servers button to select a server.

Reading Your Mail   You use the Read button to read either incoming or outgoing mail. To read a message, highlight it with the mouse or the cursor keys; then click on the Read button or press Alt-R. You can also read a message by double-clicking on the message itself.

Forwarding Mail   The Forward button lets you relay a copy of a message to another user. When you forward a message, you can also add a one-line comment to it. To forward a message, select the message and click Forward or press Alt-W.

Deleting Old Messages   The Delete button deletes messages. To delete a message, select it with the mouse or arrow keys, and click Delete or press Alt-D. You can also delete a message by selecting it and then pressing Del on the keyboard.

Saving Mail Messages   The Save As... button saves the selected message as an ASCII text (.TXT) file. To save a message, highlight the desired message with the mouse or the arrow keys, and then click Save As... or press Alt-A.

Creating a New Text Message The Text button creates a new text-based message. When you select this button, you'll see the LANtastic mail editor, as shown in Figure 9.10.

Figure 9.10

The LANtastic for Windows mail editor

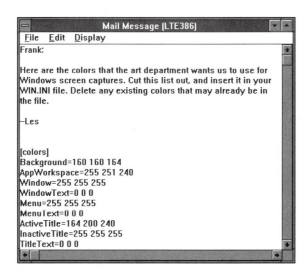

To send a message, type the message into the mail editor, and then select Send from the File menu. A mail message can be up to 16k (16,384 characters) long.

Since LANtastic uses plain text files for mail messages, you can use the mail editor's File Open command to open any plain text file up to 16k in length. Once you've opened the file, you can use the Send command to send the text as a mail message. Conversely, you can save a message to a text file using the File Save As... menu choice.

Sending a Text File via Mail The File button sends a file to another network user as a mail message. When you select this button, you'll see a file dialog box like the one in Figure 9.11.

As mentioned, you can include a one-line comment with the file. The comment will appear in the incoming mail window so the recipient knows what type of file you've sent. By default, the comment field includes the file name.

Sending a Voice Mail Message If you have an Artisoft Sounding Board or other Windows-compatible sound board installed in your system, you can send and receive voice mail messages through the LANtastic mail system.

available servers. After you've selected a server, you'll see the Queues screen, as shown in Figure 9.14.

Figure 9.14

The Queues screen, from which you add, modify, and delete queue entries and printer streams

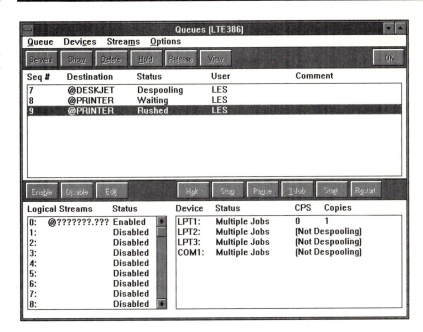

If you've used the NET.EXE printer queue management screen, this screen will look familiar; the arrangement of the information is almost identical to the DOS version. There are three windows, one each for queue entries, printer streams, and printer ports. Each window has an associated set of buttons above it and an associated pull-down menu at the top of the screen. With a few exceptions, the pull-down menus duplicate functions available on the buttons.

The Queue Window The printer queue window display shows each job, along with its sequence number, destination printer, status, user name, and an optional comment.

To manipulate any item in the printer queue, select the item with the mouse or arrow keys. When you select an individual job, the six buttons above the queue window become active. Each of these buttons performs an immediate action on the selected queue entry.

- *Servers* switches to a different server. You can use this button to see the queue entries on any server on the network, providing you have sufficient privileges on that server.

- *Show* displays detailed information about the print job.

- *Delete* deletes the selected item from the print queue.

- *Hold* places the selected print job on hold.

- *Release* releases a previously held print job for printing.

- *View* shows the contents of the queue entry. Note that most Windows applications send data to the printer in graphics mode, so when you view the contents of a Windows print job, you see the actual binary printer codes.

Three items on the Queue pull-down menu do not have corresponding buttons. Rush places the selected queue entry next in the queue, even if there are other jobs ahead of it. Save As... saves the contents of the queue entry to a file, and Make Entry creates a new printer queue entry from a file.

The Streams Window The Logical Streams display window shows each of the 20 printer streams. As in the DOS version, each stream may be enabled or disabled. To enable a stream, select it with the mouse or arrow keys, and then click the Enable button above the window. To disable a stream, select it and click the Disable button. To edit a stream's name, select the desired stream and click the Edit button.

The Device Window The Device display window shows the status, speed, and number of copies for each of the five printer devices on the server. The six buttons above the Device window allow you to control each printer device. The buttons are as follows:

- *Halt* immediately stops all printing on the selected device. The printer then remains unavailable until a Start or Restart command is issued.

- *Stop* allows the currently printing job to complete. Once the current job is finished, the printer halts.

- *Pause* stops printing temporarily. To resume printing, click the Start button.

- *One-Job* allows one job to print, and then stops printing.

- *Start* begins printing after Pause or Stop has been pressed.

- *Restart* is the same as Start, but it restarts the currently printing job from the beginning.

The Options Menu The printer queue display's Options menu at the top of the Queues screen contains only two items. Update Rate lets you tell LANtastic how often to update the printer queue display windows, and Update Now updates the display immediately.

Logging In and Out

As you saw in Chapter 5, you must be logged into a server before you can use any shared resource on it. The Connection Manager Login/Out button lets you log into and out of servers. When you select the Login/Out button, you'll see the login dialog box shown in Figure 9.15. As you may recall from Figure 9.7, this is the same dialog box you see when you click the Service button on the Drive Connections screen.

Figure 9.15

The Connection Manager login dialog box, from which you can attach or detach any server on the network

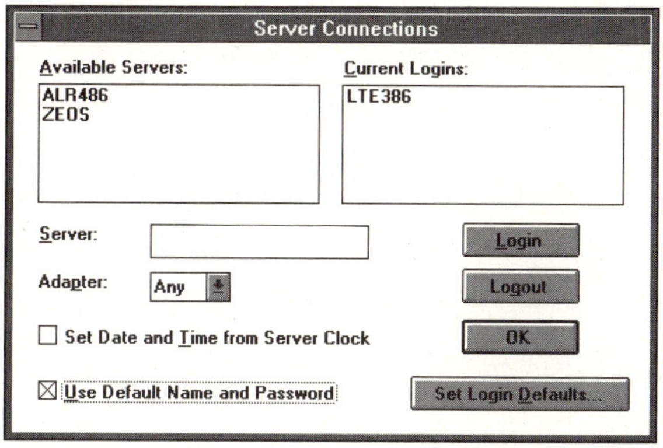

To log into a server, select from the list of available servers or type the name of the server you want in the Server box; then click the Login button. If the Set Date and Time from Server Clock box is checked, LANtastic will synchronize your PC's clock with the server's clock.

If the Use Default Name and Password box is checked, LANtastic will use the default name and password. If this box is not checked, LANtastic will prompt you to enter your user name and password. To change your default login information, click the Set Login Defaults… button and enter your user name and password.

To log out from a server, select the server from the list of current logins and click the Logout button.

Managing Your Account Settings

The Connection Manager Account button serves several purposes: It lets you view your account information, change your password, or temporarily disable your user account. To see the Account Management screen, shown in Figure 9.16, select the Account button from the Connection Manager menu.

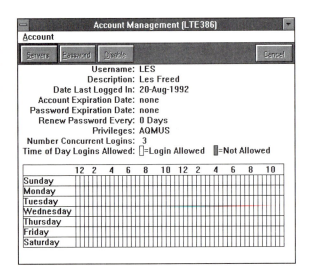

Figure 9.16

The Account Management screen, from which you can view your account settings, change your password, or disable your user account

As you can see, the Account Management screen displays detailed information about your user account. Note that you can't change any of these settings from this screen, even if you have the S system manager privilege; these settings can only be changed from the Network Manager program described later in this chapter.

If you have an account on more than one server, you can use the Server button to view your account information on another server. The current server name appears at the top of the Account Management display to let you know which server you're currently logged into.

The Password button changes your password on the current server. As a security precaution, to prevent other people from changing your password, you must enter your current password in order to change it.

The Disable button temporarily disables your user account. Again, you'll be asked to enter your password as a security measure. Before you can use this function, the number of concurrent logins for your account on the server must be set to one. If your account is set to allow more than one concurrent login, a network manager has to disable your account using the Network Manager program. Once an account is disabled, only a network manager can reactivate it.

Server Management

The last item on the Connection Manager menu, Server Mgt, takes you to the Server Management screen, from which you can monitor server usage, see who is logged into the server, and perform several management tasks on the server. You must have the S server management privilege to perform any management task on the server. Figure 9.17 shows the main Server Management screen.

Figure 9.17

The Server Management display, which shows the users logged into the server, as well as detailed information on each user's activities

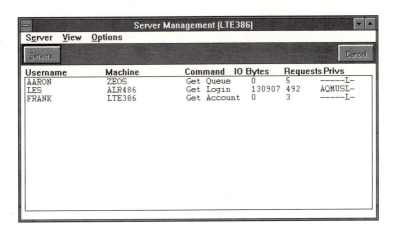

The Server Management display shows detailed information about each user logged into the server, including the user's name, the machine name, and a running total of the amount of data transferred over the network.

The Server Management screen has three pull-down menus: Server, View, and Options. The Server menu contains several commands for managing server operations. Here are the menu choices:

- *Select Server* lets you choose from a list of available servers.

- *Run...* lets you specify a command to run on the selected server. The command can be any valid DOS command.

- *Terminate User* logs the selected user off from the server. To log a user off, highlight the user's name on the Server Management screen, and then select Terminate User from the Server menu.

- *Disable Logins* prevents any additional users from logging into the selected server.

- *Shutdown...* shuts down the selected server. You can specify a delay before shutdown, and a warning message for all users on the server. As an option, you can reboot the server after the shutdown takes place.
- *Cancel Shutdown* cancels a shutdown in progress.
- *Flush Server Caches* clears the shared resource caches on the selected server.

The View menu selects between the user statistics screen shown in Figure 9.17, and a graph of server throughput that illustrates the amount of network traffic on the server, as shown in Figure 9.18.

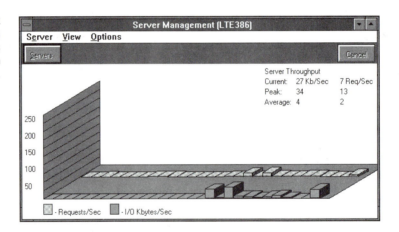

Figure 9.18

The server throughput screen displays a graph showing the server's throughput rate over a period of time.

The Options menu contains two items: Update Rate tells LANtastic how often to update the server management display, and Update Now updates the display immediately.

The Network Manager Program

The LANtastic for Windows Network Manager program is the Windows counterpart of the NET_MGR.EXE program. Like its DOS cousin, the Windows Network Manager controls all major LANtastic network management and security options from a single menu, which offers the following choices:

- *Accounts* creates, deletes, and modifies accounts for groups and individual users on the network.
- *Resources* manages shared network resources like disks and printers. From this menu, you can create, delete, or modify security privileges for each shared device.

- *Server* controls performance-related settings and configuration options for servers.
- *Audit Trail* controls network auditing.
- *Queue* clears the printer spool area or changes its location.
- *Boot Image* creates and manages the disk boot image used by diskless network workstations.
- *Password* changes or disables the master password for the current control directory.
- *Archive* backs up or restores the control directory information.
- *Control Dir* selects a control directory to use.

In this section, we'll take a close look at each of the Network Manager's functions. We'll assume you're familiar with LANtastic network management. If you're not, see Chapter 6 for detailed information on network management.

It's important to remember that all Network Manager operations affect the currently selected control directory. The name of the current control directory appears in the lower-left corner of the main Network Manager menu. To choose a different control directory or a control directory on a different server, use the Control Dir button on the main Network Manager menu.

Managing User Accounts

The Accounts button on the Network Manager menu controls user and group accounts. Figure 9.19 shows the Accounts screen.

The Individual Accounts and Group Accounts buttons near the bottom of the screen select between individual and group accounts. When you first open the Accounts window, the Individual Accounts button will be selected. To work on the group accounts list, click the Group Accounts button.

Looking at Figure 9.19, you'll notice that there are two large windows, one on each side of the screen. The Accounts window at the left displays a list of existing account; the right window is the Account Clipboard.

The Account Clipboard provides a convenient way to copy information from one user account to another. The Copy and Paste buttons copy account information between the Accounts list and the Account Clipboard. You can copy an existing user's account to the clipboard, make some changes to the account information, and then resave the account under a new name or in a different control directory. This is especially handy when you need to add several users with essentially the same privileges.

Figure 9.19

The Accounts screen. The window on the left shows existing accounts. The one on the right is the Account Clipboard, a temporary holding area for account information.

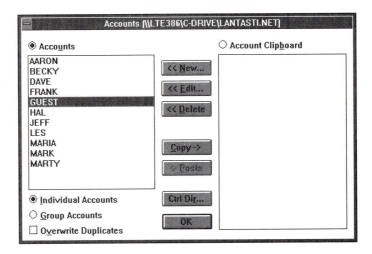

The Overwrite Duplicates check box at the bottom of the screen allows the Network Manager to replace existing account entries with entries of the same name from the Account Clipboard.

The New, Edit, and Delete buttons operate on either the current Accounts list or the Account Clipboard list. To switch between the two, click on the button for the list you want to use.

Creating a New Account   To create a new account, select either Group Accounts or Individual Accounts, and then click on New. A new account dialog box will appear, as shown in Figure 9.20.

To create the new account, enter a user name, description, and password. If necessary, you can also increase the number of concurrent logins from the default value of 1. When you've entered all the necessary information, click on the OK button.

Note that newly created accounts have no supervisor rights and no password or account expiration dates. By default, new accounts have access to the server 24 hours a day. To change any of these settings, use the Edit button on the Accounts screen.

Copying an Existing Account   When you're adding new users to a server, it's often convenient to simply copy another user's account information into the new account and then modify it as necessary. If you're adding the same user to several servers, it's equally convenient to create the user information once, and then copy the account information into the control directory on several servers.

Figure 9.20

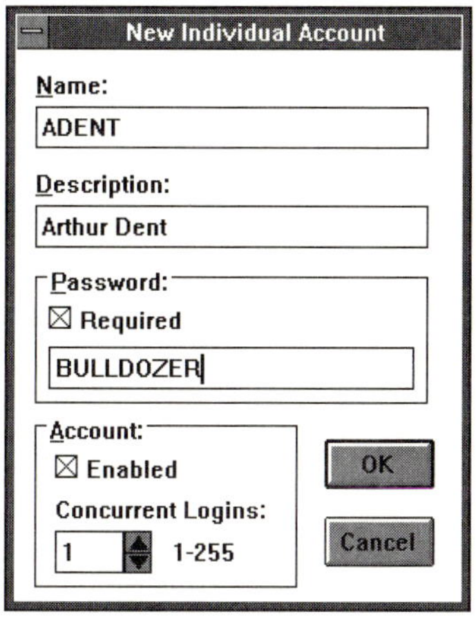

Creating a new user account

[Dialog box: New Individual Account]
- Name: ADENT
- Description: Arthur Dent
- Password: ☒ Required — BULLDOZER
- Account: ☒ Enabled
- Concurrent Logins: 1 1-255
- OK / Cancel

To copy an existing user account, follow these steps:

1. Click on the Accounts button and select the account you wish to copy from the Accounts list.

2. Click on the Copy button to copy the selected account to the Account Clipboard.

3. Click on the Account Clipboard button; then select the newly copied account from the Account Clipboard window.

4. Click the Edit button, and make any necessary changes to the account information. After you've made the changes, click the OK button.

5. Click the Paste button to copy the modified account back to the current Accounts list.

To copy an account to a different control directory, follow the procedure just outlined, but click on the Ctrl Dir… button to change control directories before you click on the Paste button.

Editing an Existing Account Once you've created a new user account, you can edit the account's parameters with the Edit button on the main Accounts screen. To edit an account, select it from either the Accounts list or the Account Clipboard, and click on the Edit button. Figure 9.21 shows the Account Parameters screen.

The Account Parameters screen displays the account name, a description, optional password expiration and account expiration dates, and the

236 Chapter 9: LANtastic and Windows

number of concurrent logins. If the account has been used, the Date Last Logged In field shows the date of the last login through the selected account.

Figure 9.21

Editing an existing user account

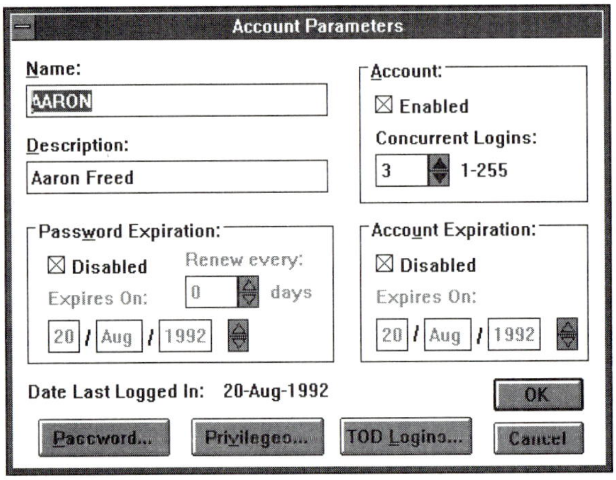

To change any settings on the main Account Parameters screen, use the mouse or keyboard to move the cursor to the setting, and then make the required change.

The three large buttons at the bottom of the screen set the password, manager privileges, and time of day logins for the account. To change a user's password, click on the Password button and enter the new password.

To set the user's manager privileges, click on the Privileges button. A list of account privileges will appear, as shown in Figure 9.22. Select the privileges you want the user to have from the list and click OK.

Figure 9.22

Setting a user's account privileges. In this example, the user has the queue manager privilege.

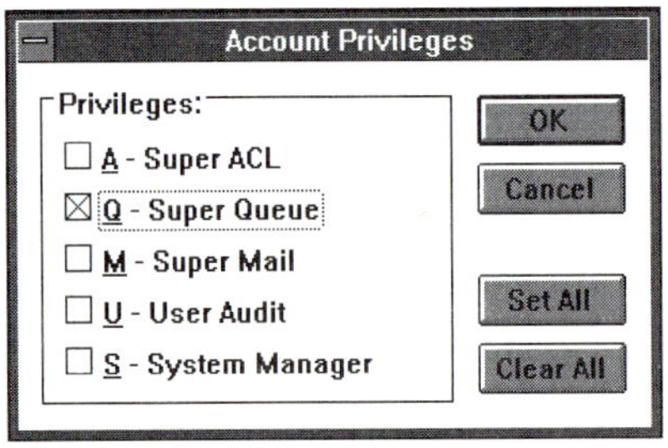

To change the allowed login times, click on the TOD Logins… button. You'll see a display like the one in Figure 9.23. The allowed login times are shown in white; disallowed times are in gray. To select a block of time, move the mouse pointer to the start of the block and press and hold the mouse button. Then move the mouse to the end of the block and release the button. Click the Allow or Disallow button to allow or disallow logins during the selected block of time. To save the new login times, click OK.

Figure 9.23

Changing the allowed login times. The gray areas indicate times when the user is not allowed to log in to the server.

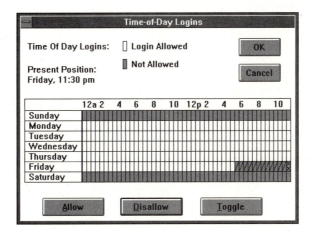

When you've finished changing a user's account, click the OK button on the Account Parameters screen to save the new settings.

Managing Shared Resources

The Windows Network Manager's Resources button lets you manage shared network resources. As with the DOS version, you manage all shared resources—printers, disks, and mail queues—from one program. When you click the Resources button, you'll see the main Resources screen, shown in Figure 9.24.

The large window on the left side of the screen shows the currently installed resources. If there are more resources than fit in the window, you can use the scroll bar on the right side of the window to scroll through the list. Our example server has five local drives: two floppies (A: and B:), a hard disk (C:), a cartridge drive (D:), and a CD-ROM player (E:).

The buttons along the right side of the screen allow you to add, delete, and modify any resource. To add a shared resource, click the Add... button at the top-right corner of the screen. You'll be prompted to enter a name and physical location for the new resource.

The Edit... button lets you set the physical path and description for disk drives, or the printer port and printer parameters for shared printers. The

Chapter 9: LANtastic and Windows

ACL... button lets you edit the access control list for the selected device, and the Icon... button allows you to change the icon assigned to the device. As you can see from our example screen, we've assigned a different icon to each shared device. The Delete button removes the selected resource from the shared devices list. If you delete a shared resource, other users will not be able to use the resource.

The Resources screen contains a Resource Clipboard, similar to the Account Clipboard in the Accounts screen. You can copy an item to the clipboard, and then edit the item and save it under a different name or in a different location. Again, this is especially useful when you're adding the same resource to several servers on the network.

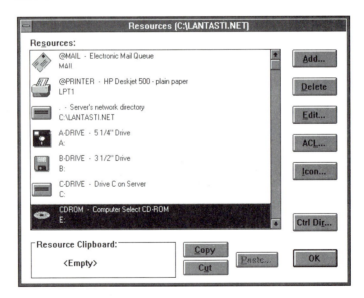

Figure 9.24

The Resources screen, which shows all the shared resources on the server. The buttons along the right side allow you to add, delete, and modify any shared resource.

Managing Server Parameters

The Network Manager's Server button manages server startup parameters. To see or change the server startup parameters, click the Server button. You'll see a display like the one in Figure 9.25.

The main Server Startup Parameters screen shows the basic configuration information for the server. Two buttons—Performance... and Auditing...—control the performance and auditing sessions for the server.

As with the DOS Network Manager, changes you make to the server startup parameters do not take effect until you shut down and restart the server.

Figure 9.25

The Network Manager Server Startup Parameters display

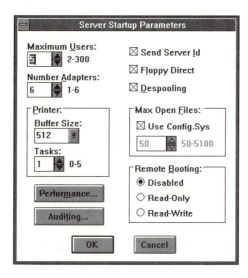

Viewing the Audit Log

If you have server auditing enabled, you can use the Audit button on the main Network Manager menu to view the server audit log. When you select the Audit Trail button, LANtastic displays the audit log for the currently selected server, as shown in Figure 9.26.

Figure 9.26

Viewing the server audit log

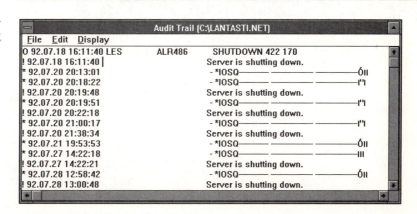

If you want to save the audit log to a text file, you can use the Save As... option on the File menu. To clear the audit log, select Clear from the same menu.

The Queue Button

The Queue button allows you to clear the printer spool area or change the location of the printer queue files. When you clear the spool area, all print jobs in the queue are deleted.

Note that you cannot clear or change the location of the spool area while the SERVER program is running.

Managing the Boot Image

The Boot Image button allows you to create, change, or delete the current diskless workstation boot image on the selected server. See Chapter 8 for detailed information on diskless workstations and the server boot image.

Changing the Control Directory Password

The Password button sets or disables the password for the currently selected control directory. As with the DOS version of LANtastic, each control directory can have a unique password assigned to it. If you choose to password protect the current control directory, you'll be asked to enter the password each time you start the Network Manager program or change control directories.

Archiving the Control Directory

The Archive button allows you to back up or restore the contents of the currently selected control directory.

When you back up a control directory, all files and subdirectories under the network control directory are copied to the archive file.

The restore operation creates a new network control directory using the control files and resources stored in the archive file. When you restore a backup control directory to an existing network control directory, files in the existing directory are not overwritten by information from the archive.

Changing the Control Directory

When you start the Network Manager program, LANtastic assumes you want to work with the resources on the currently selected control directory. The name of the current control directory appears in the bottom-left corner of the main Network Manager menu. To choose a different control directory or a control directory on a different server, use the Control Dir... button on the main Network Manager menu. If the selected control directory is password protected, you'll be prompted to enter the password.

You can also use the Control Dir... button to create a new control directory or delete an existing one.

- *What Is NetWare?*
- *The LANtastic for NetWare Software*

CHAPTER 10

LANtastic for NetWare

LANTASTIC FOR NETWARE IS A CUSTOMIZED VERSION OF LANTASTIC designed to run in conjunction with Novell's popular NetWare network operating system. LANtastic for NetWare allows you to set up a LANtastic network using the same cables and adapter boards you use for NetWare. You can even have access to NetWare servers and LANtastic servers from the same workstation, at the same time. In this chapter, we'll explain how to use LANtastic and NetWare together.

■ What Is NetWare?

Novell NetWare is a local area networking software system for IBM-standard computers running MS-DOS or OS/2, and for Apple Macintosh computers. First introduced in 1983, it has become one of several standards for PC networking, and Novell, Inc., the manufacturer of NetWare, has become one of the major powers in the PC industry.

While Novell has been in and out of many product lines from servers to diskless workstations, their revenues come almost entirely from the sale of networking software. There are several reasons for NetWare's phenomenal success, but the major one is simple: it works, and it works very well.

NetWare was formerly available in several variations known as ELS NetWare, Advanced NetWare 286, SFT NetWare 286, and NetWare 386, but recently Novell streamlined their NetWare offerings. Now they have two product lines that provide similar services—NetWare 2.*x* and NetWare 3.*x*. From the workstation end of the network, the two are nearly identical.

Novell also produces a peer-to-peer network system, NetWare Lite, that competes head-to-head with LANtastic. NetWare Lite offers many of the same features and services as LANtastic, but is not compatible with LANtastic for NetWare.

NetWare is a *server-based* system, meaning that all shared resources reside on a server. With LANtastic and other peer-to-peer networking systems, network users can share their individual printers and hard disks over the LAN. NetWare does not provide this function. All shared resources on a NetWare network must reside on a server, and all communication takes place between the server(s) and individual workstations. Thus, the server maintains complete control over all traffic on the network.

LANtastic is a NetBIOS compatible network. NetBIOS is an unofficial industry standard, originally designed by IBM for the IBM PC baseband network. The standard version of LANtastic comes with its own NetBIOS software, and will work only with its own NetBIOS. The LANtastic for NetWare package uses Novell's NetBIOS in place of Artisoft's. In essence, LANtastic for NetWare adds peer-to-peer capabilities to a server-based NetWare network.

A Quick Tour of NetWare

NetWare has two major components: the LAN server software and the workstation software. The server software runs only on the file server, and is not normally of concern to network users. Most LAN users never even see the server, and they don't need to because they can access all the files and other resources available on the LAN from their own PCs.

The workstation software comes in two parts. The first part is the low-level protocol driver called IPX. The IPX program provides the software interface between the network adapter card and the NETx redirector program. In LANtastic terms, IPX is similar to AEX.EXE, and NETx.EXE is comparable to REDIR.EXE. On many NetWare networks, the IPX services are provided by a program named IPX.COM. In 1990, Novell introduced a replacement for IPX.COM called the NetWare ODI (object device independent) driver. The ODI driver consists of several separate program files, which provide the same basic services as the older IPX.COM driver. The main difference between the two is that IPX.COM must be tailored to match each individual workstation's combination of network board type, IRQ line, and I/O address, while the ODI drivers are more flexible and require less customization for each workstation—an important consideration when a network has hundreds of workstations with dozens of configurations.

To connect to a NetWare server, follow these basic steps:

1. Load the IPX and NETx workstation software. When you load NETx, an additional disk drive will appear on your system. The drive usually contains only one file, LOGIN.EXE.

2. Switch to the network login drive, and type **LOGIN**. The LOGIN program will request a user name and password. Once you provide a valid name and password, LOGIN looks for and runs an optional *login script*, which is roughly equivalent to an AUTOEXEC.BAT file for network users; it creates network drive mappings and printer assignments automatically. Each user can have his or her own login script.

3. Once your login script has run, you're connected to the NetWare network. To create additional network drive mappings, you use a program called MAP.EXE; to create printer redirections, use the CAPTURE.EXE program.

As you can see, this process is similar in many ways to the LANtastic login process. In both cases you must load the network software, log into the network, and then create network drive mappings and printer assignments.

For more detailed information on NetWare, see the *PC Magazine Guide to Using NetWare* by Les Freed and Frank Derfler, published by Ziff-Davis Press.

■ The LANtastic for NetWare Software

The LANtastic for NetWare software includes essentially the same programs and features as the standard LANtastic package. Once it's installed, LANtastic for NetWare operates exactly like the standard LANtastic package, except it lets you connect to LANtastic and NetWare servers at the same time.

The major difference between LANtastic for NetWare and the standard LANtastic package is that LANtastic for NetWare uses Novell's NetBIOS instead of Artisoft's AI-LANBIO to communicate with the LANtastic workstations on the network. Because Novell's NetBIOS isn't 100 percent compatible with Artisoft's AI-LANBIO, there are a few caveats you should know about:

- You can't run the LANtastic for NetWare SERVER.EXE on a workstation that is running Windows 3.*x* in 386 Enhanced mode.

- To use Windows 3.*x* with LANtastic for NetWare, you should install the Windows NetWare network driver, not the LANtastic driver.

- Because of the previous requirement, LANtastic for NetWare users cannot use the LANtastic for Windows package. You can still use networked drives and printers with Windows and LANtastic for NetWare, but you must establish your LANtastic drive and printer connections before you start Windows.

- LANtastic for NetWare servers and workstations can't communicate with standard LANtastic servers and workstations, even if they're connected to the same Ethernet cable.

Installing LANtastic for NetWare

LANtastic for NetWare uses the same INSTALL program described in Chapter 4. All of the requirements outlined there apply equally to LANtastic for NetWare. In addition, you should make sure your IPX or ODI drivers are correctly configured and working properly with NetWare before you attempt to install LANtastic for NetWare. If your network board doesn't work with NetWare before you've installed LANtastic for NetWare, it certainly won't work afterwards!

Like the standard version of LANtastic, LANtastic for NetWare allows you to install as a server, a workstation, or both. If you install the LANtastic server, the installer program will create the LANTASTI.NET control directory, which will contain the default resources for your PC. If you're concerned about the security of the files on your PC, we recommend you remove the default resources and install only those you actually wish to share with other users. See Chapter 6 for more information on shared resources and network security.

After you run the LANtastic for NetWare installer program, you must log into the NetWare network and copy the program file NETBIOS.EXE from the NetWare server onto your local hard disk. The NETBIOS.EXE file can usually be found in the SYS:PUBLIC directory on any NetWare server. To copy the file to your PC, use the command

```
COPY Z:NETBIOS.EXE C:\LANTASTI
```

Before you can use LANtastic for NetWare, you may need to edit the STARTNET.BAT file created by the installer program. The exact contents of your STARTNET.BAT file will vary depending on your NetWare installation, but we've included two sample STARTNET.BET files as a guide. You can use any text editor to edit the STARTNET.BAT file, as long as it produces plain text files. The EDIT.EXE program supplied with DOS 5.0 is ideal for this purpose.

If you use NetWare regularly, you probably have a batch file that loads the NetWare workstation software for you. A typical NetWare batch file looks like one of the following examples. (Note that in this and the remaining ODI examples, we use the NE2000 NetWare hardware driver, which is compatible with Artisoft Ethernet boards. If you have a different type of network board in your PC, replace the NE2000 in the examples with the appropriate driver for your board.)

Using the ODI drivers:
```
C:
CD\NETWARE
LSL
NE2000
IPXODI
NETX
O:LOGIN
```

Using the IPX.COM driver:
```
C:
CD\NETWARE
IPX
NETX
O:LOGIN
```

If you start NetWare with one of these batch files, you can't load LANtastic for NetWare because the NetWare NETBIOS.EXE and the LANtastic REDIR.EXE and SERVER.EXE programs must load before the NetWare NETx program.

We suggest you keep your NetWare batch file to use when you want to run only NetWare, and use the LANtastic STARTNET.BAT file when you want to run NetWare and LANtastic. Remember though, if NetWare is already loaded, you must remove the NETx program from memory before you can load LANtastic. To unload NETx along with all NetWare drive and printer assignments, type **NETx /U**.

Here are some typical STARTNET.BAT files for a LANtastic server and workstation, using both the ODI drivers and the IPX drivers.

A LANtastic workstation using the IPX drivers:

```
IPX
NETBIOS
REDIR machine name
NETX
```

A LANtastic workstation using the ODI drivers:

```
LSL
NE2000
IPXODI
NETBIOS
REDIR machine name
NETX
```

A LANtastic server using the IPX drivers:

```
SHARE
IPX
NETBIOS
REDIR machine name
SERVER
NETX
```

A LANtastic server using the ODI drivers:

```
SHARE
LSL
NE2000
IPXODI
NETBIOS
REDIR machine name
SERVER
NETX
```

Note that your actual STARTNET.BAT file may contain other LANtastic commands in addition to the ones shown here, particularly NET USE commands that establish LANtastic drive mappings.

There's one final thing to check before you begin to use LANtastic for NetWare. The LANtastic INSTALL program modifies your CONFIG.SYS file to include a LASTDRIVE statement that tells DOS the letter of the last drive in your system. On an all-LANtastic network, LASTDRIVE is usually set to Z: to provide the maximum number of networkable drives.

NetWare also checks LASTDRIVE, but it uses the information in a different way. When you load the NETx redirector program, NetWare creates a new drive mapping one letter higher than the current LASTDRIVE setting. If LASTDRIVE is set to Z:, NetWare has no place to put the first network drive.

You should pick a LASTDRIVE setting to define the boundary between your NetWare drive mappings and your LANtastic drive mappings. For example, if LASTDRIVE is set to O:, LANtastic can use all available drive letters up to O:, and NetWare can use drive letters P: through Z:. This boundary isn't hard and fast. Once NETx is loaded and you've logged into the NetWare network, you can use the NetWare MAP.EXE program to create NetWare drive mappings to any drive letter.

The LASTDRIVE statement can appear anywhere in your CONFIG.SYS file, although it typically comes last. The syntax for LASTDRIVE is LASTDRIVE=*n, w*here *n* is the last drive letter.

Using LANtastic for NetWare

Once you've installed the software and edited your STARTNET.BAT and CONFIG.SYS files, you're ready to use LANtastic for NetWare. To start the networking software, type **STARTNET** from the DOS prompt.

As we just explained, the STARTNET.BAT file loads both the NetWare and the LANtastic networking software. Once STARTNET has loaded successfully, you can log into the NetWare network and use the NetWare MAP and CAPTURE commands as usual, but in addition, you can use the LANtastic Connection Manager program to create LANtastic drive and printer assignments.

If you've installed the LANtastic server, other users on your NetWare network will be able to use shared resources like disks and printers on your PC. Remember, for other users to access LANtastic shared resources, they must install the LANtastic for NetWare software on their machines. The standard NetWare workstation software cannot see or use shared resources on a LANtastic server.

As you know from Chapter 5, the LANtastic Connection Manager program controls all LANtastic drive and printer mappings. The Connection Manager can recognize NetWare drive and printer assignments, but cannot alter them. To change NetWare drive and printer mappings, you must use the NetWare MAP and CAPTURE commands. Conversely, the NetWare MAP command does not recognize LANtastic drive and printer assignments.

Veteran LANtastic users may not be familiar with NetWare commands, and vice versa. Table 10.1, which lists commonly used LANtastic commands and their NetWare equivalents, should help you translate from one networking vernacular to the other.

Chapter 10: LANtastic for NetWare

Table 10.1

LANtastic Commands and NetWare Equivalents

LANTASTIC COMMAND	NETWARE COMMAND	PURPOSE
NET use lpt*x* \\ server*qname*	CAPTURE /l=*x*, /q=*qname*	Connects local printer port *x* to printer queue *qname*
NET UNUSE LPT*x*	ENDCAP /l=*x*	Stops capturing printer port *x*
NET LOGIN	LOGIN	Logs user into server
NET LOGOUT	LOGOUT	Logs user out from server
NET USE *x*: \\ server*netdir*	MAP *x*:=server /*netdir*	Connects logical drive *x:* to network dirootory *nctdir*
NET DIR	LISTDIR	Lists directory of network files
NET PRINT *file qname*	NPRINT *file* /q=*qname*	Prints file *file* to network queue *qname*

- *Built-in Compatibility*
- *Third-Party Network Boards*
- *Network Your Network—On-Line Services*
- *LANtastic and Portable Computers*
- *Working through Problems*

CHAPTER

11

LANtastic and Third-Party Products

THE BEST NETWORK IS ONE YOU DON'T SEE. AFTER ABSORBING OUR advice about network planning and installation, you should have a network that is invisible and responsive to its users. People should feel like they're using resources attached to their own local PCs— that's seamless and invisible resource sharing. But some hardware and application programs seem to defy seamless integration. This chapter describes some successes and frustrations you might encounter as you mold your LANtastic network into a superb tool for group productivity.

■ Built-in Compatibility

LANtastic is based on Microsoft's MS-DOS. The LANtastic redirector works with processes built into DOS 3.1 and later versions to move requests for service between application programs and the network resources. Because of its firm and broad integration with DOS, and because of much careful development effort, Artisoft's network operating system works well with practically any hardware or software right out of the box.

The exceptions are a tiny sliver of the total world of personal computer products and an even smaller division of the modern and popular products you're most likely to install. Still, if you get one of these slivers under your skin it can ruin a whole day, or a hard-earned reputation! Even in a very favorable environment there are a few general incompatibilities you should watch for and some special techniques you can use to improve performance and resolve conflicts.

Anyone developing a complex computer product has to make a lot of assumptions about the environment the product will eventually be part of, and different people make different assumptions. Naturally, these assumptions don't always hold true.

Different assumptions on the part of developers lead to incompatibilities in products, but these conflicts tend to be resolved over the life of a product. LANtastic has benefited from at least four major evolutionary changes and many smaller upgrades, all of which have improved the program's compatibility.

HINT. *When in doubt, update your software. Companies create new software releases to add features and cure known problems. If you run into a clear incompatibility problem between any hardware or software products, get the latest updates of the software and look for read-only memory (ROM) chip updates for the hardware.*

Problems Common to All LANs

Because all LANs operate on the same fundamental principles, they share many of the same advantages and problems. Different categories of computer products carry their own unique seeds of network incompatibility. LAN adapter hardware suffers from IRQ and memory-address conflicts within the PC; utility programs bypass DOS and fail; databases steal RAM buffers; word processing programs crowd the network; and installation programs can wreak havoc with CONFIG.SYS files. These are problems all LANs experience, not just LANtastic.

Hardware Conflicts

Because hardware is at the most fundamental level of computer activity, hardware problems appear first and have high visibility. Software problems might appear only intermittently under specific conditions, but typically hardware problems are always apparent.

Programs like System Sleuth from Dariana, Inc. can help you identify used IRQs and avoid conflicts. But in most cases, you'll solve more hardware conflicts through trial and error than insight. You need some practical knowledge to understand that you might have a conflict between a LAN adapter set for IRQ3 and the COM2 port, but you'll probably still have to experiment to see if the adapter will work at IRQ 5 or 7 in that computer.

HINT. *Before you spend hours trying to make an adapter work in a PC, do a sanity check and try an adapter you're certain is good. We've found brand-new adapters from first-rate companies that were bad when they came out of the box.*

As computer systems become more complex the chances for conflict increase. For example, modern PCs can use extended memory above 1 megabyte, but they require some type of memory management software. A common source of conflict between hardware and system software comes from memory managers that do not exclude the memory address of the LAN adapter. In this situation, the adapter and the memory manager try to use the same piece of memory for different purposes simultaneously, and, not surprisingly, this can cause intermittent unreliable behavior.

HINT. *Don't be afraid to use trial and error to solve hardware integration problems. You can't break or burn up anything by changing IRQ and memory address settings until you find a combination that works.*

An external LAN adapter provides an excellent way to duck around adapter card installation problems—although you may pay some penalty in throughput. Artisoft's Central Station and external adapters from I.Q. Technologies, Xircom, and Megahertz provide LANtastic network connections through the existing parallel port and avoid conflicts with other products.

Software Conflicts

The worst assumption software developers can make is that their application will "own the universe" inside the computer. Applications based on this assumption bypass DOS and talk directly to the hardware, trying to change interrupt vector addresses or interrogate hardware devices. Many diagnostic and setup utility programs are built this way; their developers claim that their programs need the power to do the job.

Some diagnostic utilities designed for stand-alone operation are not compatible with networking products in general. For example, let's contrast the DOS CHKDSK utility and the popular multifunction utility program PC Tools from Central Point Software. Because CHKDSK is part of DOS, it contains code that recognizes the presence and limitations of redirected drives. In effect, you can't run CHKDSK in a client PC against a networked drive.

Like other utility packages, PC Tools runs well in any client PC alongside LANtastic, but the software doesn't differentiate between networked drives and those that are actually present on the PC. The PC Backup utility in PC Tools will back up any redirected drives from client PCs, but the functions that address the drive hardware—Compress, Rebuild, Mirror, and Undelete—will fail if you run them from a client PC against a network drive. Similarly, many commands under the PC Shell function such as Directory Maintenance and File Map won't work on networked drives in client PCs.

A product that competes with PC Tools, Norton's Disk Doctor version 6.0, exhibits similar behavior in a PC that is a LANtastic server. If you run Disk Doctor on a LANtastic server, the program reports that the File Allocation Table on the server's hard drive is bad! Don't let these programs' erroneous reports convince you that you need to change hardware.

On the up side, the PC Tools and Norton Disk Doctor functions that directly address the hardware are useful on a PC that acts as a LANtastic server when the server software isn't loaded. You can and should periodically defragment the drive when the server software isn't running to improve performance. You can also use Undelete and other DOS functions of PC Tools on the server's drive when the server isn't running because LANtastic uses DOS to write its files. The Undelete in Microsoft's DOS 5 is the same as the one in PC Tools.

The PC Shell segment of PC Tools is a good example of a program that can consume memory a LANtastic server could otherwise use for disk caching. PC Shell uses EMS (expanded memory) when it is resident and active. If you hot key into PC Shell, it automatically loads the PCSHELL.THM overlay file into any available expanded memory to hold the image of the underlying application. If EMS memory doesn't exist or is insufficient, the image is placed in a file called PCSHELL.THM on disk. The amount of expanded memory required to run PC Shell depends on how the program is loaded, but even in the recommended "tiny" configuration it takes approximately 200k of expanded memory.

Generally when you use utility programs you must separate network functions and local functions. Later in this chapter, we'll discuss special purpose network utility programs and their application to LANtastic.

Programs Out of Control

Programmers generally work in high-level computer languages such as C, COBOL, or Pascal. Highly specialized programs called *compilers* convert each statement of the programming language into a series of very detailed binary code commands that the computer executes. Because the machine-readable code they create is so detailed, compilers have lots of room for bugs. Unfortunately, some bugs only show up in the unique environment of networks.

A programmer can write perfect code and still have an imperfect program because of compiler problems. For example, a bug in a popular compiler makes some applications appear to overwrite the interrupt vector for IRQ 3 when they exit, so if the LAN adapter uses IRQ 3, exiting the application breaks the connection to the server.

LANs are sophisticated systems, and you can run into conflicts at many levels. In the past, some COBOL and Pascal compilers weren't optimized for network commands and had poor code for allowing applications to share data files simultaneously. Others tried to print by writing directly to the hardware instead of using the DOS functions.

When you're faced with problems like these, the first step is to be sure your network runs perfectly with other applications. Then contact Artisoft and the vendor of the application. There might be workarounds, like changing the IRQ of the LAN adapter, or one of the companies might have a new release that solves the problem.

LAN Utilities

There's a whole world of network utility products that work beautifully with LANtastic. In surveying the LAN utility software market, the staff of the PC Magazine LAN Labs divided the products into the following categories:

- Memory management software
- Menuing software
- Software metering
- Modem remote control
- LAN remote control
- LAN traffic reporting
- LAN traffic control (concentrator control)
- Protocol decoding

If a network program is designed according to the IBM NetBIOS standard, it will work with LANtastic. Compatibility with applications designed for NetBIOS is not usually a problem. In this section we'll take a quick look at each category of utility software.

Memory management software   In their simplest form, memory management programs allow networking software to be moved into high, extended, or expanded memory. QEMM and NetRoom are two excellent memory managers.

Menuing software   Menuing software for LANs allows a network administrator to load a series of commands into each copy of the program, which the program then sends to DOS when users make menu selections. Menuing programs are wonderful tools because they can enhance network security and simplify operation at the same time. LANtastic is compatible with all menuing programs that aren't specifically customized for another network operating system.

Software metering   Closely akin to menuing software, software metering programs track the number of copies of a program running on a LAN, and can limit access to the number an organization is licensed to use. This kind of software helps organizations avoid the abuse of licensing agreements, and is often recommended by internal auditors. Because software licensing abuse is a frequently audited item, there will continue to be a steady demand for this software in large organizations.

Modem remote control   Modem remote control software allows a PC calling over a relatively slow telephone modem link to control the actions of a CPU, or even a single multitasking session emulating a single CPU, on a PC connected to the LAN. In large organizations, this category is being subsumed into access server systems, and software companies need technical and marketing agreements with hardware companies to ensure sales of their products as part of integrated systems.

LAN remote control   LAN remote control software, like Artisoft's The Network Eye, allows one networked PC to take control of another networked PC. This software is very similar to modem remote control products, and some companies, such as DCA CrossTalk, package the two together. Products like R2LAN and Close-Up LAN compete with The Network Eye.

LAN remote control software has several applications:

- *Remote control across bridges and routers*   This task is very similar to the remote control of a PC using a modem. The goal is to access data files or other services on a remote LAN segment without burdening the relatively slow communications circuit linking the LAN segments together. Instead of using inefficient DOS commands and queries that clog the communications line, the LAN remote control program moves only screens and keystrokes, which leaves room for other data. Products for this application need very few "bells and whistles." Providing remote control with an efficient way to handle the transmission of the screen image is the critical element in this type of product.

- *Training* This is a classroom application involving students and instructor. The instructor can link to students' PCs to check their work and the students can link to the instructor's PC for a demonstration. The ability to "chat" on-screen and to use mouse pointing devices and special cursors that designate who is in control are useful elements of programs used in this role.

- *Help desk* In large and mid-sized organizations, the ability to provide "over-the-shoulder" technical assistance to people many floors or several miles away is important. The requirements for this kind of software include all those for the previous entry plus, perhaps, the ability to force a boot on the remote PC. Troubleshooting utilities, such as an integrated memory mapper, interrupt analysis tool, or system performance analyzer, are useful add-ins to a program used in this way.

- *Management control* In a role similar to the classroom application, managers can use these programs to monitor the activities of their employees. Interestingly, several countries outside the U.S. require that remote control software clearly notify the monitored party that monitoring is taking place.

LAN traffic reporting LAN traffic reporting software typically takes advantage of the reporting capabilities built into Ethernet, ARCnet, or Token-Ring adapters to gather and report on network traffic. Note that this software does not include a method of controlling network data—it only reports on network activity. EtherVision from Triticom Corporation is an excellent, low-cost traffic reporting program that works with Artisoft's LAN adapters in the NE-2000 emulation mode.

LAN traffic control (Concentrator control) LAN traffic control software typically works by monitoring a wiring concentrator used for 10BaseT, Token-Ring, or ARCnet wiring. The central location of the concentrator in the network wiring scheme makes it a perfect point from which to monitor and control network activities. The leading companies in this market, SynOptics and Cabletron, offer software that runs under Microsoft Windows with beautiful screen displays, and is capable of reporting on and controlling the network access of even a single station. The control, display, and upward reporting aspects of these products justify their premium prices.

Most of these programs use the TCP/IP protocol suite to move data between the wiring hub and the management software in a format called the Simple Network Management Protocol (SNMP). In a LANtastic network you would typically configure at least one PC with LANtastic/AI and an Artisoft LAN adapter set to the NE-2000 emulation mode so you could load either LANtastic or any popular TCP/IP package, such as PC/TCP from FTP Software, into the PC. Although this would be a part-time either/or configuration, it would satisfy most network management needs.

The full-time TCP/IP solution Artisoft recommends is Wollongong's Pathway Access release 2.0 or later with WIN/ROUTE version 2.1 or later. This approach requires a dedicated PC to act as a router between a LANtastic network and a TCP/IP network. It is more suitable for establishing a full-time link to a TCP/IP system than for using SNMP to extract information from a wiring hub.

Protocol decoding   Protocol decoding products capture the frames, tokens, or packets traversing a network, and then decode their contents, perhaps even translating them into English. These products typically take the power of a fast processor to run, and carry price tags well in excess of $10,000.

Compatibility

In general, LANtastic works well with all network-specific programs. If you want more sophisticated electronic mail capabilities you can readily add cc:Mail, Futurus Team, or Microsoft Mail. Network scheduling packages such as CaLANdar and Futurus Team also work well under LANtastic.

If you want software protection for your hardware, Unitrol's Immunity disk mirroring software is compatible with LANtastic. This product mirrors two disk drives as one, so if one drive fails, the other automatically carries on. LANtastic can also take cues from uninterruptable power supplies such as the Tripp Lite BC/LAN and Omni/LAN, and will gracefully shut down the server software and close open files if the server begins running on a UPS. There is a delay for short outages, but your data will be saved before the UPS runs down.

Non-networked Programs

Applications don't have to be specifically designed for networks to work with LANtastic. You can store the .EXE files from any application on a server and direct the program to put its document or data files in a server's subdirectory. However, if applications aren't written for network operation you may experience problems such as data loss and file conflicts. You can control all these problems by carefully configuring the location of the files on the system.

If an application isn't designed for network operation, your safest course of action is to put a separate copy of the program on a hard disk drive in each person's PC and give everyone private subdirectories on the server to hold data or text files. Because the application doesn't have the ability to allow multiple users simultaneous access to the same data files, you should keep each user's files isolated.

If you don't keep the files separate, two people could open the same file and make changes, but the last file saved would over-write all previous versions. At best, users trying to enter the same file with non-networked applications would receive confusing notifications of sharing violations.

Some programs, particularly specialized applications that have not been rewritten or modernized, don't give you a choice of what disk drive letter you use to install the program. Nor do they allow you to specify a path for data files or for the location of the executable file; they just forge ahead and try to put everything on the C: drive. Fortunately, LANtastic is very flexible, even allowing you to reassign local drive letters to a server drive; however, this action can cause you to lose the use of that local drive unless you work around the problem with the DOS SUBST command.

If you have been forced to reassign the C: drive of a client PC, you can still use the local drive by using the DOS SUBST command to "move" your C: drive to a different drive letter—in this example we'll use D:. The command is SUBST D: C:\

For good form (especially if your server is using a different DOS version), set your COMSPEC statement to point to the COMMAND.COM on the new substituted drive, like this:

```
SET COMSPEC=D:\COMMAND.COM …
NET USE C: \\Server\C-DRIVE
```

Optionally, you could later NET UNUSE the shared drive letter and regain access to your internal hardware as C:, but you wouldn't have to, because D: would now be your C: drive.

Another limitation of older programs is their inability to print to anything other than LPT1 or LPT2. The best solution to this dilemma is to run the application from a menu program that redirects the printers through NET USE commands designed specifically for that program. You can also allow people to select their printers through LANPUP, but using a menu system is closer to foolproof and requires less training.

Configuring Your File Structure

Keeping the program files on a local drive accomplishes two things: It reduces the load on the network adapter cards and file server, and it avoids conflicts in configuration and overlay files. Many programs, particularly word processing packages, use separate files called overlays to activate seldom-used functions. So selecting a function such as underlining might force the program to open an overlay file of 100k or more and search it for instructions on how to underline—creating a lot of network traffic in the process.

For example, to access functions such as Spell Check (Ctrl-F2) and List Files (F5), WordPerfect goes to a 600k overlay file in the file server, finds the right segment of the file, and brings in the code it needs to perform the requested function. All these actions can take a while, particularly if the overlay file isn't cached in the server. By the way, this isn't just a function of WordPerfect. Almost all word processing programs that attempt to limit the RAM they use, including Word and WordStar, make extensive use of overlay files.

One suggestion is to load just the overlay on as many PCs as possible. A product called Net-Aware from LANSmith Inc. will route requests for access to the overlay to the local hard disk instead of sending them to the server. Net-Aware uses rules that you establish to literally redirect the redirector so specific requests for data are met from locations you specify, which does a lot to cut down on the network traffic.

An increasing number of programs use separate configuration files that designate the type of video adapter, the I/O ports, and other setup details. The paramount example is the WIN.INI file for Microsoft Windows, but modem communications and word processing programs also have configuration files. Unless every PC in your office is virtually identical, sharing a configuration file won't work. Typically, each user needs a separate configuration file on a local drive or in a private subdirectory on the server.

The networked versions of programs like WordPerfect are quite sophisticated. WordPerfect includes setup files for specific users that can override the master setup file; however, the network administrator must take specific actions to configure the system. In general, look for special capabilities like those in the network version of WordPerfect, but try to keep large overlay files on local drives whenever possible.

Storage space on local PCs is often at a premium, so you'll want to benefit from the economy of a server's hard disk as much as possible. You can give every user a copy of the program and a place to keep the files it creates in a private subdirectory on the server. Although this setup avoids conflicts with shared configuration and overlay files, it generates more network traffic as people load programs.

In a few cases—primarily those involving electronic mail and personal information managers like Futurus Team—you might find it beneficial to store the application programs on the server and let people keep private files on their own PCs.

In summary, you can

- *Keep programs on the client PCs and put text and data files on the server*. This is a good arrangement for programs that aren't network-aware; it reduces network traffic and allows personally customized programs.

- *Keep programs and files on the server.* This arrangement is economical in the short run and relatively easy to administer, but creates a lot of network traffic. Try to keep overlays and configuration files on local drives.
- *Keep applications on the server and private files on client PCs.* This is a useful configuration for certain types of programs such as e-mail.

An increasing number of companies offer information on using their programs on a network. For example, the *WordStar 6.0 LAN Installation Guide* includes a comprehensive section detailing installation on a LANtastic network. Symantec's popular Q&A program is available in LAN packs that automatically meter the number of people using the program simultaneously, so you can provide broad access to Q&A without buying a copy for each person.

Database Programs

Database programs come in many forms. You might quickly recognize an inventory program as a DBMS, but many accounting programs and other business applications are also written in a DBMS. Most modern database programs come in network-compatible versions that allow multiple users simultaneous access to the same data file. This means more than one person can, for example, enter names and addresses into a customer file; however, one file such as Customer Name might link to several other files such as Address and Accounts Payable. In this event, the disk operating system in each PC and on the file server must keep track of many file names and pointers—and they all use RAM to keep score.

More than three or four people will be using the same database program on a network, you'll probably have to tune some parameters to give DOS enough memory to store all the information it must hold. The parameters you'll need to change would include the maximum number of simultaneously open files, the buffer capacity in a DOS program called SHARE, and the size of the buffers available to DOS for storing file names.

In a DOS-based networking system like LANtastic, you must make adjustments for shared file operation in the client PCs and in the PC acting as a server. Installation manuals typically describe a statement in the CONFIG.SYS file called FILES=. The manual will suggest a setting for each PC like FILES=20. But on the LANtastic server that hosts the files for a multiuser DBMS, you must add all the FILES= statements on all the clients, and then add about ten files for the operating system. The total goes into the CONFIG.SYS file of the server. DOS has a limit of 255 files in CONFIG.SYS; if you need more than that, set the CONFIG.SYS statement to 255 and set MAX FILES OPEN in LANtastic's NET_MGR server startup parameters to the needed value.

In a busy database installation, you should also make an entry for the DOS SHARE program in the server's CONFIG.SYS. A good place to start is with SHARE /L:1000. SHARE also has an F: parameter that the DOS documentation describes as the "file space for sharing information." Actually, the space used by the /F: parameter stores the full path name of every open file, plus a bit of overhead. If you exceed this file space, DOS returns error 36 (decimal) documented as "System resources exhausted," which may sound like you're running out of disk space when you aren't. Worse, very few applications handle this condition gracefully. If strange error messages appear or applications mysteriously hang when you try to run reports or when many people are using the same application, try setting the following line in the server's CONFIG.SYS and see if things improve.

```
SHARE /F:9999 /L:1000
```

These parameters will take some RAM from applications, but you can experiment with lower settings once you've isolated the problem. Always watch the installation programs for new programs carefully. Many add a FILES or SHARE statement to the CONFIG.SYS entries. If there are two SHARE statements in the same CONFIG.SYS, the second one will return the error message "Share already loaded." A poorly designed installation program can override your carefully crafted network configuration.

DOS and Other Environments

Because LANtastic uses DOS, it is fully compatible with Microsoft's latest releases. For example, the MS-DOS shell (DOSSHELL) includes a task switcher that allows you to swap between DOS applications. Since it uses the same task switching conventions as Microsoft Windows in Real mode, it is possible to use the DOS shell task switcher on a nondedicated LANtastic server.

Microsoft has licensed several disk utilities from Central Point Software (maker of PC Tools), including UNFORMAT, UNDELETE, and MIRROR. MIRROR is not disk mirroring software; it stores information about the hard drive, and can also track file deletions for later use by UNDELETE and UNFORMAT. When the server software is running, MIRROR, UNDELETE, and UNFORMAT cannot be used on a server's drives, either locally or through the network from a workstation. If MIRROR is included in the AUTOEXEC.BAT file on a server it can be used to take a "snapshot" of the hard disk(s) at boot time. If the SERVER.EXE program is loaded from AUTOEXEC.BAT, MIRROR must be run before the SERVER command, and cannot load in its TSR form.

Some environments are not hospitable to LANtastic. For example, the LANtastic server software is not compatible with older versions of Novell's DR DOS (before 6.0). Similarly, the server software conflicts with multitasking program environments like DESQview, and is not compatible with OS/2.

You must take some very careful steps to run the LANtastic client software (or any network client software) under the DESQview multitasking environment. Specifically, you have to load all the networking software before you load DESQview, which means you'll lose some RAM you could otherwise use to run programs in each DESQview window.

LANtastic and OS/2

You can run the LANtastic client software under IBM's OS/2 version 2.0, but you must take the steps described in the OS/2 manual to configure the hardware and software. With the initial release of OS/2 2.0 you have to put the LAN adapter card into 8-bit mode before you can run the LANtastic client software in a DOS session.

You can install LANtastic on a machine that runs OS/2 over either the High Performance File System (HPFS) or the DOS FAT file system. Open the OS/2 System folder from the desktop and select the Command Prompts folder. Choose a windowed or full-screen DOS session from within this folder. Once the session has started, you can install LANtastic in a client configuration. After you've installed the LANtastic files, you must complete these steps before you run any LANtastic program:

1. Make a DOS boot diskette, and then create a boot image of it.

   A. At a machine running DOS, format a diskette with the command

   ```
   FORMAT A: /S
   ```

   B. On the boot diskette, create a CONFIG.SYS file that contains the following statements:

   ```
   DEVICE=FSFILTER.SYS
   FILES=50
   BUFFERS=30
   LASTDRIVE=Z
   ```

   C. Create an AUTOEXEC.BAT file on the boot diskette, and include these lines:

   ```
   PATH=C:\LANTASTI;C:\DOS;C:\
   C:
   STARTNET
   ```

266 Chapter 11: LANtastic and Third-Party Products

- D. Copy the file FSFILTER.SYS to the boot diskette from the C:\OS2\MDOS directory on the OS/2 machine. Here is the complete list of files that must be on the boot diskette:
  COMMAND.COM
  AUTOEXEC.BAT
  CONFIG.SYS
  FSFILTER.SYS

- E. To create a boot image, place the boot diskette in the appropriate drive on the OS/2 PC; then open a DOS or OS/2 window and t the command

  `VMDISK A: C:\DOS\DOS_BOOT.IMG`

(See the OS/2 Master Help Index for details on using the VMDISK command.)

2. Create the specific version boot DOS session icon.

    A. In the Command Prompts folder, position the mouse cursor over the DOS Window icon and press the right mouse button.

    B. Select the Copy option from the menu that appears; then type **DOS Boot Image** or another description in the New Name field.

    C. Press the Copy button to create the new icon.

    D. Click the right mouse button on the new icon, and then click on the right-pointing arrow button next to the Open selection.

    E. Choose the Settings selection from the list that appears; be sure the Path and file name field contains an asterisk (*).

    F. Select the Session page and click on the DOS Settings button. Choose the DOS Startup Drive selection from the Settings list and type the following in the Value field:

    `C:\DOS\DOS_BOOT.IMG`

    G. Click on the Save button. This will put you back on the Settings page.

    H. Return to the System folder by double-clicking on the title-bar icon (the button with a graphic on it in the upper-left corner of the window). Now double-clicking on the DOS Boot Image icon will bring up a DOS window and start LANtastic.

Once you've completed these steps, you can use LANtastic from within the DOS session, just as you would at a DOS-based workstation. Note that disk redirections made within a LANtastic session are only accessible from within that session and not from anywhere else in OS/2 or from other DOS windows.

■ Third-Party Network Boards

So far in this chapter, we've dealt with adding products onto LANtastic. If you have an existing, non-LANtastic network, you may find yourself in the reverse situation: wanting to add LANtastic to your LAN.

Artisoft designed the standard LANtastic operating system to run over Artisoft hardware. This all-Artisoft combination gives you Artisoft's well-known fast throughput and low RAM consumption; however, Artisoft's LAN adapters can also emulate a Novell NE-2000 Ethernet adapter, which means Artisoft's boards work very well with practically any other network operating system including Novell's NetWare, various versions of Microsoft's LAN Manager, TCP/IP, and Banyan's VINES. While the same Artisoft hardware works with LANtastic and with products from other companies, it takes a special version of the LANtastic software to run over other makes of LAN adapters.

The LANtastic redirector and server modules depend on another piece of software—the Network Basic Input/Output System (NetBIOS)—to carry requests for service and data between the LAN adapter cards on the network. NetBIOS was developed as an interface between the old IBM PC Network Program (PCNP, superseded by PC LAN) and network interface cards provided by a company named Sytek.

The impulse behind the original NetBIOS was to provide the glue that would stick the standard parts of the network operating system to a specific make and model of LAN adapter card. Any NetBIOS software module presents a standardized, unchanging face to the networking software. But the other side of the module is customized to work with a specific type and version of networking hardware. NetBIOS software modules typically come on a diskette provided with the LAN adapter.

When the IBM/Sytek team designed the NetBIOS interface to the network operating system, they defined a number of functions and calls for system communications, and LANtastic's NetBIOS conforms to those specifications. Unfortunately, many NetBIOS programs on the market either don't meet all the specifications or include special proprietary network calls.

To help solve this problem, Artisoft markets a product called LANtastic/AI (Adapter Independent) that is designed to work over a variety of NetBIOS packages used on adapters marketed by over 20 manufacturers. Although these 20 companies represent a large share of the market, they're less than a majority, so there are still practical limitations on the brands and types of adapters you can use with LANtastic. Specifically, you can't use

LANtastic/AI with many of the Ethernet adapters from 3Com Corporation, though it does work with the popular 3Com 3C503.

The LANtastic/AI package includes NetBIOS software and driver modules you can use on many different adapters, particularly those that emulate the NE-2000. The list includes adapters from Accton Technology, CNet Technology, Novell, and Tiara Computer Systems. A driver called NEX000.EXE provides good performance with all these adapters. The /AI package also provides customized interface software for some adapters like the 3Com 3C503, the Intel EtherExpress16, and the Western Digital WD80XX line. Programs named 3C503.EXE, EXP16LAN.EXE, and WD8003.EXE provide a way for these boards to communicate with the LANtastic server and redirector software.

In practice, installing LANtastic/AI over these adapters isn't much different from installing it over Artisoft's adapters. Few adapters offer the wide choice of IRQ and memory assignments you'll find in Artisoft's products, so you may have less flexibility during the installation. The LANtastic/AI diskette includes drivers for specific brands of ARCnet adapters from companies like Standard Microsystems and Thomas-Conrad.

In addition, there are other, more complex, options for LANtastic/AI. You can, for example, use the /AI package to run LANtastic over IBM's Token-Ring adapters. Although LANtastic and Token-Ring may not seem like a natural mix, peer-to-peer networking software offers several advantages over the dedicated-server network operating systems typically associated with Token-Ring. You might choose LANtastic because it can easily back up all the drives on all networked PCs at a central point, or because it allows you to share CD-ROM drives, plotters, and other high-cost devices—or you may simply inherit Token-Ring from a previous tenant!

Note that Artisoft doesn't supply a specific interface program for IBM's Token-Ring adapter in LANtastic/AI. Since IBM helped write the specification, the IBM PC LAN Support program version 1.1 or higher works fine as an interface between LANtastic and the IBM hardware, but you must get this program from IBM and load it before you load the LANtastic/AI software.

You can work out something similar with other brands of Token-Ring adapters, ARCnet adapters, and even Ethernet adapters that have their own NetBIOS support programs. Contact Artisoft technical support for the latest information on compatibility between LANtastic/AI and the adapter and NetBIOS you want to use.

■ Network Your Network—On-Line Services

If you have a modem and communication software, you should know about the many on-line services available to you. If you don't have a modem, these services may be your reason to get one. On-line services allow you to communicate with hardware and software vendors, other LANtastic users, and thousands of computer users around the world.

CompuServe

CompuServe is one of the oldest and largest on-line information services in the United States. It offers an incredible array of products and services including on-line shopping, news and sports, electronic mail, stock, bond, and commodity price quotes, weather forecasts (including color radar), and hundreds of other services. You connect to CompuServe via a modem, usually through a local telephone call. CompuServe offers several billing plans, including a $7.95 per month "basic" account. CompuServe supports 9600 bps modems in most major cities, but you can also use a 2400 bps or 1200 bps modem. To connect to the service, you need a modem, communication software, and a CompuServe account. CompuServe sign-up kits are available at most computer retailers, software stores, and larger bookstores.

Artisoft includes a free CompuServe sign-up kit with every Artisoft product. The kit entitles you to a free introductory CompuServe membership, a $15 credit for future CompuServe use, and a subscription to *CompuServe* magazine. For more information on CompuServe, call 800/848-8199 (U.S. and Canada only). In the United Kingdom, ring 0800/289-378. In other countries, dial 01-614/457-0802 or 44-272/255-111.

The Forums

Of all the services available on CompuServe, the forums are probably the most useful for PC users. A forum consists of two major sections: a message section and a file section. In the message section, you can leave messages for other users, and read messages to and from other users. Forum discussions are open to all users, and you will find messages from people with all levels of computer expertise. Don't feel shy about leaving a message or asking a question; everyone is there to help, and your message will usually receive a prompt answer.

One of the wonderful things about the forums is that they are open 24 hours a day, 7 days a week. If you have a problem with your network or an application program, you can usually get help from another user. You can also search the message database for messages on topics of interest to you. For example, if you're having a problem with the DOS5 shell, you can go to the Microsoft system software forum and search for all messages containing the word "DOS" in the title. By reading these messages, you may be able to determine the cause of your problem.

In addition to the message section, each forum contains a library of files that are available for downloading. In the libraries, you'll find utility programs, shareware applications, bug fixes, and technical bulletins from hardware and software vendors.

Many major hardware and software vendors maintain a forum on CompuServe. Table 11.1 lists a few of the key forums you'll find on the service.

Table 11.1

Key CompuServe Forums

COMPUSERVE SOFTWARE FORUMS	
Forum	**Products Covered**
Adobe	Adobe fonts, PostScript, Illustrator
Aldus	PageMaker, Freehand
Artisoft	All Artisoft Products, including LANtastic
Ask3Com	3Com networking products
Autodesk	AutoCAD, Generic CAD, Autosketch
Borland	All Borland products, including languages
Central Point	PC Tools, CP Backup, Copy II PC
CrossTalk	CrossTalk Communicator, Remote2, CrossTalk for Windows
DATASTORM	Procomm family of products
Digital Research	DR DOS
Hayes	Smartcom
IBM OS/2	IBM OS/2 and applications
Lotus Development	1-2-3, Ami Pro, other Lotus products
Microsoft	All Microsoft products, including languages and applications
Norton/Symantec	Norton Utilities, Q&A
Novell NetWire	All Novell products
WordPerfect	All WordPerfect products
WordStar	WordStar, Legacy

Table 11.1

(continued)

COMPUSERVE HARDWARE FORUMS	
Forum	**Products Covered**
Apple Macintosh	Apple Macintosh computers and applications
Artisoft	All Artisoft hardware products
Ask3Com	3Com network products
DEC Users Network	DEC PCs, VAX
Epson	Epson laptops and printers
Hayes	Hayes modems
Hewlett-Packard	HP Personal computers, scanners, and printers
IBM Users Network	IBM PCs and compatibles
Intel Corporation	Intel PC expansion products
Practical Peripherals	PPI modems
Tandy Users Network	Tandy PCs
Texas Instruments	TI PCs and printers
Toshiba	Toshiba laptops and printers
Zenith Data Systems	Zenith PCs and accessories

The Artisoft Forum

Artisoft's CompuServe forum is of particular interest to LANtastic users. The forum is staffed by Artisoft employees, so you can get information on LANtastic and Artisoft hardware products directly from the source. The forum is very active; you can use it to exchange messages with LANtastic users around the world.

In addition to the message database, Artisoft maintains a large file area containing press releases, technical bulletins, utility programs, and software patches. The forum staff are very good about keeping the forum file libraries up-to-date.

ZiffNet

ZiffNet is an on-line service similar to CompuServe. It contains several sections, each sponsored by one of the Ziff-Davis family of computer magazines, which includes *PC Magazine*, *PC Week*, *PC Computing*, and *MacUser*. ZiffNet actually operates on CompuServe's computers, and is available through CompuServe. From any CompuServe prompt, type **GO ZNT**. The main ZiffNet menu will appear, as shown in Figure 11.1.

Figure 11.1

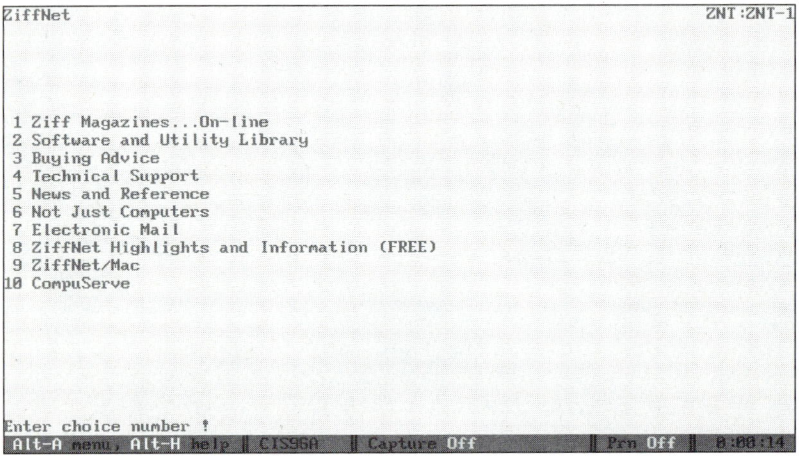

The main ZiffNet Menu, from which you can download files, enter one of the magazine forums, or read product reviews

```
ZiffNet                                                    ZNT:ZNT-1



 1 Ziff Magazines...On-line
 2 Software and Utility Library
 3 Buying Advice
 4 Technical Support
 5 News and Reference
 6 Not Just Computers
 7 Electronic Mail
 8 ZiffNet Highlights and Information (FREE)
 9 ZiffNet/Mac
10 CompuServe




Enter choice number !
Alt-A menu, Alt-H help  | CIS96A  | Capture Off   | Prn Off | 0:00:14
```

The menu changes from week to week. As you can see, a wealth of information is available. The PC MagNet section contains the full *PC Magazine* utility library, an index of all product reviews, and several forums. Figure 11.2 shows the main PC MagNet menu.

PC MagNet includes several forums, each with a particular focus. The Editorial forum is frequently host to discussions of current industry trends and recent product announcements. The Utilities forum contains messages about the *PC Magazine* utility programs. The Programming forum is the place to go for pointers on programming, and the After Hours forum is devoted to recreational computing.

■ LANtastic and Portable Computers

Laptop and notebook computers have become increasingly powerful, portable, and affordable over the last few years. In speed, storage, and memory capacity, many laptops now rival their desk-bound counterparts. The growing popularity of portable computers has led several manufacturers to develop external network adapters designed specifically for them. Since most portables don't have expansion slots, these adapters usually attach to the laptop's parallel printer port, and they offer surprisingly good performance.

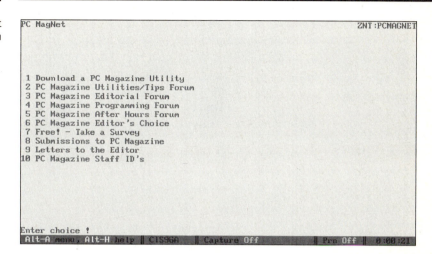

Figure 11.2

The PC MagNet main menu

If you want to add a laptop to a LANtastic network, you might also consider purchasing Artisoft's Central Station. The Central Station provides a LAN-to-laptop connection, and can also operate as a print server or remote access server. (See Chapter 8 for more information on the Central Station.)

We've even seen laptops used as portable file servers, servicing a network of other portable computers. At a recent trade show, a major software vendor was demonstrating its product on a small stage. They were using a desktop PC and a notebook computer as workstations to run the program, and both machines were attached to large monitors so the audience could see. Under the stage, we spotted the glow of a Compaq LTE 386 notebook, resting on a briefcase. A closer look revealed that the notebook was acting as the file server for the LAN.

By the way, external LAN adapters are also useful on computers that have lots of internal expansion slots available. They provide a great way to make temporary connections when you don't want to open a PC, and they prevent IRQ and memory address conflicts. They're also a nice troubleshooting tool. Because external adapters typically work the first time, they can help isolate problems in the cable, computer, or LAN adapter card.

Xircom, D-Link Systems, IQ Technologies, and other companies make external LAN adapters for laptop computers. Xircom and IQ Technologies' products allow you to use the parallel port and still retain access to a printer.

Such devices range in price from about $400 for ARCnet products to over $800 for products supporting Token-Ring, and most of them will work with the /AI version of LANtastic.

■ Working through Problems

Although incompatibility problems are quite rare, when they do occur they can be frustrating. Remember that Artisoft offers free technical support through telephone lines, an electronic bulletin board, and a very effective forum on CompuServe. Some of these problems may resemble a tangled skein of yarn to you, but Artisoft's experts have seen most of them before and can probably offer a solution.

■ Glossary

access control list (ACL)   A list of shared resources and their associated user rights. LANtastic maintains an ACL for each shared resource on each server.

access protocol   The traffic rules that LAN workstations abide by to avoid data collisions when sending signals over shared network media; also referred to as the *media access control (MAC) protocol*. Common examples are carrier sense multiple access (CSMA) and token passing.

address   A unique memory location. Network interface cards often use shared memory address locations to move data from the card to the PC's processor.

AFP (AppleTalk File Protocol)   Apple's network protocol, used to provide access between file servers and clients in an AppleShare network. Also used by Novell's products for the Macintosh.

AppleTalk   An Apple networking system able to transfer data at a rate of 230 kilobytes per second over shielded twisted-pair wire.

ARCnet (Attached Resources Computing Network)   A networking architecture (marketed by Datapoint and other vendors) using a token-passing bus architecture, usually on coaxial cable. It is generally implemented in the chips and connectors on the network adapter card.

background program   A program that performs its functions while the operator is working with a second, different program.

base address   The first address in a series of addresses in memory, often used to describe the beginning of a network interface card's I/O space.

baseband   A network that transmits signals as a pulse rather than as variations in a carrier signal.

benchmark   A test program used to determine system speed and performance.

boot PROM   A read-only memory chip that allows the workstation to communicate with the file server and to read a DOS boot program from the server. Stations can operate on the network without having a disk drive.

broadband A network that carries information riding on carrier waves rather than directly as pulses, providing greater capacity at the cost of higher complexity.

broadcast To send a message to all stations or an entire class of stations connected to the network.

buffer A temporary storage space. Data may be stored in a buffer before it is transmitted or as it is received. A buffer may be used to compensate between the differences in the speed of transmission and the speed of processing.

bus topology A "broadcast" arrangement in which all network stations receive the same message through the cable at the same time.

byte A group of eight bits.

cache An amount of RAM set aside to hold data that network stations are likely to access again. The second access, which finds the data in RAM, is very fast.

channel A path between sender and receiver that carries one stream of information (a two-way path is a *circuit*).

character One letter, number, or special code.

client/server computing A computing system in which processing can be distributed among "clients" on the network that request information and one or more network "servers" that store data, let clients share data and programs, help with printing operations, and so on. The system accommodates stand-alone applications (such as word processors), applications that require data from the server (such as spreadsheets), applications that use server capabilities to exchange information among users (as with electronic mail), and applications that provide true client/server teamwork (such as databases—especially those based on Structured Query Language, or SQL). Without client/server capabilities, a server downloads an entire database to a client machine for processing; SQL database applications divide the work, allowing the database to stay on the server.

coax or coaxial cable A type of network media. Coaxial cable contains a copper inner conductor surrounded by plastic insulation and then a woven copper or foil shield. It is commonly used to carry radio-frequency signals, such as those used in cable television and Ethernet networks.

CPU (central processing unit) The functional "brain" of a computer. The element that does the actual adding and subtracting of 0s and 1s that is essential to computing.

crosstalk The spillover of a signal from one channel to another, which is very disruptive. Usually, careful adjustment of the circuits will eliminate crosstalk.

CSMA (carrier sense multiple access) A media-sharing scheme in which stations listen in to what's happening on the network media; if the cable is not in use, the station is permitted to transmit its message. CSMA is often combined with a means of performing collision detection, hence *CSMA/CD*.

cursor The marker indicating the place on the video screen where the next character will appear.

driver A software program that interfaces between portions of the LAN software and the hardware on the network interface card.

EISA (Extended Industry Standard Architecture) A PC bus system that is an alternative to IBM's Micro Channel Architecture (MCA). The EISA architecture, backed by an industry consortium headed by Compaq, is compatible with the IBM AT bus; MCA is not.

Ethernet A network cable and access protocol scheme originally developed by Xerox, but now marketed by many companies, including Artisoft.

fiber optics A data transmission method that uses light pulses sent over glass cables.

file server A type of server that holds files in private and shared subdirectories for LAN users. *See also* server.

gateway A shared portal from a local area network into a larger information resource such as a large packet-switched information network or a mainframe computer.

IEEE 802 A set of standards for the physical and electrical connections for local area networks, developed by the IEEE (Institute of Electrical and Electronic Engineers).

IEEE 802.3 10BaseT An evolving IEEE standard describing 10Mb-per-second twisted-pair Ethernet wiring. This wiring requires a wiring hub and is useful for installing network monitoring and control devices.

interrupt A signal that suspends a program temporarily, transferring control to the operating system when input or output is required. Interrupts have priority levels, and higher priority interrupts take precedence in processing.

I/O Input-output.

IPX (Internet Packet Exchange) NetWare's native transport protocol, used to move data between server and/or workstation programs running on different network nodes. IPX packets are not related to packets used in Ethernet and similar systems, or to the tokens used in Token-Ring.

IRQ (interrupt request) A computer instruction that interrupts a program for an I/O task. It often is executed through specifically channeled electrical circuits.

jumper A plastic-and-metal shorting bar that slides over two or more electrical contacts to set certain conditions.

k Abbreviation for kilo, meaning 1,000; for example, a 1.2-kbps circuit operates at 1,200 bits per second. When used as a measurement of memory, one k equals 1,024 bytes.

local Programs, files, peripherals, and computational power accessed directly in the user's own machine rather than through the network.

local area network (LAN) Connected computers in the same building.

LocalTalk The 230.4-kilobit-per-second media-access method developed by Apple Computer, Inc. for use with its Macintosh computer.

locking A method of protecting shared data. When an application program opens a file, file locking either prevents simultaneous access by a second program or limits such access to read only. DOS versions 3.0 and later allow an application to lock a range of bytes in a file for various purposes. Since DBMS programs interpret this range of bytes as a record, this is called *record locking*.

MCA (Micro Channel Architecture) The basis for the IBM MicroChannel bus used in high-end models of IBM's PS/2 series of personal computers.

media The cabling or wiring used to carry network signals. Typical examples are coax, fiber-optic, and twisted-pair wire. Plural of *medium*.

modem (modulator-demodulator) A device that translates between electrical signals and some other means of signaling. Typically, a modem translates between direct-current signals from a computer or terminal and analog signals sent over telephone lines. Other modems handle radio frequencies and light waves.

NetBIOS (Network Basic Input/Output System) A layer of software originally developed by IBM and Sytek to link a network operating system with specific hardware. It also can open communications between workstations on a network at the session layer. Today, many vendors either provide a version of NetBIOS to interface with their hardware or emulate its session-layer communications services in their network products.

NetWare A series of network operating systems and related products made by Novell, Inc.

network A continuing connection between two or more computers that facilitates the sharing of files and resources.

ODI (Open Data-Link Interface) A standard interface for transport protocols, allowing them to share a single network card without any conflicts.

on-line Connected to a network or host computer system.

Open Systems Interconnection (OSI) reference model A model for networks developed by the International Standards Organization, dividing the network functions into seven connected layers. Each layer builds on the services provided by those under it.

OS/2 (Operating System/2) An operating system developed by IBM and Microsoft for use with Intel's 80286 and 80386 microprocessors. Unlike its predecessor, DOS, OS/2 is a multitasking operating system.

peer-to-peer resource sharing A software architecture that lets any station contribute resources to the network while still running local application programs.

print server A computer on the network that makes one or more attached printers available to other users. The server usually requires a hard disk to spool the print jobs while they wait in a queue for the printer.

print spooler The software that sends a file to a shared printer over a network, even when the printer is busy. The file is saved in temporary storage and then printed when the printer becomes available.

protocol A specification that describes the rules and procedures products should follow to perform activities on a network, such as transmitting data. Protocols allow products from different vendors to communicate on the same network.

queue A list formed by items waiting for service in a system. An example is a print queue of documents to be printed in an electronic publishing system.

RAM (random access memory) Also known as *read-write memory*; usually able to accept user programs.

record locking The exclusion of other users from accessing (or sometimes just writing to) a record in a file while a first user is accessing that record.

redirector A software module that is loaded into every network workstation. It captures application programs' requests for file- and equipment-sharing services and routes them through the network.

RF (radio frequency) A generic term referring to the technology used in radio, television, cable, and broadband networks. It uses electromagnetic waveforms, usually in the megahertz (MHz) range, for transmission.

ring A network connection method that routes messages through each station on the network in turn. Most ring networks use a token-passing protocol, which allows the station to put a message on the network when it receives a special bit pattern.

ROM (read-only memory) Memory that can hold data indefinitely, even without power. ROMs commonly are used in PCs to store the essential "boot" program required to read DOS from the boot disk.

server Any computer on a network that makes file, print, or communications services available to other network stations.

serial port An I/O port that transmits data out one bit at a time, in contrast to a *parallel port*, which transmits multiple (usually eight) bits simultaneously. RS-232-C is a common serial signaling protocol.

star topology A network connection method that brings all links to a central node.

T-connector A coaxial connector, shaped like a T, that connects two thin Ethernet cables and has an additional connector for a network interface card.

terminator A resistor used at both ends of an Ethernet cable to ensure that signals do not reflect back and cause errors. It is usually attached to an electrical ground at one end.

thick Ethernet A cabling system that uses large-diameter, stiff cable to connect transceivers. The transceivers connect to the nodes through flexible multiwire cable. Thick Ethernet is also widely known as *FYGH cable: frozen yellow garden hose*.

thin Ethernet   A cabling system that uses a thin, flexible coaxial cable to connect each node to the next node in line.

token passing   An access protocol in which a special message (token) circulates among the network nodes, giving them permission to transmit.

Token-Ring   Refers to the wire and the access protocol scheme whereby stations relay packets around in a logical ring configuration. This architecture is described in the IEEE 802.3 standards.

topology   The map of the network. The physical topology describes how the wires or cables are laid out, and the logical or electrical topology describes how the messages flow.

twisted pair Ethernet   *See* IEEE 802.3 10BaseT

twisted-pair wiring   Cable comprised of two wires twisted together at six turns per inch to provide electrical self-shielding. Some telephone wire—but by not all—is twisted-pair.

wiring hub   A cabinet, usually mounted in a wiring closet, that holds connection modules for various kinds of cabling. The hub contains electronic circuits that retime and repeat the signals on the cable. The hub may also contain a microprocessor board that monitors and reports network activity.

■ Index

* (asterisk) used with group account names, 114
@ (at-sign) preceding print queue names, 115
^ (caret) preceding macros, 177
! (exclamation point) preceding macros, 176
! command-line macros, 177–178
? (question mark) default printer stream, 137
? (question mark) preceding macros, 177
? command-line macros, 178
/NOCR option, 163
10BaseT standard, 4
2Mbps adapters, 38–39

A

access control, 108
Access Control List (ACL), 108
    editing keys, 121
    privilege, 112
    rights, 116
access privileges, 89, 92
access rights, checking, 103
access server, 42–43
account entries, replacing in Windows, 233
account privileges, setting, 111–113
accounts
    comparing users to groups, 114
    controlling, 110
    copying in Windows, 234–235
    deleting, 172
    displaying information about, 174
    editing in Windows, 235–237
    managing in Windows, 232
    manipulating in Windows, 218
    reactivating when disabled in Windows, 230
account settings
    controlling, 173–174
    managing in Windows, 229–230

ACL (Access Control List), 108
    adding and changing entries, 120–122
    editing for selected devices in Windows, 238
    rights, 116
ACLs for printers, 124
ACOM.EXE, 198–200
ACS (Asynchronous Communication Server), 189
active hubs, 21
adapter cards, 2, 13
Adapter Drivers to Install option, 70
adapter installation, guidelines for, 65
adapters
    AE-3 Ethernet, 38–39
    and data rates, 14
    and operating system compatibility, 16
    for Sounding Board, 44
    2Mbps, 38–39
    troubleshooting, 255
    using with diskless workstations, 183
address range, swapping with LIM EMS 4.0, 76
AE-3 Ethernet adapter, 38–39
AFP (Apple network protocol), 275
alerts (special messages) sent by MIBs, 19
alias, creating for pathname, 158
ALONE, 31
ANSI.SYS, loading, 185
ANSI standard for STP signaling, 8
APPC (Advanced Program to Program Communications), 17
Apple network protocol (AFP), 275
archiving the control directory in Windows, 240
ARCnet (Attached Resource Computing Network), 18
    cabling, 8
    and data rates, 18
A-REDIR program, 192

arranging programs, 262–263
ArtiCom, 36
    ACS package, 190–191
    application program, 198–200
    server default port settings, 194–197
ArtiScribe, 46
Artisoft adapters, 2
Artisoft forum, 271
ASCII escape characters, 128
A-SERVER.EXE, 197
asterisk (*) used with group account names, 114
at-sign (@) preceding print queue names, 115
ATTACH command-line option (NET.EXE), 153
Attached Resource Computing Network (ARCnet), 18
Attachment Unit Interface (AUI), 15
audio format conversion, 45
audio messages, sending in Windows, 224–226
AUDIT command-line option (NET.EXE), 153
auditing, controlling in Windows, 233
audit logs
    entries, 133
    and security problems, 134
    viewing in Windows, 239
audit parameters, 136
Audit Trail Maintenance, option, 110
audit trails, 109
AUI (Attachment Unit Interface), 15
AUTOEXEC.BAT, 80
    and diskless workstations, 182
    warning about Windows installation, 211, 212
AUTOEXEC.BAT files, creating for the boot disk, 185–187
autologin, returning default with a macro, 178

B

backing up control directory information in Windows, 233
backup, 60
BACKUP command-line option (NET_MGR), 170–171
baluns, 15
batch files
    creating with command-line interface, 152
    and NetWare, 247, 248
    and PAUSE command-line option, 161
blocking access with record locking, 90
bootable disk, preparing, 184
boot file, 182–183
boot image, 110, 233, 240
boot image file, creating, 187–188
Boot Image Maintenance option, 110
booting preparations, 183
boot ROMs, installing, 183
buffers, creating, 186
bus-mastering circuitry, 13

C

cable types, 7, 8
cabling, 2
    for ARCnet, 18
    building and fire code considerations for, 4
    coaxial, 8, 9
    fiber-optic, 9–11
    fiber-optic guidelines, 55
    standards, 53–54
    STP, 7–8
    UTP, 3, 4–7
caches, 29
    clearing on the selected server in Windows, 232
    closing and resetting, 157
CALL, using to execute unique batch files, 187
cards
    for adapters, 13
    for hubs, 20
caret (^) preceding macros, 177
carriage return, omitting from command string, 163
cassette tape icon, 222

Index **285**

CD-ROM Drive field, using with disk resources, 119
CD ROM drives, sharing, 31, 201–202
CD ROM and standard LANtastic, 29
Central Station, 42–43
    connecting with, 202–203
    and print servers, 137
CHANGEPW command-line option (NET.EXE), 154
changing passwords, 103
characters, returning for installed LANtastic programs, 177
character strings, displaying on screen, 156–157
Chat with Another User option, 91
CHAT command-line option (NET.EXE), 153–154
Chat feature, 30, 103
chatting with users in Windows, 226
classroom training application, 259
classroom training and TNE, 37
client and server capability, LANtastic for NetWare, 33–34
client size considerations, 56
client software and RAM, 22
CLOCK command-line option (NET.EXE), 154
CMP (Communications Plenum Cable), specifications, 4
CMR (Communications Riser Cable) specifications, 4
coaxial cable, 8–9
COM2 serial port and IRQ line, 65, 67
command-line macros, 177–178
command-line mode for Connection Manager, 90
commands
    for LANtastic and NetWare, 250
    running on selected servers in Windows, 231
    sending to server, 163–164
Comment column in printer queue, 99
comments, adding to voice mail messages in Windows, 226
communication program (ACOM), 198

compatibility
    of adapter and operating system, 16
    and LANtastic/AI, 33
    and LANtastic for NetWare, 35
    problems, 265
    of wiring hubs, 19
compilers defined, 257
CompuServe billing plans, 269
CompuServe forums, 270–271
concentrator control, 259–260
CONFIG.SYS, 70
    and diskless workstations, 182
    warning about Windows installation, 211, 212
CONFIG.SYS files, creating for the boot disk, 185–186
configuration, 29, 110
configuration files, separating, 262
Connection Manager
    connecting network disk with, 152
    display for Windows, 218
    main menu, 91–92
    modes, 90
Connection Manager Drive Connections display, 220
Connection Manager Printer Connections display, 222
connections, making and breaking in Windows, 218
connectors, costs for fiber-optic cabling, 10
contention protocol and Ethernet, 16
control directory
    making backup of, 171
    restoring, 173
    selecting, 110
    selecting in Windows, 233
Control Directory Maintenance option, 110
control directory for Network Manager, 109
control directory password, changing in Windows, 240
Control Directory setting, 70
controlling access, 108
controlling LAN segment flow, 17
controlling networked PCs, 258
controlling network printers, 91

286 Index

conversion, audio format, 45
COPY command-line option (NET.EXE), 154–155
COPY command-line option (NET_MGR), 171–172
copying information between user accounts in Windows, 233
Copy option in printer queue, 99
cost of installation, 2
costs
    of adapters, 13, 14
    of ArtiCom, 36
    of baluns, 15
    of cards, 38, 39
    of Central Station, 42–43
    of coaxial cable, 8
    of connectors, 8
    of external LAN adapters, 274
    of fiber-optic cabling, 10, 11
    of hubs, 20, 21
    of installing UTP, 5
    of LAN adapters, 24
    of LANtastic, 23
    of LANtastic for NetWare, 34
    of LANtastic for Windows, 31
    of LANtastic Z, 35
    of media filters, 15
    of metering products, 147
    of modems, 189
    of Peer-Hub, 40
    for protocol decoding products, 260
    of Sounding Board and ArtiSound Recorder, 44
    of TNE, 37
    for Token-Ring, 18
    of Type 1 and Type 6 cable, 8
    of wiring hubs, 19
CREATE command-line option (NET_MGR), 172
creating audit entries, 153
creating buffers, 186
creating messages in Windows, 223
crosstalk and cabling, 54
CSMA/CD, 16
customizing menu systems, 59

D

database programs, 263–264
data carrying and cabling, 9
data rates
    and adapters, 14
    and ARCnet, 18
    and coaxial cable, 9
    and fiber-optic cabling, 10, 11
    and LANtastic Z, 35
    of STP, 8
    and Token-Ring, 17, 18
    of UTP, 6
data rates for modems, 189
date, returning with a macro, 177
Date and Time fields, 134
day, returning with a macro, 177
DDE interfaces, exchanging messages with, 31
default autologin, returning with a macro, 178
default port settings for ArtiCom server, 194–197
default printer, selecting in Windows, 215
default resources, 70
defaults, handling with Net pull-down menu, 219
defaults for adapter installation, 65
default user name, 95
default values for server settings, 131–133
defining streams, maximum allowed, 138
DELETE command-line option (NET_MGR), 172
Deleted status in printer queue, 98
Delete option in printer queue, 99
deleting messages in Windows, 223
deleting from the print queue in Windows, 228
denying user rights, 121
Description field, using with disk resources, 119
Despooling status in printer queue, 98
Destination column of printer queue, 98
DETACH command-line option (NET.EXE), 155

deterministic media-access control system, 17
diagnostic utilities, 256
Dial-Up Connection, 204–205
digital dictation system, 46
DIR command-line option (NET.EXE), 155
directory, listing in NetWare, 250
Disable button in Windows, 230
DISABLE command-line option (NET.EXE), 156
disabling print streams, 138
DISCON reason code, 134
Disk Drive Connections setting, 70
disk drives
    adding, 94
    adding and removing in Windows, 218
    managing in Windows, 219–221
    selecting, 93
    setting path for in Windows, 237–238
    using, 93–94
disk files
    printing, 141
    sending to other users, 103
diskless network workstations, 110
diskless workstations
    and AUTOEXEC.BAT, 182
    and CONFIG.SYS, 182
    and increased security, 182
    and running Windows, 208
disk management, 110
disk redirection, canceling, 169
disk resources
    adding, 118–119
    modifying, 119–122
disk space
    and downloadable fonts, 144
    requirements for loading Windows, 210
    requirements for Sounding Board, 44–45
displaying files and drives in Windows, 215
displaying print job information in Windows, 228
DMA (Direct Memory Access), 67
DMA channels, using with the Sounding Board, 188

DOS
    file limit, 263
    requirements, 29
    SHARE program, 264
    used on servers, 22
DOS 5 and disk drive handling, 24
DOS-based server software, RAM requirement for, 23
DOS batch files, using with LANtastic, 175–176
DOS-drive setup, 34
DOS environment variable, setting, 167–168
downloadable printer fonts, managing, 143–145
drive connections
    creating in Windows, 220, 221
    removing in Windows, 221
drive and directory, returning with a macro, 177
drive letter, selecting, 93
drive mapping
    adding in Windows, 213
    and NETx, 248–249
drivers, accessing to run Windows, 208
driver software, 22
driver stack, using to communicate with adapters, 23
drives. *See also* disk drives
    adding and removing, 91
    display in Windows, 220

E

ECHO command-line option (NET.EXE), 156–157
echoing characters with a macro, 178
editing keys for ACL, 121
EEMS (Extended Expanded Memory Specification), 76
EEPROM, storing Central Station code in, 204
EISA adapters, 65
electricians, 55
electronic mail, 91. *See also* mail messages and messages
EMM386.EXE, 80

EMS expansion technique, 75–76
Enhanced Parallel Port (EPP), 14
envelope icon, 222
EPP (Enhanced Parallel Port), 14
error message, returning with a macro, 177
escape sequences, 128
Ethernet, 16–17
    cabling, 8
    and signaling rates, 16
exclamation point (!) preceding macros, 176
EXPAND command-line option
    (NET.EXE), 157
expanded memory, 75–76
external adapters, 14
external LAN adapters, 42, 255

F

F: SHARE parameter, 264
FDDI (Fiber Distribution Data Interface), 10
fiber-optic cabling, 9–11
    and data rates, 10, 11
    guidelines for selection of, 55
file libraries on forums, 269–270
file limit for DOS, 263
files
    copying on a server, 154–155
    discontinuing redirection of, 155
    printing to queues in NetWare, 250
    printing through print queue, 162
    sending to a printer, 141
FILES= statement in CONFIG.SYS file, 263
file server, installing Windows from, 209
files for Windows program SETUP, 210–211
file sharing, 89–90
FLUSH command-line option (NET.EXE), 157
font file size, managing, 144
fonts, managing, 143–145
formats for networking, 23
forums (CompuServe), 269
forwarding messages in Windows, 223
frames as messages on Token-Ring, 17
frames as data packets, 22

G

Group Account Management option, 110
group accounts
    comparing to user accounts, 114
    controlling, 110
    managing, 113–114

H

Halt print device option, 140
hardware conflicts, 255
hardware interrupts, 56
Held status in printer queue, 98
HELP command-line option (NET.EXE), 158
Help pull-down menu in Windows, 219
high-DOS memory, filling in unused areas of, 76
high memory, loading client software into, 22
HIMEM.SYS, 80, 211
Hold option in printer queue, 100
HP printers, 97
hubs. *See also* wiring hubs
    active and passive, 21
    Peer-Hub, 40–42
    and port capacity, 19, 20

I

I/O address, selecting, 67–68
I/O mapping, 64–65
IBM 3270 terminal cabling, 8
IBM Type 3 specification, 4
icons, using to designate network resources, 32
Immediate status in printer queue, 98
index for printer streams, 138
INDIRECT command-line option (NET.EXE), 158
Individual Account Management option, 110
INSTALL.EXE, 185
installation
    of boot ROMs, 183
    of connectors, 10
    cost of, 2

Index **289**

and inventory, 50
of LANtastic for Central Station, 203
of LANtastic on OS/2 systems, 265–267
of LANtastic for Windows, 216–217
of NetWare, 246–249
of networked applications, 147–148
of Windows from the network, 208
of workstation software, 184–185
Installation Directory, 69
Install Default Resources setting, 70
INT14, 191–192
internal adapters, 14
Internetwork Packet Exchange, 23
interrupts, 65
inventory sheets, 50
IP (Internet Protocol), 23
IPX drivers and batch files, 248
IPX (Internetwork Packet Exchange), 23
IPX (NetWare workstation software), 245
IRQ lines, 39, 65–67
IRQ locations, scanning, 51
ISA adapters, 65

K

keyboard access in Windows, 219
keyboard conversations, 91, 103, 218, 226

L

LAN metering software, 146–147
LANPUP, 30
LAN remote control software, 258
LANs, 2
LANtastic
   commands, 250
   costs per node, 29
   forms of, 28
   incompatibility, 265
   mail and logins, 100
   for NetWare, 33–35
   as peer-to-peer system, 88
   program group, 217
   recommended adapters, 2
LANtastic/AI, 33
LANtastic for NetWare. *See* NetWare

LANtastic for Windows, 31–32, 216–217
LANtastic Z, 35
laptops and LANtastic, 35, 272–274
laser printers
   guideline for loading, 57
   protecting with UPS, 144
LASTDRIVE, 70
LASTDRIVE statement and NetWare, 248
legal aspects of networking, 145–146
License Packs for shared software, 146
licensing agreements for software, 146
LIM (Lotus/Intel/Microsoft), 75
linking laptops with LANtastic Z, 35
linking Macintosh computers, 24
linking PCs to mini- and mainframes, 17
loading
   ANSI.SYS, 185
   Windows files from the network, 210
local drives
   advantages of keeping program files on, 261
   connecting to shared resources, 153
   redirecting, 169–170
local hard disk
   installing Windows on, 209
   and running Windows, 212
Local Path field, using with disk resources, 119
local printers, connecting to printer queue in NetWare, 250
logging in, 90
logging into and out of servers in Windows, 229
logging users out from a server, 168
logical drives, 89, 250
logical shared port connections, controlling, 198
Logical Streams display window, 228
LOGIN.BAT, 152
login command-line macro, 177
LOGIN command-line option (NET.EXE), 158
Login and Logout Connection Manager options, 103
Login or Logout option, 92

logins
    enabling and disabling, 166
    setting for users, 170
LOGINS on server, 72
login times
    changing, 113
    changing in Windows, 236–237
LOGOUT command-line option (NET.EXE), 159
LPT command-line option (NET.EXE), 169–170

M

MAC (Media Access Control), 15
Machine field, 134
machine name, returning with a macro, 177
Machine Type menu option, 69
MAC protocol, 275
macro defined, 176
macros and LANtastic for Windows, 31
mail
    accessing in Windows, 218
    reading in Windows, 223
MAIL command-line option (NET.EXE), 160
mail editor, 102–103
mail manager privilege, 112
mail messages
    checking for, 161
    reading, 101
    sending, 102
mail message types in Windows, 222
Mail Services option, 91
managed hubs, 19
Management Information Base (MIB), 19
manager privileges, setting in Windows, 236
match any name character (-), 114, 120
MCA adapters, 65
Media Access Control (MAC), 15
media filters, 15
memory
    and LANtastic for NetWare, 35
    limits, 72–75
    mapping, 64–65

organization, 74
reducing requirements, 38
requirements for ArtiCom, 190
requirements for running with Windows, 208
memory address, selecting, 67–68
memory management software, 258
memory management terms, 78
memory managers, 82–84
memory map diagram sample, 77
memory-resident programs, 36
menuing software, 258
menu mode for Connection Manager, 90
menu systems, 59
MESSAGE command-line option (NET.EXE), 160–161
message exchange, 30
message icons in Windows, 222
messages
    handling with Net pull-down menu, 219
    recalling, 163
    sending, 160
MIB (Management Information Base), 19
mirroring software, 260
modems
    access, 190
    recommendations, for LANtastic Z, 35
    remote control software, 258
    sharing, 197–198
    supported by CompuServe, 269
monitoring network activity, 259
Monitor and Manage Server Activity, 92
multimedia extensions, 44
multiple resources and printers, 123
multitasking, 24
music, adding with Sounding Board, 44

N

name for printer streams, 138
NAME environment variable, 186
naming services, 24
National Electric Code, 4
NDIS (Network Driver Interface Specification), 16

Index

NET.EXE, 90
NET.EXE command line, 152
NET.EXE commands, displaying, 158
NetBIOS, 23
    background, 267
    and NetWare, 246
    standard and network compatibility, 257–258
NETBIOS address, returning with a macro, 177
NET CHAT, 103
NET PRINT command, 141
Net pull-down menu in Windows, 219
NET UNUSE command, 141
NET USE command, 141
NetWare
    and batch files, 247, 248
    commands, 250
    installing, 246–249
NetWare Lite, 244
NetWare server, connecting, 245
network account, monitoring status of, 92
Network Adapter Installed option, 70
Network Disk Drives and Printers option, 91
Network Driver Interface Specification (NDIS), 16
network drives, using with Windows, 213
networked applications, installing, 147–148
Network Eye (TNE), 36–38
networking applications, pros of, 145
networking formats, 23
networking software, 2, 22
Network Interface Cards (NICs), 12
Network Manager menu, 115, 118
Network Manager menu options, 110
network resources
    accessing via modem, 204–205
    monitoring use of, 92
Network Startup Batch File, 69
networks
    applications, 2
    boards (third-party) for, 267–268
    communications protocols defined, 2
    compatibility, 257–258
    disks, 115
    displaying directories for, 155–156
    failure and coaxial wiring, 9
    mail queues, 115
    printers, 115, 213–215
    programs, adding to a program group, 215
    saving configurations with Net pull-down menu, 219
    security, 59
    signaling speeds, 6
    survey form, 51
    traffic, 209
network software, 19
NETx redirector and NetWare, 247, 248–249
new accounts, creating in Windows, 233
Next Scanner, 5
NIC (network interface card), 64
NICs (Network Interface Cards), 12
nodes, 2, 29
non-DOS systems, RAM requirement for, 23
non-networked programs, 260–261
NORMAL reason code, 134
NOS (Network Operating System), 28
notebook computers and LANtastic, 272–274
Number of Concurrent Logins field, 112–113

O

ODI (Open Device Interface), 16
ODI driver for NetWare, 245
ODI drivers and batch files, 248
Off-LAN communications defined, 2
One-Job print device option, 140
Open Device Interface (ODI), 16
operating system and adapter compatibility, 16
OS/2 and LANtastic, 265–267
overlay files
    loading on local drives, 58
    suggestions for loading, 262

P

packet (frame), 22
page frame, 76
PairScanner, 5
Paradox, vendor monitoring of, 146
parallel ports, 95
parameters, changing for databases, 263
passive hubs, 21
password, 90
    changing, 92, 103
    changing for user accounts, 154
    controlling use of, 110
    managing in Windows, 233
Password button in Windows, 230
password for control directory, changing in Windows, 240
Password Maintenance option, 110
password protection, 110
pathname, expanding, 157
pathname of NET.EXE program, returning with a macro, 177
pathnames, entering for new disk resources, 118–119
PAUSE command-line option (NET.EXE), 161
Pause print device option, 140
PBX (Private Branch Exchange) phone systems, 4
PC dedication as network server, 31
PCM (Pulse Code Modulation), 45
PCs, controlling on a network, 258
PDS (Premise Distribution System) plans, 4
Peer-Hub, 40–42
peer-to-peer system, 88
performance, controlling, 110
Perform Installation option, 70
phone systems, PBX, 4
physical drives, 88–89
physical topology, 5
planning system requirements, 53
playing back audio, 188
plenum cable, 4
pop-up messages
    enabling and disabling, 160–161
    handling with Net pull-down menu, 219
    sending, 164
portable computers and LANtastic, 272–274
ports
    capacity and hubs, 19, 20
    and Central Station, 42
    connecting to network printer queue in Windows, 214
    disabling with Peer-Hub, 41
    information screen, 194
    selecting in ArtiCom, 200
    settings for ArtiCom server, 194–197
POSTBOX command-line option (NET.EXE), 161
power outages, reconfiguring with Peer-Hub, 41
PRINT command-line option (NET.EXE), 162
print devices, controlling, 139–140
printer assignments and SETUP in Windows, 212
Printer Connections setting, 70
printer devices, displaying information about in Windows, 228
printer ports
    redirecting, 169–170
    stopping capture of in NetWare, 250
Printer Queue Management option, 91
printer queues, 137
    controlling, 99–100, 162–163
    controlling in Windows, 218
    display, 97–99
printer queue window in Windows, 227–228
printer redirection, canceling, 169
printer resources
    adding, 123
    deleting, 124
    modifying, 123–124
    settings, 125–127
printers, 57–58
    adding, 91, 95–96
    adding and removing in Windows, 218
    correct selection of, 97
    definition, 30
    direction, 142
    escape sequences, 128

fonts, 143–145
managing, 110
managing in Windows, 221–222
mapping, 34
monitoring with Central Station, 43
and multiple resources, 123
network capacity of, 95
output, 159–160
port availability, 123
redirecting, 141
removing, 91
rights, 124
selecting default in Windows, 215
status, 99
using on network with Windows, 213–215
Printer Server, 204
printer server, using Central Station as, 43
printer setup strings, 128–130
printer spool area
    clearing in Windows, 233
    controlling in Windows, 240
printer streams, 99, 137–139
    displaying in Windows, 228
    managing, 167
printer timeout interval, handling with Net pull-down menu, 219
printing
    to a file, 140–141
    incoming jobs, 98
    multiple copies, 141–142
    restricting, 138
    stopping in Windows, 228
print jobs
    placing on hold and releasing in Windows, 228
    separating with streams, 143
print preview, 96
print queue files, specifying location of, 110
print queues, 95
print server, 136
privileges, access, 89
Privileges field of Individual Account Management menu, 112
program arrangement suggestions, 262–263

program files for Windows SETUP, 210–211
programs, adding to Windows display, 215
PROM (programmable read-only memory), 183
prompting users, 152
prompt messages, printing with macro, 178
protected mode, 75
protecting shared data, 278
protocol decoding, 260

Q

Q&A, vendor monitoring of, 146
QEMM-386, 84
QIC (quarter-inch tape cartridge) systems, 60
question mark (?) default printer stream, 137
question mark (?) preceding macros, 177
QUEUE command-line option (NET.EXE), 162–163
queue entry, displaying in Windows, 228
Queue Maintenance option, 110
queue management screen in Windows, 226–227
queue manager privilege, 100, 112
queue managers, 97, 139
queue names, descriptive, 143

R

RAM
    and client software, 22
    requirements for Central Station, 43
    and server software, 23
    and startup parameters, 130
reactivating disabled accounts in Windows, 230
real mode, 75
Reason field and codes, 134
RECEIVE command-line option (NET.EXE), 163
recording audio, 188–189
recording mail messages in Windows, 225
record locking, 89–90
REDIR command, 72
redirecting printers, 141

redirection of files, discontinuing, 155
redirector software, 22
Release option in printer queue, 100
remote booting preparations, 183
remote control software applications, 258–259
remote PC control, 50
remote viewing with TNE, 36–37
remote workstations, accessing with TNE, 37
reporting capabilities, 259
reporting scheme, SNMP, 19
resources
    managing in Windows, 232
    redrawing in Windows, 221
resources for LANs, 24
restarting printers in Windows, 228
restarting Windows, 217
Restart print device option, 140
RESTORE command-line option (NET_MGR), 172
restoring drives to local, 169
restricting printing, 138
RG cable types, 8
rights, access, 103
ROM, 280
ROM BIOS chips, benefit of compressing, 84
ROM shadowing, 84
routers, 17
RUN command-line option (NET.EXE), 163–164
Rush option in printer queue, 100
Rush status in printer queue, 99

S

safety and performance for cabling, 54
saving messages in Windows, 223
scanning for viruses, 59
security, 59
security level and diskless workstations, 182
security levels, 103–109
security privileges, controlling, 110
security problems and audit logs, 134
SEND command-line option (NET.EXE), 164
sending messages in Windows, 223
Sequence # column of printer queue, 98
serial ports, 95, 194
SERVER.EXE, 130
server auditing, controlling, 134
server-based systems, NetWare, 244
Server Startup Parameters option, 110, 130
servers
    access in Windows, 218
    categories, 21–22
    changing in queue window, 228
    changing in Windows, 223
    and client capability, LANtastic for NetWare, 33–34
    connections, 92
    directory structure, 58–60
    establishing connection to, 158–159
    logging onto in Windows, 220
    logging out of, 159
    management display, updating in Windows, 232
    management in Windows, 231–232
    parameters, 131–133, 238
    PC dedication as, 31
    requirements, 55–57
    software and RAM, 23
    selecting, 93
    selecting in Windows, 231
    shutting down, 166
    shutting down in Windows, 232
    and workstation compatibility, ArtiCom, 36
SET command-line option (NET_MGR), 173–174
settings
    for serial ports, changing, 194
    for servers, managing in Windows, 233
    showing status of, 164–165
setting the workstation clock, 154
Setup File option, 128
SETUP program files for Windows, 210–211
Setup String option, 128, 129
setup strings for printers, 128–130

shared disk resources, 115, 117–118, 122
shared ports, creating batch files for, 200–201
Shared Resource Management option, 115, 118
shared resources
    controlling, 115
    creating for CD-ROM drives, 201–202
    types, 115
Shared Resources Management option, 110
SHOW command-line option (NET.EXE), 164–165
SHOW command-line option (NET_MGR), 174
Show option in printer queue, 100
shutdown, canceling for server in Windows, 232
SHUTDOWN command-line option (NET.EXE), 166
SHUTDOWN reason code, 134
signaling, ANSI standard for STP, 8
signaling rates
    and Ethernet, 16
    and Token-Ring, 21
signaling scheme, SNMP, 19
signaling speeds, 6
signal types, 15
silver satin flat cable, 4
Simple Network Management Protocol (SNMP), 19
slide shows and voice, 44
SLOGINS command-line option (NET.EXE), 166
SNMP (Simple Network Management Protocol), 19
software
    client RAM for, 22
    conflicts, 255–256
    interrupts, 14, 191–192
    licensing agreements, 146
    metering, 258
    for networks, 22
    piracy, 145
software protection, 260
Sounding Board, 43–46

hardware, 188–189
software, 189
speakers, 188
speed. *See also* data rates
    for ARCnet, 18
    and external adapters, 14
    and UTP, 6
speeding data transfer, 67
spooling, 95
stack software set, 22
standards for cabling, 53–54
starting Windows, 217
STARTNET.BAT, 69, 70–72, 247, 248
STARTNET.BAT configured for Central Station, 203
Start print device option, 140
startup parameters, controlling in Windows, 238
StationWare applications, 203–205
Status column of printer queue, 98
stopping printing in Windows, 228
Stop print device option, 140
storage on tapes, 60
STP (Shielded Twisted-Pair) wire, 7–8
STP and data rates, 8
STREAM command-line option (NET.EXE), 167
streams, enabling in Windows, 137, 228
STRING command-line option (NET.EXE), 167–168
string macros, 176–178
strings, displaying on screen, 156–157
subdirectories for servers, 58
surveying networks, 51
swap files for running Windows, 209
swapping address range, 76
system analyzer programs, 78–79
system configuration, 29
system manager control, 89
system manager privilege, 112

T

T-connectors used with Thinnet, 9
technical support, 28, 274
Teflon-coated cable, 4

TERMINATE command-line option (NET.EXE), 168
text, returning with a macro, 177
text editor programs, using with ASCII escape characters, 128, 129–130
text files, sending via Mail in Windows, 224
thick Ethernet cabling, 8
Thinnet cabling, disadvantages of, 8–9
third-party network boards, 267–268
throughput. *See also* data rates
   for adapters, 14
   comparisons, 17
   on Ethernet, 16–17
time, returning with a macro, 178
Time of Day Logins field, 113
TIMEOUT reason code, 134
TNE (Network Eye), 36–38
TNE as a training tool, 37
Token-Ring, 17–18
   and data rates, 17, 18
   and signaling rate, 21
   and STP, 7–8
tracking software on LANs, 258
traffic reporting and control, 259–260
traffic rules, 275
training classroom application, 259
training and TNE, 37
transceiver, using to change wiring, 15
troubleshooting utilities, 259
Type audit log codes, 134
types of signals, 15

U

UL (Underwriters Laboratory), 54
Unix
   used on servers, 22
   using to handle large files, 24
UNLINK command-line option (NET.EXE), 169
UNUSE command-line option (NET.EXE), 169
updating printer queue display windows, 229
UPS (uninterruptable power supply), 56
UPS reason code, 134
USE command-line option (NET.EXE), 169–170
User Account Management, 92
User Account Management Connection Manager option, 103
user accounts
   comparing to group accounts, 114
   copying, 171–172
   copying information between, 233
   creating, 110, 172
   disabling, 103, 156
   managing in Windows, 233–234
user audit privilege, 112
User column in printer queue, 99
USER command-line option (NET.EXE), 170
user name, 90
Username field, 134
users
   logging off from the server in Windows, 231
   logging into and out of server in NetWare, 250
   preventing from logging onto the selected server in Windows, 231
user security, 108
UTP (Unshielded Twisted-Pair) wiring, 3, 4–7. *See also* wiring

V

VA (volt/amps), 56–57
values for audit parameters, 136
vendors for cabling, 4
viewing network printers, 91
View option in printer queue, 100
viruses and security, 59
V in mailbox, 101
voice files, recording and playing back, 46
voice mail, 103
voice mail messages, sending in Windows, 224–226
voice messages, 44, 101

W

Waiting status in printer queue, 99

Index **297**

WAVE files, 45
WaveLAN, 11
Windows
   driver for Sounding Board, 189
   and LANtastic, 31–32
   memory requirements, 208
   on a shared server, 56
   using master copy for installation, 209–212
   WAVE files, 45
Windows Connection Manager display, 218
wire lengths, and UTP, 6
wireless LANs, 3, 11–12
wire pairs, analyzing, 5
wiring, changing with transceiver, 15. *See also* cabling
wiring centers, gathering data in, 19
wiring closet, 18, 20
wiring concentrators, monitoring, 259–260
wiring contractors, 55
wiring hub, 18–19
wiring hub for Token-Ring, 17
wiring patterns, 5
WNET.INI and system flexibility, 32
workstation clock, setting, 154
workstation and server compatibility, ArtiCom, 36
workstation software, installing, 184–185

Z

ZiffNet, 272